Legends of the
CALIFORNIA BANDIDOS

LEGENDS OF THE
CALIFORNIA
BANDIDOS

By

Angus MacLean

Illustrations by Ione MacLean Bowman

Pioneer Publishing - Fresno - 1977

ISBN 0-914330-09-8

iv

TABLE OF CONTENTS

INTRODUCTION

These stories are not just spur-of-the-moment concoctions, written on short notice to "fill out" a book. They represent an accumulation over a period of years.

When my grandfather, Dr. Thomas C. Still, brought his family into El Pueblo de San Luis Obispo in the fall of 1867, the vigilante hangings of members of the Linares Gang less than a decade earlier was still a very live subject of conversation, as was the somewhat earlier "visit" from Joaquin Murrieta and his band who "took over" the Mission gardens as their camp ground for several days.

Then in 1872, when Grandpa moved his family to Ortiga Springs in Eastern San Luis Obispo County, at that time very thinly settled, Tiburcio Vasquez and his band were very live indeed. In fact, one of the bandits' retreats was in what was then known as Vasquez Canyon, less than thirty miles from Ortiga Springs.

In 1879, following the discovery of gold in Vasquez Canyon, Grandpa moved his family there, and as the only doctor readily available, he had many calls to treat the native Spanish Californians and the more recent arrivals from south of the border who made up a large proportion of the prospectors roaming the hills. And at times these included men wanted by the law.

The Still family of my mother's generation all learned to speak Spanish at an early age, and many of their closest associates during those early years were Spanish Californians, giving the Still family a close insight into the people and their problems during those years of transition from the earlier Spanish traditions to the Anglo culture.

From Monterey to Ventura, Central California was the last stronghold of the Spanish Californians in Alta California, hence a logical retreat for men of "Mexican" origin wanted by "gringo" lawmen. Thus most of the legends of the Salinas Valley and environs deal largely with the California *bandidos* rather than their "American" counterparts.

From this distance in time, it is hard to separate the *revolucionario* from the *bandido*. In fact, many of the south-of-the-border bandits of the gold rush years would seem to have gotten their start in the insurrections down in Mexico, before transferring their talents to Alta California.

As to the source of these stories: At an age when most kids were being nurtured on such childhood classics as "Who Killed Cock Robin" and "Jack the Giant-Killer," I was absorbing these old tales of bandits and vigilante "justice." In fact, some of these stories might be called "family history"—like the time Grandpa was called out of bed to cut a bullet from the shoulder of Librado Corona. Also, the somber tale of the demon-haunted demise of Pascual Benadero who had so villainously "framed" his stepson into a vigilante hanging.

During the postwar depression of the 1920s, many of the old-timers made pilgrimages back to the La Panza district, camping for a time at the Still ranch. My uncles, Will, Othor, and Mentley Still, knew many of these men from earlier years, and of course tales of bandidos and buried loot were bound to come up. My own memory encompasses a number of these men, including some "reformed bandidos;" hence these tales of an earlier day registered with me more than they might have done otherwise.

For many years my mother, Dabirma Still MacLean, wrote a column of community gossip for local papers, and was induced to add a little "frontier history" from time to time. Over the years she gathered quite a bit of material from old-timers then living. She made an effort to collect anecdotes of the early-day bandits, and some of her notes and correspondence survived the years. This material figures in some of these stories.

I am also indebted to my uncle, Mentley Still, for much of the detail in several of these anecdotes. He had a keen retentive mind and remembered many of the stories from an earlier day.

In more recent years I have tried to overlap these tales of old-timers with what I could find in the way of historic material. In some cases (like the vigilante action in San Luis Obispo in 1858) there were written accounts at the time of the incidents, offering a base for analysis. However, all too often under frontier conditions, very little was recorded at the time, leaving the recounting of events to what could be pieced together from the memories of people long after the event took place.

In presenting these legends, I have used the story approach, since this allows a greater insight into a time and a people, an example being the story of Luciano Tapia, known also as El Mesteño (The Wild One).

Frankly, I have used a little artistic license in presenting the story of Luciano Tapia; yet in essence, this story squares in all details with recorded accounts of the incident, bolstered by tradition as handed down by early-day residents of San Luis Obispo. However, just the cold record of Luciano Tapia as having been amongst the "miscreants" hanged by the vigilantes back there in 1858 loses most of the pathos in an account of what would seem to have been an inherently decent young man caught up in the manipulations of a ruthless gang.

Then there is the phantom Joaquin Murrieta, with so little really known about him that many "experts" had discounted him completely as but a figment of fiction. Yet, Murrieta lived and took on substance in the folklore of the Spanish Californians.

In the case of Tiburcio Vasquez, there are cold hard police records of arrests, convictions, prison sentences, and the final degradation of being hanged as proof that Vasquez once existed. Yet, somehow, more than these records, it takes the legends which grew up around him to give him life.

In dealing with stories handed down from the past, one is bound to get various versions, often contradictory. In presenting these stories, I have in some cases presented one version in preference to others; at other times elements of several versions have been incorporated into one story. Too much of "maybe it was, and maybe it wasn't" makes for dull reading, but I think the reader will readily see how I made my choice.

Where names have been an integral part of the legend, those names have been used. However, in many cases, names get lost with the passing years; so in some instances, I have given names to characters. It is hard to put life into nameless beings.

Frankly, to a degree, I have stretched my own imagination a bit in trying to put life into these stories. Call them legends if you will—call them yarns if you prefer. And if pedantic "history" gets trampled under foot at times in the telling, *Le suplico a Ud. que me perdone.*

Part I
THE LINARES GANG

Some sidelights on the vigilante action of 1858,
in San Luis Opispo.

HANGED AS A MISCREANT

"Shall we have some sport with these two dogs before we slaughter them?" Froilan Servin was eager in his anticipation. "First, let us use the knife on them!" He displayed his keen-edged knife and laughed derisively. "They are but dogs, so why not give them the treatment of dogs!"

Froilan's three companions rode on in glum silence, not a one deigning a comment, though all three knew this was no idle jest on the part of the rowdy young desperado.

"You do not look forward to the sport, Mesteño?" Froilan asked. "Why must you always be so chicken-hearted, amigo? Any other one of our compadres would be eager for the sport, now that we have the dogs in our power! Pio or Huero would cheerfully use the knife on them if they were here! They have done so often enough in the past!"

Luciano Tapia, known also as El Mesteño (The Wild One), did not answer; for the thought of the sport almost made him sick to the stomach. He had in the past witnessed the "sport," as his comrades in banditry so glibly referred to the slow torture slayings of helpless captives—too many times! And the picture of the wretches writhing in agony before death at long last released them from their suffering was burned deeply in his mind.

"If cutting them does not appeal to you, we could gouge their eyes out with chamiza splinters, then turn them loose," Froilan suggested. "Thus blinded, they could not dodge us as we trampled them down with our horses. Or we could rope them and drag them over the stones and splintered brush—the way Grijalva and Valenzuela find so amusing!"

Two other young men rode in trembling silence, hearing Froilan's enthusiastic plans for their finish, yet helpless to defend themselves against their captors.

Bareheaded, barefooted, clothed only in loose-fitting britches, their bare shoulders and backs sun-tanned to a burnished mahogany tone, Ysidro Silvas and Luis Morillo had been cutting wild-grass hay in the meadow back there at the Frenchmen's camp only a few short hours ago, and at that time there had been no thought of trouble. Now, with their hands tied behind their backs and their feet tied securely under their horses' bellies, the two young peons were being led to their death, and each knew that pleading would be useless. Both well knew the ruthlessness of the Linares gang and shuddered, knowing in their hearts that for the victims of the outlaw band death all too often came slowly, after long hours of torture. Froilan Servin's words were not just idle ramblings.

Never once questioning the right of his superiors to give the orders, yet sick at heart that he himself had been chosen to carry those orders out, Luciano El Mesteño looked the two prisoners over, and he thought: They are as I am, a man born to the soil, and not of the gentility. But is that a fault? They have harmed no one. They are friends, *paisanos* (fellow countrymen). Then why must they die?

Yet, even as his mind asked the question, his mind knew the answer: These two young peons had seen a murder committed, and they must not live to tell of that murder.

Back there at the Frenchmen's camp, Monsieur Jose Borel lay dead, and Monsieur Bartolo Baratie (and perhaps Baratie's pretty young wife also) was soon to die.

Back there two nights ago, El Mesteño, Froilan, and six companions had spent the night as guests of the two Frenchmen who had welcomed them hospitably, and the evening had gone by pleasantly enough. The more youthful members of the party had besported themselves as boys will, laughing, joking, and wrestling in friendly competition with these two young peons, now their prisoners.

The older men had lounged around the fireplace, talking, joking, and taking a few drinks from the Frenchmen's wine jug.

Unfortunately, through some slip of the tongue on the part of one of his hosts, Rafael Herrada, the leader of the outlaw band, had learned that the Frenchmen had some gold hidden in their household goods. Their things were still packed in trunks and boxes, for Borel and Baratie were but recent arrivals in San Luis Obispo County, scarcely ten days in their new home along the San Juan River.

This thoughtless disclosure on the part of the Frenchmen was to cost them their lives, for the ruthless Huero Rafael had no scruples where gold was concerned. To slaughter his kindly hosts for their money would give El Huero no qualms of conscience.

Huero would keep the Baraties alive only long enough to find out from them where their gold had been hidden, then they too would be killed, for no one must be left alive to tell of a crime committed. This silencing of witnesses was an unswerving motto of Jack Powers, now the mastermind of the gang. Dead men cannot testify against you!

Nicknamed Huero (fair complexioned), Rafael Herrada always adhered to this policy; for "El Huero" was Jack Powers' trusted friend as well as his lieutenant in the outlaw band.

Luciano El Mesteño's grim reverie was interrupted by a voice near at hand. "Do not kill us, Luciano. We have not harmed you." Luis Morillo spoke haltingly. "We will go far—will not give you any trouble if you free us."

Luciano looked at the youth tied securely to the horse he himself was leading, and in his own soul, the Mesteño was sorely troubled.

Two days ago, Luciano Tapia had met Luis Morillo for the first time; but in that short time, Luciano had come to look upon Luis as a friend. They had wrestled together and had found friendship in the roughhouse play of youth. And now he, Luciano, must slaughter this friend, or he himself would suffer dire consequences.

Jack Powers and his two lieutenants, Rafael Herrada and Pio Linares, were harsh in their discipline should anyone cross them up. Slow but certain death had been the punishment for some who had so brought the wrath of these leaders upon them—those whose misdeeds had been costly to Powers. For lesser crimes against the gang, floggings and occasionally the marking knife and the hot branding iron had been used at the whim of Powers or one of his lieutenants.

It was a strong hold that this gang held over the country between Monterey and Santa Barbara; for the native Californianos would not call in outside aid in controlling the gang's activities. Furthermore, because most of the raids had been directed against the gringo newcomers—unwelcome outsiders—the Californianos would not turn against their own people. Even the more responsible members of old Spanish-California families tended to ignore the raids as long as these raids did not affect them. Also, it was a known fact that several members of the gang were from influential families, so that blood ties were involved.

As for Jack Powers, his own part in the gang's activities was not yet as widely known, for he posed as a cattle buyer and sportsman, and though he had for the past few years been masterminding the gang, he himself seldom joined in the actual holdups. For the most part, it was either Pio Linares or Rafael Herrada who led the men in a raid; and since both Pio and Rafael were from influential Spanish-California families, crimes that either one was involved in would go unpunished.

Not often did gang members rebel against orders given by one of the leaders, for they knew the consequences. Luciano thought back over the three years he had been with the gang and recalled those who had displeased Jack Powers or one of the lieutenants. Reviewing these memories, Luciano shuddered, knowing he himself would suffer a like fate should he incur the displeasure of his superiors.

"Luciano, did you hear me?" The plaintive voice of Luis brought Luciano back to the present. "Luciano, I have never harmed you. Let me go. I beg of you, do not kill me!"

The hopelessness, the fear, the wistful pleading look in the eyes of Luis Morillo smote the latent conscience of El Mesteño. He looked away, for he could not look into the eyes of Luis as he answered, "It is either your life, or mine, Luis. You know I cannot free you! If I did, my own life would be forfeit!"

"Friend Luciano, promise me this then: Kill me yourself! Do not turn me over to *him*!" With a tilt of his head, Luis indicated Froilan Servin, who was leading the horse on which Ysidro Silvas was bound. "I fear what he has in mind — "

Luciano nodded. Death at the hands of the loutish Froilan would be slow and painful. In his heart Luciano knew that the least he could do for these unfortunate captives was to spare them from the sadistic pleasures of the over-eager Froilan.

Grimly Luciano steeled himself to do the slaughtering when the time for the slaughter came. Nor could there be any gain in postponing that which must be done.

"This will be far enough!" Luciano dreaded this stop, but he saw no gain in delaying it any longer. The two captives and their executioners had come about five miles from the Frenchmen's camp and were now along the flats of the San Juan River.

Luciano wrapped the end of the lead-rope around the horn of his own saddle to hold the horse on which Luis was tied, dismounted, then dropped the reins of his own horse to the ground to assure his standing still.

Froilan Sevin clumsily followed suit, eager for the sport he hoped would be in store.

Luciano untied the rope binding Luis' feet, then jerked the captive to the ground, wrists still tied behind his back.

In hopeless desperation over his plight, Luis made one last effort to escape. A quick wrench as his feet hit the ground and Luis slipped from Luciano's grasp, then bounded away, frantically trying to make good his own escape. Though his hands were still bound, making running awkward, fear more than compensated for this handicap.

For a time it looked as though Luis would outrun Luciano, but desperation gave Luciano speed also, and in time he was able to overtake his quarry.

In lieu of a belt, Luis had used a small horsehair rope wrapped several times around his middle, then looped through itself, to hold his britches up. In grabbing for his captive, Luciano found the bare shoulders and ribs of the young paisano slippery from sweat, so he caught hold of this rope belt as he tried to restrain the still frantically struggling lad.

Luciano tripped and fell, but managed to keep a hold on the rope, dragging Luis down with him. Then Luciano was upon Luis, straddling him, holding him down as he bound his ankles with the horsehair rope, hogtying him as he would a *becerro* being tied down for the branding.

The slow-witted Froilan lumbered up, eager for the sport he had been contemplating ever since being assigned as one of the executioners.

Wrists and ankles securely bound, Luis Morillo lay still, helpless to defend himself, vulnerable to the mutilations which Froilan had in mind before finally finishing him off. For Luis well knew the reputation of the outlaw band, knew that torture before death was a common ritual of the Linares Gang, and he could read the gloating pleasure mirrored on Froilan's face.

"*Hijo del asno!* Give me that knife!" Luciano spoke sharply to Froilan. "You will do as I tell you!"

It was characteristic of these two young bandits, each of a similar age and neither outranking the other in the gang, that Luciano should take charge, while Froilan sullenly did as Luciano ordered.

"You are like Pio!" Froilan grumbled. "You want to keep all the sport for yourself!" However, he relinquished the knife to Luciano without further protest.

What must be done must be done! And Froilan's knife would serve the grim needs of the execution! No gain in going back to the horses for the rifle! This Luciano told himself, within his own mind; but his lips were tightly sealed lest he cry. To kill a man, a man who was bound and helpless... to kill a friend...

Luciano knelt, his knees firmly holding the hapless Luis down so that his flinching would not bungle the execution. Then Luciano explored Luis' throat with his fingers, while his eyes avoided those of his captive.

Here! Just below the jawbone! Plunge the knife in here, then jerk it across the throat, severing the jugular vein, the gullet, and the windpipe, all in one quick stroke. With animals, this was the method commonly used in butchering. It should serve the purpose now.

Luciano placed his hand firmly on Luis' chin and held his head to expose the throat for that final stroke of the knife. Resolutely he raised the knife, but he could not plunge it in.

To kill a man in the heat of anger, or in the excitement of battle; this Luciano could do, and could do it without any qualms of conscience. But to slaughter a man bound and helpless... In spite of his wild upbringing, this Luciano Tapia found most repugnant.

Or should he just turn the captives over to Froilan, then ride away and forget the whole matter? Froilan would enjoy the assignment. But this alternative was even more repugnant to Luciano than the other, for he had in the past seen the tortures perpetrated on helpless captives by members of the gang, and he knew Froilan had no scruples against torture killings.

*   *   *

"Callarse la boca, hijo del asno!" Luciano's tone was amiable as he addressed his grumbling companion. "Shut your mouth, son of a jackass, and keep it shut!"

"But, Mesteño, when our companions find out that you let the prisoners go, they will be very angry with you!" the son-of-a-jackass said. "You know the penalty..."

"If our comrades find out that we released the prisoners unharmed, I shall tell them that it was your stupid blundering that allowed their escape! They will believe me, for it is not without cause that you are called son-of-a-jackass!"

Luciano laughed heartily at Froilan's discomfort, then added another dig: "Amigo, keep your mouth shut, or you yourself may even yet experience that treatment you would have so cheerfully worked on another!"

Yet, in his heart, Luciano knew that it would be himself, not the stupid Froilan, who would bear the brunt of their superior's displeasure should the release of the two condemned peons be discovered.

"I wonder if El Capitan Huero has been able to extract from the Frenchman the hiding place of his gold?" Froilan remarked.

"That we will find out when we get back to the Frenchmen's camp," Luciano answered. "Come! The business here is finished! There is no gain in delaying our return."

*   *   *

"Three portion of gold for Jack Powers, *mi patron*—my bosom friend who calls me his trusted right arm; three portions of gold for me, Rafael Herrada, trusted lieutenant and adroit leader in today's most profitable enterprise; one portion of gold each to Desidro, Miguel, Jesus, Santos, and El Mesteño, for their parts in today's operation; one-third of a portion to Pio—*not* the three portions which would have been his as a lieutenant had he taken part in today's business; one-third of a portion to the loutish Froilan—he is worth no more, and too much gold in his possession could be dangerous; and finally, one-third of a portion to la Señora de Linares, for her silent tongue and her generous hospitality."

Pio Linares had gotten cold feet and had run out on his companions just before the actual raid on the Frenchmen's camp, hence he could hardly expect a full cut in the loot; as for la Señora de Linares, Pio's wife, Huero Rafael saw the wisdom of keeping in her good graces; for her house just outside the Pueblo de San Luis Obispo had furnished an excellent hideout for Huero and other members of the gang many times in the past.

Thinking of Pio Linares, his fellow lieutenant, Rafael Herrada, nicknamed "Huero" (fair-complexioned) laughed boisterously. Pio, with his almost psychotic fears of capture, amused Huero no end. Not that Pio Linares was a coward—Pio could face death daringly and had done so many times in the past.

What Pio Linares really feared was capture, capture by friends of some of his victims, capture which might bring a certain treatment, a treatment which Pio had himself administered to other men without compunction.

When first the knowledge of the Frenchmen's gold had been brought to his attention, Pio Linares had been quite enthusiastic about the whole venture; but when certain of the men involved balked at killing a woman, a native Californian like themselves, Pio had developed misgivings. Fearing that Madame Baratie might be spared in spite of his own demands that all persons at the Frenchmen's camp be silenced permanently, and that the woman might later point him out, Linares had left the raiding party just before the raid on the Frenchmen's camp, and he had returned to San Luis Obispo, that he might have an alibi.

Huero Rafael, whose own hands had been bloodied many times in the past, feared neither capture nor punishment. Had not his friend, Jack Powers, with his knowledge of gringo laws, kept members of the gang immune from all vengeful hands!

Take that instance last fall, the killing of the two Basco cattle-buyers, Pedro Obiesa and M. Graciano, for the gold they had carried with them that they might carry on their business.

A drunken bar-clinger, one Juan Pedro Oliveras, had talked too much, had mentioned overhearing a conversation not meant for his ears, and in so doing had incriminated Juan Herrada who in turn, when confronted by the authorities, had incriminated others, including Jack Powers, Huero himself, Pio Linares, and one Nieves Robles as being the ones who had done in the Basco-French cattle-buyers on the Nacimiento.

Robles, the only one named who could immediately be located, was picked up by the authorities, jailed, and booked for trial. But did Jack Powers, who had also been named in that killing, panic and run out on his compadres? He did not!

Jack Powers and Huero Rafael had been safely away, up in San Francisco, spending their share of the loot, when a highly perturbed Pio Linares located them and told them of Robles' having been jailed, and how others suspected of having taken part in the Nacimiento killings had been named and were now on the wanted list.

Instead of prudently removing himself from his old haunts, Jack Powers had brazenly returned to San Luis Obispo, where he himself stood accused of the same crime as Robles, had sought Robles out in his jail cell, had advised him as to how he should plead, and had gotten a lawyer to defend him when the case came to trial.

In the farce of a trial which followed, Nieves Robles was released, and once safely past the risk of conviction due to that "double jeopardy" rule in gringo law, Robles bragged openly of his own part in killing the two Basque cattle-buyers, quoting a quaint folk jingle:

> Ladron qui mata a ladron
> Merecer cien años de perdon
> The thief who kills a thief
> Deserves a hundred years relief (from purgatory)

The claim of the Californians was that since Graciano and Obiesa were dealers in stolen cattle, they deserved to be killed.

With Nieves Robles out of jail and talking too much, Powers advised him to take his bragging tongue elsewhere for a time, on a little vacation. And with Robles gone, the double murder had been forgotten by most, or at least it had been relegated to the limbo of "unsolved crimes."

Yes, Huero Rafael Herrada was complacently free of all worries as as he counted out the gold on that fateful May 12th, in the year 1858, there at the camp of the slain Frenchmen, Jose Borel and Bartolo Baratie, men who so recently had come to the San Juan from Oakland.

Tall, handsome, blond, highly intelligent, Rafael Herrada had often passed himself off as a gringo, for he had early and easily mastered the gringo language. Calling himself Raphael Money, Huero had often accompanied Jack Powers on his "business trips," and gringos who did not know Huero personally were usually impressed by his courtly manners and easy speech.

So far, no one outside the gang members themselves realized that Jack Powers, with a land claim near Santa Barbara, and often seen in the gambling halls of San Francisco and Los Angeles, was in any way connected with the notorious Linares Gang of highwaymen. Nor had Rafael Herrada himself come under suspicion.

"Mi capitan, I shot the man as you requested, but I could not bring myself to shoot the woman..." Somewhat apologetically Santo Peralta made his report to his superior, knowing that subordinates who failed to carry out orders could be in for real trouble.

Just behind Peralta, and leading Madame Baratie with a firm grip on her arm, Desidro Grijalva made his appearance. These two men

had been designated by Huero Rafael to "take care of" Bartolo Baratie
and his wife, and they had taken the unfortunate couple to a willow
thicket some distance from the house for the execution. But they had
only partially carried out that order.

Huero looked toward the woman who, weeping forlornly, had
buried her face in her rebozo, and with callous disregard for the
woman in her grief, he ordered, "Jerk that rag from her face!"

Grijalva complied, and Huero Rafael gave the woman an appraising
look before speaking.

"To slaughter one so fair *would* be a crime—and we commit no
crimes here!" Huero laughed boisterously at his own humor, then
scowled. "Too many orders have been disregarded of late, and this
must stop! If not, we may have to do a little disciplining again! Keep
that in mind, amigos! Keep *that* in mind! In good time, I shall decide
who kills this woman, and he *shall* kill her! The next man who is slack
in his assigned duties will pay heavily for his insubordination!"

To this, Grijalva and Peralta said nothing. Both men knew this was
no idle threat, and neither wanted to risk incurring further displeasure.

"El Mesteño and Froilan should be back soon from their sport with
those wretches they took to dispose of," Grijalva hazarded. "Let them
kill the woman."

"I had thought of that," Huero said, having returned to his jovial
mood, and at the moment of no mind to pick a quarrel with his men.
"We shall see! We shall see!"

"The lady is far too beautiful to slaughter! I know of a much better
solution!" Luciano El Mesteño winked suggestively at his captain. "I
know of a hut far back in the mountains. Give the woman to me, and I
will take her to where she can cause no one any trouble!"

"Amigo, you are a man after my own heart!" Rafael Huero leered
knowingly, then burst into ribald laughter. "You shall have the
woman, Mesteño! However, when you are through with her, do not
turn her loose to talk!"

Rafael Huero was pleased with this solution. The men would all be
satisfied, for none wanted the job of killing the woman, and it was a
code of honor within the gang that a woman so claimed by a member
of the gang must be kept silent by that member, by whatsoever means
he chose.

"Here is your share of the gold, Mesteño. And enjoy your pleasures
to the utmost, amigo!" Huero slapped the Mesteño on the shoulder in

a comradely gesture. "A virile young stallion like yourself will be the better for the experience!" Huero laughed heartily. "The woman is yours! And, Mesteño, I envy you the excitement of breaking her in!"

El Capitan Rafael Herrada gave no thought to the woman, her feelings, her fears—as he gave her to a man she knew only by sight, knew only by the name El Mesteño (The Wild One).

"I leave the woman here with you, Mesteño," Huero said. "Take from the Frenchmen's supplies whatever you need, and go your way when you get ready." Then Huero turned to the other members of the gang: "Come, men, we have work to do! That garrulous old windbag over on the Camate will be telling around all over the country that we spent last night with him unless we shut his damn mouth for him! Remember, amigos, the gringos are still up in arms over the death of those two Bascos last fall, and any other killing which could be traced to us might prove to be more than even El Patron Powers could handle!"

With his comrades gone, Luciano El Mesteño looked at the woman, saw that she was comely and young, and temptation was strong within the wayward soul of the young man known as The Wild One. The woman was his! He had in front of his comrades claimed her, openly, as part of the loot he was entitled to claim. Why should he not take her to some remote camp, have his will of her? Other men did and they were not thought the less of for having done so.

Luciano the Mesteño was truly a virile young stallion, and desire was strong within him. Yet, looking at Madame Baratie (a Californian of English-Spanish birth), Luciano knew here was no *puta de la cantina,* no lightsome lady for a man to take at his own pleasure, then relinquish to some other man. Here was a young woman of high birth and virtue, a young woman who up till now had led a sheltered life.

The woebegone but prideful face of the girl as she silently awaited what to her would be a living death smote the wayward soul of the man who was known as The Wild One, and brought forth from him an inherent gallantry which conquered desire. Luciano could not bear to see that hopeless look in the girl's eyes.

"Señora, give me your word that you will not betray me should we meet strangers along the way, and I will see that you get safely back to your own people."

Looking into the eyes of the young outlaw, the girl saw the change, saw lust change to compassion, and she sensed that this man was different from his companions. Here was no remorseless wolf who preyed without conscience on those whose misfortune it was to cross his path. This young man was like the mustangs he was named for, wild and free. But it was the wildness of environment, not of inherent viciousness.

Impulsively the girl held out her hand. "I will do as you say. I place myself at your mercy."

"I will not harm you," Luciano promised as he took the girl's hand in his own. "My word of honor."

"And I will not betray you," the girl vowed. "My word of honor."

Luciano Tapia—The Wild One—made camp for two, and in his own mind was a strong awareness of the girl who was to share that camp with him, a lonely secluded camp here along the flatlands of the San Juan River. And within the vital young body of El Mesteño was a raging lust-filled desire, and only his word of honor stood in his way.

Honor amongst outlaws? Honor, that its word be binding when lustful desire was so strong? This Wild One had no training of honor, only a crude clumsy code of his own devising; and yet, here is the true yardstick of manhood: that a man have the manhood to hold true to his own code—not blindly to abide by the code set down by others.

It had been late in the afternoon when El Mesteño and Madame Baratie left the Frenchmen's camp, the scene of the brutal murder of two men. For Luciano had had to take the time to run in the Frenchmen's horses, that he might get a mount for the woman. Then with the horses coralled, Madame Baratie had indicated the mare which had been her accustomed mount since coming to San Luis Obispo County. So Luciano had saddled the mare with the sidesaddle which ladies of the time used.

Then, because his own horse was leg-weary and going lame from the long runs after wild horses, Luciano chose a strong well-muscled black gelding from the Frenchmen's *caballada*, for he knew his own life might well depend on the stamina of his mount.

With the horses saddled and ready for the trip, Luciano had hurriedly taken such provisions as he could carry from the supplies in the storeroom of the Frenchmen's house, rolled them in a blanket, then tied the roll behind the cantle of his own saddle. Then, having assisted the girl to her saddle, Luciano had led the way as the two rode from the scene of the double murder. For neither could face a night spent in this death-haunted camp.

It had been with high hopes that the girl had come to the isolated ranch on the San Juan scarcely ten days before, to share the future with a husband who, though older than she, had won her affections. And now, that husband lay dead in a willow thicket back of the house she was leaving.

Neither the man nor the girl spoke much as they ate their evening meal, yet each was keenly aware of the other. Neither ate much, for the brutal events of the day had robbed them of hunger; yet each knew that eating was essential, for they must have strength for the long grueling journey that was ahead of them.

They both knew they dare not take the old Mission Trail known as El Camino Real up through the Salinas Valley, for there was too much chance that they would be seen and recognized, and El Capitan Huero must never know that the Mesteño was disregarding his instructions to take the woman far back into the mountains, away from any chance she might try to escape.

Luciano knew the only chance they had would be to cross the Temblor Mountains, then take El Camino Viejo. That ancient trace along the east side of the Diablo Range was the only alternate route northward; and Luciano knew that even this route must be traversed with caution. For most of those who did travel this bleak inland trail were outlaws who for reasons of their own did not wish to be seen.

Since the handshake which had bound their exchange of promises, the girl had meekly followed the man's lead, never once questioning his plans nor his motives; yet in her heart the girl knew her peril, sensed the lustful desire within the man, knew that his way of life had required little in the way of self-discipline. Yet, in spite of this, she somehow trusted his word of honor, trusted his inherent manhood.

Temptation spoke strongly to El Mesteño, as he laid the saddle-blankets on the ground, to form a crude bed. A bed to be shared with a softly yielding woman here in the river flats, surrounded by lonely windswept hills?

Why not! Here was no wildcat woman who must be tamed before the taking. Here was a girl of gentle raising, and her spirit was well nigh broken by the tragedy of the day.

Luciano knew that if he insisted, he could have his will with the girl. Then, why not? Other men did so, and they were not thought less of for so doing.

"Señora, your bed is ready." Luciano indicated the blankets. "We have a long day's ride tomorrow, and you will need the rest."

All the blankets for one bed? The girl's eyes spoke the question that she dared not ask. What else could she expect? Here was a man who took what he wanted without asking, an outlaw traveling with a notorious band, and her woman's soul told her what this man wanted.

"You will need the blankets for warmth. I do not. I have slept on the ground many times in the past." The man had read the question in the eyes of the woman, and he had answered as though she had spoken. "Here! Take this knife! You will feel safer with it close to your hand in the darkness."

Luciano held out to the girl the knife he had taken from Froilan earlier in the day. Then a wistful little-boy note crept into his voice as he added, "But you have nothing to fear. I gave you my word of honor."

"Thank you for offering me the knife, Luciano, but I know that I shall not need it while you are here to protect me," the girl answered. "I will feel safer if you yourself keep the knife, in case of some danger in the night."

And in her gentle trust, the girl had her greatest protection, for that trust strengthened the first chivalrous impulse which had prompted the untamed youth to offer assistance to a girl he had never even seen until just a few days back.

*   *   *

Grimly, doggedly grim, the horsemen followed the faint trace known as El Camino Viejo, having picked up the trail of Luciano Tapia, known also as El Mesteño. As ruthless in their righteous vengeance as the most ruthless men of Jack Powers' gang, these horsemen—these gringos—were in no mood for leniency as they set about ridding the world of miscreants and malefactors. Two men had already dangled from their ropes back there in the glaring sunshine along the dusty streets of El Pueblo de San Luis Obispo, had strangled their last gasping breath through their rope-throttled throats as they swung from the iron grillwork of the old jail-house gate.

More men were to dangle, strangling, there on the old iron jail-house gate, strangling for sins they had so freely confessed ere the vengeful noose tightened; were to die ingloriously ere vigilante justice was at last satisfied.

Cynically Dame Fortune had turned her back on the villainous band of highwaymen, had at last turned her back on Jack Powers and his gang whom she had heretofore favored even though their crimes had been grievous. With wry cunning had fickle Fortune done the unforeseen, the unforeseeable.

Ysidro Silvas and Luis Morillo, whose lives had been spared by Luciano, had not gone into hiding; neither had they fallen into the hands of Jack Powers and his men, nor had they fallen into the hands of Powers' lackeys, the law-enforcement men of San Luis Obispo County. Instead of going into hiding, Silvas and Morillo had gone to El Rancho Huer-Huero and there had told their grim tale of slaughter and robbery to David Mallagh, the Irish sea captain whose fearless wisdom had made him an acknowledged leader amongst the gringo newcomers, and forthwith Captain Mallagh had set about bringing the murderers to justice.

A search of the nightspots in San Luis Obispo had been made, the local sheriff in charge of this search, and with Silvas along to point out suspects. Santos Peralta, joyously celebrating in *la cantina* with money he could not readily account for, had been identified by Silvas as one of the men who had taken part in the murders, and Peralta was then arrested by the sheriff and taken to the local jail. This arrest was made under pressure by the "Americans."

Santos Peralta, who had so callously shot and killed the wounded Baratie under Rafael Huero's orders back there at the Frenchmen's camp, had confessed as the vigilantes' rope was placed around his neck—had confessed to everyone else's sins, but not to his own.

Peralta had told how the Mesteño had claimed the woman as his own—as a part of the spoils of the raid, damning The Wild One in the eyes of the *Americanos*. Then as chance would have it, a traveler had spoken of seeing a man and a woman answering the description of El Mesteño and Madame Baratie make an overnight stop in Las Polvarderas, on their way north along El Camino Viejo. So a hastily-formed posse of vigilantes had set out from San Luis Obispo, trying to pick up the trail of El Mesteño and his presumed captive.

Thus, unknowingly, El Mesteño, who was returning to San Luis Obispo County, was riding to meet Fate, even as Fate, personified by the vigilantes, was riding to meet El Mesteño.

*   *   *

Seated by his lonely campfire in the gathering dusk of evening as it settled down over the vast San Joaquin Valley, Luciano Tapia, called El Mesteño, thought back over the swift happenings of the last ten days. Meanwhile, the black gelding which Luciano had taken from the Frenchmen's *caballada* cropped contentedly at the sparse grass of the windswept plain, for a horse cares little who his master is as long as that master is humane.

For the first time in his lonely life, Luciano felt lonesome—forlorn and alone, though often in the past he had been alone. Keenly did the young man miss the presence of the girl, the companionship—the physical presence—of the girl.

In that week the two had traveled together, Luciano had come to know love—the honest love that a man may know for the one woman precious to him. Nevertheless, not once during that week of continuous association did Luciano speak of that love to the girl; an inner sensitiveness told him that the tragedy which she had gone through had, for the time being at least, frozen within her soul all responsiveness, had left her with only a passive acceptance of Fate.

Throughout that week of traveling together, Luciano had known that he could have taken the girl—could have had his will of her, could have kept her, meekly submissive, for as long as he wished. But to have done so, he would have possessed only the spiritless shell of the woman, and it had been the spirited whole that he had wanted.

Yes, for Luciano the Mesteño the week of travel up along El Camino Viejo had been one of repressed desires, foreign to his willful nature. And yet, in a way, the reward for his own restraint had been most soul-satisfying to this mustang youth. The trusting gratitude in the eyes of the girl as she said goodbye there in the house of Chavez had been Luciano's reward, and he knew within his own soul that the respect and gratitude of the girl had been the reward he most wanted.

Having reached the mission town of San Juan Bautista, Luciano had left the girl at the home of one Chavez, with instructions that she be placed on the first stage leaving for Oakland, where she had relatives who could see to her future. Then, on an impulse as he said goodbye, Luciano had given the girl the gold which Rafael Herrada had portioned out to him as his share of the loot, retaining only $20 in coin for his own immediate needs.

Then the channel of Luciano's thoughts changed as almost sheepishly he reviewed in his mind that episode of the two peons condemned to death, and his own seeming weakness in freeing them unharmed. Why must he always be so squeamish! Why had he turned sick to the stomach at the thought of a deliberate killing?

To hold a place in this wild land, a man must be strong! Yet, when given a responsibility by his superiors within the outlaw band, he had sickened, and he had failed to carry out those orders.

Was it the fear of his own death that made him fear the death of another? Was it a dread of pain to himself that made him dread pain for another? Would he have been stronger—more of a man—to have slaughtered the two hapless youths? Or, not wishing to kill them himself, to have turned them over to Froilan?

The robbery of aliens Luciano could understand, for were not these newcomers robbing the native Californianos of their land? Killing in self-defense, or in anger, Luciano could understand also, for was not this the way of all life! But, the wanton slaughter of defenseless men —

There had been that incident last fall, the robbery and murder of those two Bascos, Graciano and Obiesa, shot from their saddles while out looking for stray horses, then dragged to death at the end of the bandits' reatas. Nor had they been the only victims of the bloodthirsty gang.

Only a few weeks back, there had been that party of five travelers, taken off guard in their camp along the Nacimiento; five men who had amiably invited certain members of the gang to join them for supper; five men who had carelessly laid aside their guns for the evening.

The bones of those too-trustful wayfarers even now lay bleaching in the sun, or moldered in the shade of the dense willow thickets of the Nacimiento. And the deaths of those five men had not been pleasant to witness.

Nor had these atrocities been the only ones committed by the gang; Pio Linares and his cutthroat followers had been waylaying travelers along El Camino Real, between San Luis Obispo and Monterey, for over ten years, robbing and all too often killing their victims, with torture and mutilations reminiscent of Apache methods all too common.

While professing to view the gang's activities with pious horror, there were those amongst the native Californianos who were not above using the gang to further their own personal ends—like that incident of a couple of years back, of the young Texas cowboy who had so foolishly courted the pretty daughter of one of San Luis Obispo's leading citizens. Though the young Texan had courted the girl openly and honorably, his attentions had been resented by the girl's father, who had ordered the Texan away. Then, when the Texan had attempted to contact the girl without the father's knowledge, the father had called upon Pio Linares and his band of ruffians to discourage the Texan in his unwanted attentions by whatever means they saw fit.

Linares and several members of his rowdy pack had waylaid the Texan as he rode along an isolated trail some distance from town, and they had roped him and dragged him from the saddle, overpowering him before he could do anything to defend himself. And Linares' method of bringing home to the hated gringos that their attention to California women would not be tolerated by the Californianos had been brutally effective.

The Texan cowboy had survived his ordeal, but he could not identify his assailants, for they had all been masked. And though the Texan's friends had been unable to bring the local lawmen into any form of investigation, the incident had not been forgotten, and even yet was a festering source of resentment on the part of the gringos.

Nor had this harsh treatment of men not in the gang's good graces been confined to members of alien races only. Discipline of those *paisanos* who had run afoul of the wishes of Jack Powers, or the whims of either of his lieutenants, could be equally severe.

Luciano, in his mind, reviewed the events of the three years he had been with the gang—and the picture his mind conjured was not reassuring.

There had been the case of Jorge Gomez, nicknamed Gansaron Zompo, a member of the gang for many years, whose duties had been to supply the gang with provisions at such times as it seemed prudent to remain in hiding. But Gansaron had been greedy, and he had tried to short-change Huero on one order he had been commissioned to buy.

As a penalty for his cupidity, Gansaron had been stripped to the waist and tied, arms outstretched, to the poles of a corral. Then he had been given fifty lashes with a horse-whip across his bare back and shoulders. Gansaron had lain unconscious for several hours after the flogging, his back a sodden blood-clotted mess of whip-cut skin, which had left permanent scars.

But Gansaron had come off easy at that, for death, slow and painful, could have been the penalty for such a crime against the gang—like the unfortunate Ruiz.

While in San Jose, Miguel Ruiz, also a member of the gang, had, for a price, given information which could have badly upset the gang's hold on the strip of El Camino Real between Monterey and Santa Barbara had not Powers found out in time to circumvent this attempt to wrest control from him.

The traitorous Ruiz had been waylaid, then taken deep into the back country, and there he had been given a mock trial and sentenced to die. As a pack of dogs worrying a coyote, the gang had had their sport with the doomed wretch, ripping the clothing from his body, then gouging him with splintered sticks and laying the quirt to him. Then they had given the screaming wretch an apparent chance to escape by running off through the chaparral, stark naked though he was.

But that seeming escape had been but a cruel ruse, for Jesus Valenzuela, an expert with the reata, had mounted his horse, then set out in pursuit of the fleeing Ruiz. Jesus had roped Ruiz, then dragged him, but had kept the horse to a slow lope that the sport not be over too soon.

The agonized shrieks of the doomed man had grown weaker, then at last stopped, and the body, at first wildly flailing, had grown limp in death. Only then did Jesus stop his horse, to remove his reata from the rope-skinned ankles of his victim, whose body was left unburied for the buzzards to strip the flesh from the bones.

Wryly Luciano thought of the probable penalty should his own dereliction to duty in freeing the condemned Morillo and Silvas be discovered by some member of the gang. That penalty would depend on many things. The temper of Jack Powers at the time the matter was brought to his attention and the degree of damage to his plans through a subordinate's disregard of orders were the factors most likely to shape the punishment.

Luciano shuddered, then shrugged. What will be will be! Why worry over a contingency which would probably never take place! Ysidro Silvas and Luis Morillo were not fools! By now, they should be long gone and well hidden. Surely they would not risk their own lives by showing their faces anywhere within the range of the gang's activities! They knew, as did everyone else, that Jack Powers controlled the law-enforcement agencies in both Santa Barbara and San Luis Obispo Counties.

The only chance for life that either Silvas or Morillo had would be in fast flight and a far distant hiding place; and surely they would not risk their own lives!

That he himself should run and hide had never once entered Luciano's mind. This was characteristic of the nature of the young man. Had he been of a more cautious nature, he would have recognized the prudence of making himself scarce. From San Juan Bautista it would have been a simple matter to have headed northeast, into the obscurity of the gold fields, with their constantly moving population, where a man who wished to lose his identity could easily do so. But he was from the southlands, and northern California held no appeal to him.

Luciano's reverie was interrupted when the black horse, tethered nearby, raised his head and nickered, signifying the approach of someone, or something.

Luciano gazed into the gathering gloom of nightfall, but at first could neither hear nor see anything to have caught the horse's attention. Then the faint sound of hoofbeats; then shadowy forms converging as horses with riders surrounded the camp. And for Luciano: first apprehension, fearing the newcomers were avenging agents of the gang; then relief.

These riders coming into the light of the campfire were but gringos! Not to be taken seriously!

"Señores, dismount. I will make for you some fresh coffee." Luciano spoke politely, but in Spanish; for his mastery of the English tongue was slight. "Some tortillas, if you wish — "

"Buster, it is *you* we want! Not your tortillas, or coffee!" The leader of the vigilantes spoke in English, his own use of the native language being limited. "That black horse you have tied there—he was one belonging to the Frenchmen you and your henchmen killed!"

"Why—what is it that you want of me?" The bewildered young man could see this was no chance meeting, and not being able to comprehend the accusation, he was at a loss to explain. "I have done nothing — "

"Innercent!" sneered one of the posse. "I ain't never yet seen a damn greaser what weren't as innercent as a fresh-foaled babe when ketched wi' the goods on 'im!"

"Hang the bastard here'n now!" This was from another member of the band. "Them shysters back in San Luis will jest turn 'im loose!"

Another posse-man snickered, then said, "Use his own rope! We don't want fer to dirty our'n!"

To say the least, Luciano's mastery of English was faulty, and the Spanish of most of the men of the posse left much to be desired; so perhaps this lack of adequate communication might excuse the vigilantes for what may, to a later-day reviewer, seem a flagrant miscarriage of justice:

Luciano Tapia, known also as El Mesteño, was taken back to El Pueblo de San Luis Obispo, and there he was hanged by the vigilantes. Hanged, dangling, from the old jail-house gate. Hanged until he strangled, there in the sunshine of the dusty little town. Hung there on that iron gate until he gasped his last breath. Hanged as a ne'er-do-well, a useless malefactor—a miscreant; hanged as a horse-thief—that black gelding found tethered near Luciano's camp had been identified by several as being one of the horses which had been purchased previously by the murdered Frenchmen; hanged as a despoiler of women—the vigilantes having either failed to understand the young man's explanation that he had taken Madame Baratie to a place of safety; or else, understanding, they did not believe but chose instead to believe the worst alternative.

*   *   *

AUTHOR'S NOTE: This story rates as about two-thirds "history" and about one-third "legend" (and practically no fiction at all— fiction only to the extent of "emoting" the characters), for in his letters to the San Francisco *Bulletin,* written during the time of the vigilante action in San Luis Obispo, Walter Murray, a resident of San Luis Obispo, gave precise details of the whole of the French Camp incident.

Luciano Tapia's part in this drama is given by Mr. Murray: El Mesteño's release, unharmed, of the two peons whom he had been ordered to kill; of his claim to the woman, to be taken to some remote hideout, and of his subsequent chivalrous action where the woman was concerned; of his capture by the vigilantes; and of his hanging as a "malefactor."

Madame Baratie was later located among friends in Oakland; and she was induced to return to San Luis Obispo to give her account of the murders. She told of being present when her husband, wounded and unarmed, was shot down by Peralta, and how she herself had placed her husband's hat and cloak over his body before she was forced to go back to the house.

Madame Baratie verified Luciano's story of their trip, saying the young outlaw had offered to take her to where she could get transportation back to Oakland where she would be among friends if she would promise not to betray him, and how he had honorably carried out that promise. But the truth came too late for El Mesteño. He had already been hanged.

Sardonically, Fate had played a wry joke on Jack Powers, his pal Rafael Herrada, their cohort Pio Linares, and the outlaw gang that he captained, a gang whose brutal crimes had gone unpunished for so many years. For it was not the brutality of these crimes which had brought about the downfall of the gang. Instead, it had been that one act of compassion, when he who was called The Wild One freed the two peons he had been ordered to slaughter, which ended the gang's long reign of terror. For it had been the chain reaction following that initial identification of Santos Peralta by Ysidro Silvas that disrupted the gang. And so, because he had freed Silvas, starting that chain reaction, Luciano El Mesteño was hanged.

And now, having touched upon this gang's activities in this tale from the long ago, perhaps a portion of this chapter should be given over to what the old-timers of San Luis Obispo County referred to as The Linares Gang.

THE LINARES GANG

Back in the days of the Franciscan fathers, it had been the custom of travelers coming up from Sonora to stop over in El Pueblo de San Luis Obispo, and while there to go to the Mission and give thanks to The Holy Virgin for their safe arrival; or when returning to Sonora, to stop again at the Mission, to pray that the Saints be with them on that long perilous journey back across El Camino del Diablo.

Although the Mission San Luis Obispo had been "secularized" in the years of Mexico's rule, the powers that be had "graciously granted permission" for one priest to reside in a back room of the Mission that he might care for the spiritual needs of the town, and to perform such needful ceremonies as weddings, christenings, and funerals. Thus, although the Mission had been stripped of its ranch lands, the church itself continued to be a shrine for trail-weary travelers coming into town.

Then came the discovery of gold up near Sacramento, and once word reached the southland, gold-seekers came in ever-increasing numbers, from Mexico and Central America, up through Sonora, then by way of San Diego, then on up the coast, passing through San Luis Obispo, on their way to the gold fields of the northern Sierras.

"Alcalde" Jesus Luna (so local legend has it) saw in these travel-weary wayfarers sheep to be shorn; and so he decreed that these travelers passing through San Luis Obispo must pay one peso per head for the "privilege" of praying in the Mission sanctuary. Nor could these travelers avoid paying this tax by by-passing the town; for Alcalde Luna had his "enforcers" to discourage this "neglect towards pious obligations."

With caravans of Sonorans, often numbering several hundred persons to a band, coming up through California along El Camino Real quite regularly, Alcalde Luna had a most profitable racket over several years; and (so legend has it) Pio Linares became one of Luna's "lieutenants," leading a pack of ruffians who harassed those travelers who tried to avoid the tax by by-passing the town. If old-timers' accounts are to be believed, Linares used sadistic and brutal methods to discourage those travelers unwilling to pay this arbitrary toll. The hot branding iron and the marking knife were favorites, with one or two of the immigrant bands' more defiant members being singled out as a warning to the others.

Although San Luis Obispo had officially become a county (with 336 residents, according to the 1850 census) following California's admission as a state in 1850, and though an "American type" of government had been set up for the county at that time, the residents were largely Californians—citizens under the treaty with Mexico, and Mexican nationals who could claim United States citizenship simply by lying about the date they had crossed the border. So, in Central California, old ways were still prevailing in 1858, the year the French Camp murders took place.

In his letters, Walter Murray complained that "Americans were but a corporal's guard," with almost no authority to enforce the law, and the "Californians" made no effort to bring criminals to justice as long as the victims were *hueros* (people of light complexion).

Embittered by wrongs, both real and imaginary, committed by the aliens who had swarmed over the Mother Lode Country in the decade following the discovery of gold in 1848, even the more responsible Californianos were inclined to look the other way when a crime was committed, as long as the victims of the bandits were the hated foreigners. Also, it was a known fact that several members of the gangs infesting El Camino Real were from influential families; hence family loyalties were involved.

Known members of these gangs all too often sat on juries when their compadres were brought to trial, making of such trials a travesty of justice.

Walter Murray wrote: "Scarcely a month has passed without the disappearance of some traveler, or the finding of dead bodies or skeletons on the roads leading north or south from here...As many as four bodies have been found on the road at one time...It seemed as though there was an organized band of murderers, with spies posted..." (to tell of men who might be carrying money on their persons, especially cattle buyers who perforce must carry money to do business, and men from the mines who might have acquired some wealth).

In time Jesus Luna was replaced as *alcalde* (old records would seem to give his office as that of justice of the peace in the years after San Luis Obispo officially became a county under the laws of the United States). Shortly thereafter (about 1856), Luna went into partnership with an American named George Fearless on a small ranch along the Nacimiento River, and a few months later Fearless disappeared under suspicious circumstances.

Luna sold his partner's personal effects, along with both partners' equity in the ranchito, then took off for "the New Mexico Territory," with the "Americans" of San Luis Obispo County resentful that no effort had been made by the "Californians" to hold Luna for questioning. Then, somewhat later, a body believed to be that of Fearless was found on the ranch, but by then Luna was long gone.

It was about the time Jesus Luna "skipped the country," ending his influence with the Linares gang, that the soldier of fortune Jack Powers and his *brazo derecho* (right arm) Rafael Herrada first made

their appearance on the San Luis Obispo scene, and shortly thereafter these two men formed an alliance with Pio Linares and his band
of cutthroats.

With the astute Powers masterminding the gang's activities, yet
managing to keep up the role of respectable businessman, the gang's
scope was greatly enlarged, taking in most of El Camino Real between Monterey and Santa Barbara. Unsuspected by the people they
came in contact with, Powers and Huero Rafael mingled at gather-
ings; and no doubt they were able to gather much information on the
travel plans of men who perforce must carry money on their persons.

As for Pio Linares himself, it would seem he had launched upon a
career of crime at a tender age; for it was said he was taking part in
holdups while still in his teens. He claimed to have taken part in
several "revolutions" during those years of Mexico's internal troubles.
Perhaps. Perhaps he was just bragging.

In time Pio Linares had formed a band of his own, a self-styled
"captain amongst the young Californians," and he openly bragged of
starting another revolution, to "free California from the gringos." He
was notorious even among his fellow countrymen for his sadistic
practices. If one is to judge by the word-of-mouth accounts of old-
timers, Californiano as well as "American," the methods followed by
the gang in their slaughter of holdup victims were gruesomely brutal,
subjecting their victims to torture and mutilations before finishing
them off.

Thus was set the stage for the vigilante action of 1858. The newspapers of the time gave statewide coverage to the French Camp
murders, along with the "silencing" of Jack Gilkey, and the subsequent vigilante action in which six men were hanged and one shot
(and one posse-man killed, and at least three other men of the posse
seriously wounded by the bandits).

In letters by Walter Murray of San Luis Obispo to the San Francisco *Bulletin*, details of these crimes (the Nacimiento murders of M.
Graciano and Pedro Obiesa, the Basque cattle dealers, on December
1, 1857; the French Camp murders of M. Jose Borel and Bartolo
Baratie on May 12, 1858; and the killing of Jack Gilkey on the
Camate that same evening), and of the subsequent vigilante action
are given, and these accounts would seem to be accurate; for they
were written about the time of the vigilante "trials" of the captured
men (June 1858).

These letters by Walter Murray were reprinted in Myron Angel's *History of San Luis Obispo County*, first published in 1883.

As to Pio Linares: Walter Murray tells us that following disclosure of the French Camp murders by Morillo and Silvas, a posse formed and went to the ranchito owned by Pio Linares, situated just outside town, and there, from a point of concealment, Silvas pointed out certain of the men involved in the murders of the Frenchmen. Unfortunately, before the posse could close in on them, several of the men identified by Silvas escaped through a ravine in back of the house.

Pio Linares, his wife, his brother, and an unidentified man remained in the house where they had barricaded themselves, prepared to "shoot it out" with the posse.

The lawmen (for in this instance the posse was headed by the local sheriff, with a legal warrant) set fire to the thatch roof of the house, and shortly Pio's wife, his brother, and the other man came out of the building. But Pio himself remained inside the burning house.

As to Pio Linares' morbid fear of capture and what capture might bring him, Walter Murray tells us (and here I will quote verbatim):

Well, Linares' reply made to his wife, his brother, and another man—all of whom were allowed freely to pass and repass by the Sheriff and his posse—made to their urgent solicitations that he should surrender, was simply this: *"No! yo no salgo me!..."* No! I'll not go out! They'll...me! The editor of the *Clamor* can supply the blank. It is fit only for assassins and their defenders.

Just what was this fate so fearful that Pio Linares would rather be roasted alive in the burning house, or be shot to death while attempting escape, rather than risk capture by those who had set out to avenge his victims? Amigos, we will never know. For the editor of *El Clamor Publico* (a Spanish language, anti-gringo newspaper of the time) has been dead for lo these many years and cannot now tell us.

Pio Linares, however, did escape from that burning building, and for a time he remained free. His wife, under the ruse of pleading with him to surrender, placed herself in such a position that Pio, using her as a shield, made good his escape into the ravine used earlier by certain of his confederates.

Julian Garcia, "a brave fellow," pursued Linares into the ravine, and in the cross-fire Julian was seriously wounded. Fortunately, he survived his wounds, and in later years, Don Julian Garcia was one of San Luis Obispo County's most beloved and respected citizens.

Although he had escaped capture at this time, Pio Linares and certain of this confederates were later cornered in a willow thicket on the Los Osos Ranch, about ten miles from town.

In the exchange of gunfire, John Matlock, a member of the posse, was killed, and two other men were seriously wounded by the outlaws. Then a chance bullet fired into the thicket hit Linares in the head, killing him. And seeing their "capitan" fall, Miguel Blanco and Desidro Grijalva surrendered.

Blanco, who had shot Borel on the French Camp, and Grijalva, who had shot and wounded Jack Gilkey on the Camate (Gilkey had been "finished off" by Jesus Valenzuela, who had roped him, then dragged him to death) were taken back to San Luis Obispo and there given a summary trial. They "confessed" and were hanged by the vigilantes.

Later evidence would seem to indicate that Huero Rafael, and possibly other members of the gang, were in hiding in the *monte* (thicket) at the time but managed to escape detection and had gone their way after the posse had left with their captives.

Apprised of the fact that Santos Peralta had been picked up by the vigilantes, had "confessed" and been hanged, Jack Powers, who had masterminded the activities of the gang, quite prudently removed himself to parts unknown, leaving his compadres to "face the music" without his assistance.

There are various versions of Jack Powers' eventual demise. In the Myron Angel book, we are told that Powers escaped into Sonora, but that a few years later some Yaqui Indians whom he had defrauded roped him and dragged him to a slow death out in the desert, then left the body for the coyotes and buzzards to clean the flesh from the bones.

There was, however, another version of Jack Powers' earthy exit as told by certain old-timers, and that story went something like this:

Jack Powers and certain of his cohorts got into a hassle over some issue, and his vexed compadres took Powers and threw him into a pen where a bunch of hungry hogs were waiting to be fed, whereupon the voracious porkers "ate him alive."

The vengeance of the vigilantes had been swift and uncomprising. Within one month, almost to the day, from that fateful May 12th when Jose Borel, Bartolo Baratie, and Jack Gilkey had been murdered, six men had been hanged there in the sleepy little town of San

Luis Obispo—had died in the bright June sunshine in that eventful year of 1858—and one man had kicked his last kick in a willow thicket, a bullet having shattered his brain. For Pio Linares, who had feared capture and what capture might bring to him, had chosen death to surrender, had fought with the ferocity of desperation until a chance bullet brought him down.

These seven men were dead, and six more men, named as having taken part in either the Nacimiento murder of the two Basques or the French Camp murders, were in hiding—hiding like rats routed from a burning barn.

Santos Peralta, Miguel Blanco, Desidro Grijalva, and Luciano Tapia, all named by their confederates as having taken part in the French Camp murders, were hanged, as was Jose Antonio Garcia, who was involved in the Nacimiento murders. Pio Linares, named as having taken part in both crimes, had been shot while resisting arrest.

Jack Powers, Huero Rafael Herrada, Jesus Valenzuela, Nieves Robles, Froilan Servin, and a man identified only as Eduviquez, all named by their fellow conspirators as having been involved in these crimes—as those fellow conspirators were being hanged—were in hiding.

Somewhat later, Nieves Robles was picked up in Los Angeles, returned to San Luis Obispo, given a hasty "trial," and hanged, bringing the number of "miscreants" hanged by the vigilantes up to seven.

Still later, Froilan Servin was picked up; but by then the vigilantes had been disbanded; and so Froilan was tried in a formal court of law, and in a compromise verdict was given a prison sentence.

Amigos, you say that I say seven men had been hanged by the vigilantes, and yet I have here mentioned only six names of the men who were hanged—and how come?

Amigos, the hanging of Joaquin Valenzuela, alias Joaquin Oco-moreña, deserves a whole story by itself. And anyway, Joaquin Valenzuela had not been involved in any of the above-mentioned crimes. We are told he was hanged "as a warning to all miscreants."

But, enough of that here. Read:

The Pearls of Wisdom

THE PEARLS OF WISDOM

"*Amigos y paisanos!* Friends and fellow countrymen!—and you also, my estimable gringo compatriots! For I bear you no ill will, even though you have robbed me of mine liberty and the pursuit of happiness, and even now are preparing to take from me mine worthless misspent life, still, I bear you no ill will. Compatriots and friends, I ask of you one boon only: Bring here to me *mi patron* Señor Jacky Powers, that I may confer with him before you hang me."

"Your patron saint Sir Jackal Powers won't be getting *you* off the hook, the way he did that boastful killer Nieves Robles!" a member of the vigilantes said. "El Patron Powers is even now skulking off through the sagebrush, his tail 't'wixt his kyotie laigs, trying to save his own mangy hide!"

"Ah-h-h-h!" sighed the condemned man. "Woe is me! I had counted on the wisdom of El Señor Jacky Powers, *mi patron!*" Then an inspiration struck him: "Amigos, a man about to be hanged should be allowed to confess his sins!—for the cleansing of his own soul, and as a warning to other malefactors to mend their ways!"

The vigilantes were not unreasonable men, and this request did not seem unreasonable. "Confess, amigo, confess," said one of the band. "For the cleansing of your own soul, and as a warning to other malefactors to mend their ways!"

"I have many sins to confess!" Joaquin Valenzuela, *bandido muy mucho malo* and badman notorious, standing on an upended whiskey barrel beneath the iron grillwork of the old jail-house gate, might well be wishing to cleanse his soul, for the reata draped across the gate's arch had its noose around his neck. "I have many sins to confess! Many, many sins," Joaquin stated dramatically, but under his breath he said, "Sins enough to keep this noose from tightening for many a long hour!"

"Sure! Let's hear your sins, amigo!" one of the vigilantes said amiably. "Might be interesting."

"*Amigos y paisanos!*—and you also, my estimable gringo compatriots! My sins are grievous! Let mine miserable misspent life, cut short in the fullness of manhood, be a warning to you all!" Joaquin looked his audience over with an appraising eye. So much eloquence—so dramatic a confession—was indeed having its effect. Never before had Joaquin Valenzuela held captive so large and so appreciative an audience. He went on, "Amigos, I humbly beg of you that you listen to *all* my confessions! Do not cut them short! It is for the cleansing of mine soul, and as a warning to all malefactors!"

The gringo vigilantes grinned knowingly, for they could see through Joaquin's ruse. But, Hell! Let the cuss confess! Reprehensible reprobate though he was, still his audacity brought forth admiration.

Joaquin went on, "Which of mine many sins should I confess first?" The audience snickered.

"It is true that I have robbed, and I have killed!" The voice of Valenzuela trembled as the shame of his misdeeds smote his conscience. "But I swear, it was only to feed my poor hungry wife and children, impoverished by the gringos."

"Wife and children!" someone sneered. "You living here in San Luis Obispo with a harlot! Your wife and children left elsewhere, abandoned by you, to shift for themselves!"

"Wives and children should not stand in the way of true love!" Joaquin stated. "Mine true love *la puta mi dulciana* should come first! As virile he-men yourselves, you surely can understand that!"

The snickers went the rounds. Then someone said, "That little Smith girl, Annie—what excuse can you give for the kidnapping of a child from her parents? And for the later killing of her father!"

"La muchachita Ana Smith? I did but rescue her from her doltish parents, that she might grow up in the graces of a Spanish lady. And the fate of Señor Smith? Irate papas are ruthless. It was his life, or mine!" Joaquin sighed, then went on, "But all these crimes are in the past! For one whole year now, I have lived an exemplary life! Señores! Surely! Surely, as a reformed character, my worthless life should be spared, that I may redeem mine miserable misspent life with good works!"

Joaquin Valenzuela looked expectantly at the throng of people gathered to watch the hanging. Such interested faces! So much eloquence had had its effect on the gathering, and the rogue was almost hopeful of a reprieve. But one of the vigilantes amiably doused that hope. "Your miserable misspent life will do more good if we hang you, as a warning to other miscreants!"

"But—but now I am a reformed character—"

"Reformed character!" One skeptical onlooker disbelieved audibly. "What of those two men you shot? And the other two that you carved up so efficiently that they died? Four dead men, and all within the last six months!"

"Those he-dogs! Those reprehensible despoilers of women! They would have seduced mine true love *la puta mi dulciana* hadst I not taken action against them! Surely, as virile he-men yourselves, you canst understand the outrage to my manly pride! Mine need to avenge this dishonor!"

"What aboot them stoled hawsses found in yore c'rral?"

"Those horses found in my corral were not stolen! They were borrowed—not stolen!" Joaquin stated emphatically. "Surely you yourselves borrow horses from your friends—do you not? I consider you all my friends, hence I borrow from you!"

"Those cattle you butchered within the last year! Explain that! Reformed character!"

"If a few valueless *orejanos* succumbed to my reata and knife, it was to feed the destitute—not for my personal gain!" Joaquin explained. "This was but Christian of me!"

"Too much time is being wasted!" an impatient member of the vigilantes snapped. "Let's get on with the hanging!"

"I have not yet confessed all my sins!" Joaquin stated sorrowfully. "I have many *many* sins yet to confess!"

"Confess them in two minutes!" the leader of the vigilantes said. "For in two minutes you shall hang!"

"Amigos, paisanos, and fellow compatriots! Listen most carefully to these pearls of wisdom, from the lips of a man who is about to die! I humbly beg pardon of you, my friends and fellow countrymen, for the grievous wrongs I have done throughout the years of mine misspent life, and mine inglorious death here on this iron gallows, be a warning to all who may here witness mine ignominious death! And to all malefactors amongst you, I now give you this warning! This final pearl of wisdom! Never! Never! NEVER tell your secrets to anyone! Not even to your own closest friends and fellow countrymen! *Porque asi se pierde!*"

"Amigo, paisano, and estimable fellow compatriot! Those pearls of wisdom should warn all miscreants here present that a life of crime ends on the gallows! And you have already confessed enough sins to get you through the Pearly Gates!" an unregenerate sinner remarked. "So! Saint Peter, here comes your next customer!" And with that irreverent sally, the rowdy kicked the upended barrel from under Joaquin's feet, sending one of California's most colorful outlaws to the Great Hereafter. For Joaquin Valenzuela (alias Ocomoreña), hanged in San Luis Obispo in 1858, was at least two of "the five Joaquins" named in Governor Bigler's orders to Harry Love and his Rangers, and around whom the legend of Joaquin Murrieta has been woven..

*   *   *

AUTHOR'S NOTE: Amigos y paisanos, you doubt my veracity? You say, what hokum! What malarkey! You say miscreants do not so freely confess their derelictions? You say such confessions come only in Perry Mason stories? You say such pearls of wisdom do not come from the lips of a man about to be hanged?

Friends and fellow countrymen, here is an account of the hanging of Joaquin Valenzuela, written shortly after the hanging took place (from a letter written June 6, 1858, by Walter Murray of San Luis Obispo, to the editor of the *San Francisco Bulletin*) under the heading: CAPTURE OF ONE OF THE "FIVE JOAQUINS"—HANGED BY THE PEOPLE IN BROAD DAYLIGHT.

The party (of Vigilantes) that went in pursuit spent a week of fruitless search in the hills. The murderers being well mounted, easily eluded them. At the Rancho San Emilio (San Emigdio), however, they took one Joaquin Valenzuela, alias Joaquin Ocomorenia, who was identified by several persons as one of the five Joaquins, who were mentioned in the Act of 1853, authorizing the raising of Harry Love's company of rangers. This man is also an accomplice of Jack Powers, spoke of him as his patron, and is a man steeped to the lips in guilt. He is well known at the mouth of the River Merced, and on the San Joaquin, and owes justice a score which fifty lives can never repay. He was hung in full sight of the whole people of San Luis Obispo, in broad daylight, by the voice and assistance of all the respectable men of the county, and died acknowledging his guilt, asking pardon of his friends, and warning all malefactors not to tell their secrets, even to their own countrymen. "*Porque asi se pierde*" said he—that is: "Thus you lose yourself."

In another report on the actions of The Vigilance Committee of San Luis Obispo, Walter Murray goes on:

Now we come to the innocent Joaquin Valenzuela. This man had never been charged with either the Nacimiento or the San Juan (French Camp) murders. But he was an acquaintance and comrade of the murderers— brother to one (Jesus Valenzuela), chum to another (Pio Linares), and was proven before the committee to be as full of crime as an egg is full of meat. In 1853 he was a partner of Joaquin Murieta—the veritable Joaquin. It is notorious that he was one of the five Joaquins upon whose heads Governor Bigler set a price, and to catch whom Capt. Harry Love's Company of mounted rangers was organized.

Walter Murray goes on to say: "Just before that time he (Valenzuela) kidnapped an American child, Anne, daughter of an American named Smith, and brought her down to the San Joaquin River, where he and his Mexican female partner brought her up to learn Spanish and hate the Gringos. The Americans living there took the child away, and advertised for her relatives."

The little girl's father came to the San Joaquin to claim his daughter. He was met by Valenzuela, who offered to take him across the river in the ferry. Smith disappeared, and it was assumed that Valenzuela had killed him. Later, a skeleton thought to be that of Smith was found along the river, not far from the ferry.

Another crime ascribed to Joaquin Valenzuela was that he and certain confederates stole cattle and horses from ranchers on the Central Coast, drove them eastward through "the tulares," and then on to the mines in the Sierras where they were sold to the miners, who did not ask too many questions.

We are told that Valenzuela became a "captain of a band of robbers" in Santa Barbara County, committing several robberies there. "He is a miscreant of the deepest dye, a hardened sinner, the very type of a criminal."

At least twice in his letters Murray mentions the name Ocomorenia as an alias of Valenzuela, and Valenzuela's presumed earlier association with Joaquin Murrieta is touched upon.

Instead of being an "innocent man torn from the bosom of his family by a mob and done to death," as certain of the newspapers of the time reported, we are told by Mr. Murray: "Instead of living with his wife, whoever that lady may be, he kept an abandoned Mexican prostitute, for whose sake two men have been stabbed, and two (others) shot within the last six months."

And now, ere we close this chapter, say *Adios, amigo, Rest in peace* to Joaquin Valenzuela—one little sidelight on the legend of the Joaquins of the San Joaquin Valley. Just a splintery little sidelight it is true, and yet . . .

Amongst the native Californianos, the legend has come down with surprising frequency that the pickled head which had for so many years been on display as being the head of the great Joaquin Murrieta was not in fact the head of *el bandido notorio*. Instead, many Californians insisted that the head on display was that of a wild-horse runner who at the time of his death had been in the employ of Chico Martinez, who over many years had been engaged in the capture and sale of mustangs running wild in the Gabilan Range of mountains west of the San Joaquin Valley. And here is the way the legend runs:

A group of mesteñeros were camped in La Cañada de Cantua and had just finished breakfast when Harry Love and his Rangers rode up.

"Is one among you Joaquin?" asked the captain of the Rangers.

"*Si! Si! Señores! Si!* I am Joaquin," spoke up one of the mesteñeros.

Whereupon the rangers of Harry Love shot this Joaquin, then chopped off his head. And the name ascribed to this young mesteñero was Joaquin Valenzuela.

This story has come down through the years, both by word-of-mouth and in print. It was in fact circulated widely during the time that pickled head, purportedly that of Joaquin Murrieta, was on display, and even the newspapers of the time printed the story. The head on display was viewed by Californianos who had known Murrieta personally, and many of these denied flatly that the head in the pickle jar was that of Joaquin Murrieta. True, their denial could have come from a desire to embarrass the gringos, though this hardly seems likely had the head actually been that of Murrieta.

This brings up an interesting question: Was the head that was on display actually the head of Joaquin Murrieta? And if not, then whose head was it? Some unfortunate paisano whose misfortune it had been to have been christened Joaquin? Was this head, in fact, the head of some other Joaquin Valenzuela who had come to this untimely end, an innocuous wild-horse runner, not a bad bandido? Could be. Both the given name Joaquin and the surname Valenzuela were quite common in California back in those years.

Or could it be that our Joaquin Valenzuela cheerfully lent his own name to the head of another, that his own foxy head might stay in place a while longer? Could be. Our Joaquin was a sly desert wolf, and I wouldn't put anything past him.

And so, to Joaquin Valenzuela: *Adios, amigo paisano! Vaya con Dios!* Truly wert thou an unprincipled miscreant! And yet—the world is by far a duller place without thee!

Part II
THE
CALIFORNIA BANDIDO

Something of the historic background of the California bandido.

Also

Some comments on Joaquin Murrieta. Was he for real? Or was the fabulous Joaquin but a figment from the fertile brain of a writer of fiction?

THE CALIFORNIA BANDIDO

Because this series of yarns from out of the past does perhaps encompass the Spanish-California bandits more than it does outlaws of other racial origins, something of the historic background of these California bandidos might here be in order.

In treating the subject, many writers in the past have tended to oversimplify the issue, have presented the raids by the bandidos and the retaliations against them as a political conflict between the "Californians" and the "Americans," coloring the incidents in a partisan manner, with the "good guys" all on one side and the "bad guys" all on the other side. This presentation, however, hardly squares with the facts. Actually, the California bandido was a fact of life long before the Americano entered the scene, going back into those first years of the Spanish occupancy in Alta California.

The master plan devised by Carlos III, King of Spain, and his advisors had called for, First: The establishment of army outposts in strategic positions along the coast of Alta California, to ward off those foreign powers which had been casting covetous eyes on this undeveloped west coast of the continent, claimed by Spain but un-occupied; Second: The building of missions, hopefully to bring the natives of Alta California under Spanish control—their immortal souls being of secondary consideration as far as the heads of state were concerned; and Third: The establishment of civilian colonies in Alta California, to be recruited from the by now more or less civilized settlements of New Spain, to insure a loyal Spanish citizenry in the new province.

The army outposts were established with military precision—from the start, Spain's conquest of the New World had been based on her military strength; the California Missions were founded—and certainly the selfless dedication of those first Franciscan Fathers who laid the cornerstones for the chain of missions in Alta California deserves the respect of Catholic and non-Catholic alike; but when it came to bringing in those early civilian colonies—well, the best laid schemes of mice and kings can sometimes go haywire.

For the most part, the citizens of New Spain were very unenthusiastic about the whole plan. Their attitude was, let someone else go trailing away off there in the hostile wilderness! Me, I'll stay home where there is security and plenty to eat!

To get recruits for these outposts of civilization, the governors in New Spain resorted to a combination of threats and cajolery. Citizens at outs with those then in power were given a choice: a transfer of abode to one of the colonies in Alta California—or rot in jail!

To those persons who would agree to move to the colonies, the Spanish government promised amnesty and a guaranteed dole until "such time as the colonies are self-supporting."

Certainly among those first colonists there were many who were looking for a new chance and an honest living in the new land; but also, there was a riffraff fringe, too lazy to work or make any effort to become self-supporting, and who in time became a burden to both the army outposts and to the missions, which had been set up primarily for the conversion of the California Indians.

Along with these ne'er-do-wells, whose greatest crime was slothfulness, there had also been an infiltration of cutthroats and degenerates who had taken advantage of the legal amnesty granted to prisoners who would transfer their talents to the scattered and poorly policed new settlements.

Unlike the colonies of the British, the French, and the Dutch on the East Coast, where whole family groups migrated to the colonies to form settlements that were a transplant of their own Old World culture, the settlements of New Spain were largely military bases.

High-ranking army officers and officials of the Spanish government could afford to bring their wives and other members of their families to fortifications in the New World, and in time there developed a top culture of aristocrats whose way of life was that of the aristocracy of Old Spain. On the other hand, the Spanish foot soldier seldom had either the wherewithal or a place of sufficient security to bring a wife or other kinsfolk from his home province in Spain; for the common soldier was subject to short-notice transfers to other posts, and those in charge gave little thought to his private life.

Craving the pleasures of women companions, these foot soldiers not infrequently took Indian wives, sometimes taking these primitive wives with them when they were transferred to new encampments, sometimes simply abandoning the current "wife" and taking a new one in the new location.

Some of these men with Indian wives legalized the union, and when their tour of duty in the army was ended, they settled down in the New World to take a place in developing the new land, raising their offspring in the traditions of Old Spain. Other men, however, simply abandoned their Indian wives and half-breed children when their tour of duty was over, and returned to Old Spain, to marry there, beget other children, and forget their New World families.

Younger soldiers, starting their tour of duty in the New World, found the half-breed daughters of their predecessors comely and already somewhat indoctrinated into the Spanish way of life; and so these girls of mixed blood were often chosen as the native consorts by these soldiers, thus bringing an added strain of Spanish blood into the melting pot, in time producing offspring whose appearance, temperament, and tastes were more Spanish than Indian. Add to these mixed-blood families of the soldiers the not-infrequent offspring of the aristocrats from Indian servant girls, along with the wild oats of lusty young caballeros, and over a period of nearly three hundred years there developed in New Spain a class of citizenry which had a goodly percentage of Spanish blood on an Indian base, and who followed the customs of the Spanish people rather than those of the Indians.

In time young men of this mixed blood became an important source for army recruitment; they were available, hardy, acclimated, and had a knowledge of the country, whereas the soldiers brought from Spain were often at a disadvantage until they learned the new land. This, however, posed a problem in itself, for by Spanish law, the Indians were considered a sub-species, somewhat lower than human, and by Spanish law the Indians had been forbidden the use of both firearms and horses.

The mission padres perforce had had to ignore that legal prohibition against the Indians using horses and teach their more proficient neophytes the vaquero's art; for they found very few of the *gente de razon* willing to take on this arduous chore without some assurance of wages, and wages to civilians was something the missions could ill afford in those earlier years.

Under the benign tutelage of the mission priests, the California Indians developed real skill in the various work schedules required of them. Nonetheless, even the most liberal of the Spanish padres considered the Indians incapable of self-government, a race of "children" over whom a perpetual guardianship must be kept.

There is a bit of grim irony in the legal terms used by the governing powers of New Spain to differentiate the sub-humans from the humans: *gente sin razon* (people without reason) for the Indians, who had almost no legal rights at all; and *gente de razon* (people of reason) for those with enough Spanish blood to have human intelligence and hence to be trusted with firearms and horses.

Where the line of demarcation was drawn for any given man often depended on that man's loyalty to his superiors. The line could be drawn on the rating of his sire, if that sire had any Spanish blood at all (allowing some men with a fairly large proportion of Indian blood to be *gente de razon*) for as long as that man remained loyal to his superiors. Conversely, a man of mixed blood might be rated as disloyal to his Spanish superiors (sending that man over into the mongrel fringe of outcasts, even though he might have a goodly proportion of Spanish blood).

From the very start of colonization in Alta California, there was a cross-section transplant of the population of the older settlements, from Mexico, Central America, and South America, bringing with them customs developed over nearly three hundred years.

The Franciscan padres brought Indian neophytes up from the older missions in Mexico and Central America to help train the "heathen" tribes of Alta California, hopeful that these "civilized" Indians from the older settlements, being of kindred blood, would inspire the new converts to conform to church discipline. The *gente de razon* was represented in the foot soldiers and the colonists sent into California by the Spanish governors. And over these men of humble circumstance, the Spanish aristocracy came as the ruling class, first as army personnel, then later as land owners, ushering in the golden era of huge land grants and the vast ranchos of romantic legend.

Here again was a somewhat ironic situation in that Spain, which was professing to bring civilization to the heathen of Alta California, was also bringing a fiercely class-conscious code. On the top level was the ruling class, almost exclusively of pure Spanish blood. On the next level down was a colonization of the *gente de razon,* holding something of citizenship rights and bringing with them something of the Spanish culture, even though many of these people were of mixed Spanish-Indian blood. Next down the scale were the Indians and half-breeds who had come up from the south, and who in nearly three hundred years of contact with the Spaniards had absorbed some of the Spanish culture and who looked with contempt on the "heathens" of Alta California. And low man on the totem pole was the native California Indian, whose culture had been far more primitive than had been the cultures of the Indians to the south and east.

Always in New Spain, transplanted to California, there had been a fiercely guarded caste system, those higher up determined to hold down those of a lower class. It was a system that was bound to breed outlawry.

From the start, the governing class in New Spain had looked askance on the "civilized" Indians returning to the wild, for they feared that a knowledge of the white man's weapons and ways could make them dangerous foes. Indians from the wild might be enticed into the mission fold by food and shelter during times of famine, but woe unto this Indian should he attempt to return to his old way of life once the time of famine was past.

Tales told by old-timers of the brutal treatment of runaway Indians by the soldiers sent out to capture them are grim indeed. For a first offender—if he were lucky—a flogging with a rawhide lash could be the punishment. For the "troublemaker" and the chronic runaway neophyte, the punishment could be severe. The red-hot branding iron and the marking knife were upon occasion used as a punishment for some infraction, a permanent reminder to all that opposition to the new order would not be tolerated.

There were old accounts of insubordinate Indians who had struck a superior having a hand chopped off with a sword or machete. The runaway Indian who resisted recapture was shot down without compunction, for he was considered little more than an animal. Under these circumstances it is understandable that the runaway Indian was hard to catch. Very early these runaways learned to avoid the villages of the natives, for these were too easily found by the soldiers.

In time these runaways of the native Indian strains were joined by renegades from the far south, Indians and half-breeds of Mexican tribes who, having come into Alta California as workers, found themselves at odds with those in authority, and chose to disappear into the hinterlands rather then risk punishment. To these in time were added men of the *gente de razon* who, having run afoul of the law, found they had to *vamos muy pronto*. Thus, almost from the first settlement in Alta California, there were outlaw packs roving the hills and living by their wits, by any means possible.

In time raids on the older settlements to run off cattle and horses became a common occurrence; and no doubt many of the raids and killings ascribed to "wild Indians" were in fact perpetrated by these renegades. And all too often it was the innocent who paid the price for the guilty.

From old-timers have come many tales of brutal retaliations against native Indian encampments for some crime committed by a roving band whose identity was never established.

For the most part, the native California Indians—the Salinan, the the Chumash, the Chane, the Tachi, the Tulareño, and other tribes of Central California—were a simple non-aggressive people, in a culture so primitive that they had scarcely reached the big-game hunter stage, living chiefly on fish, mollusks, lizards, insects, and such wild plants, herbs, and nuts as the seasons afforded.

They had greeted the first white men with respectful awe, and it took the "civilizing" influence of the white man to bring out the savage in them.

*   *   *

Fifty years passed from the time of the founding of those first missions in Alta California, rather tranquil years under the benign influence of the Franciscan Fathers, though the seeds of many drastic future changes had already been sown. The California missions now numbered their Indian neophytes in the hundreds, with some of the missions boasting of several thousand converted Indians living within their sphere of influence. Several of these missions had holdings so vast no attempt was ever made to mark their boundaries.

Cattle were not saleable but hides were, so great *matanzas* were held periodically to slaughter cattle (and even horses) for their hides alone, the meat being left for the coyotes and buzzards.

It had been fifty years since the founding of those first missions, and for the most part those dedicated padres who had founded the missions with much personal sacrifice had gone to their Heavenly Reward. A new generation controlled the mission wealth, men all too often more interested in the wealth of the Church than they were in churchly responsibilities. A worldly man of God can be as corrupt as any other, and already there were grumblings both in Mexico and in California over the Church's holding so much of the best land in California under its control.

To add to this resentment against the Church, there was much bitterness in Mexico, and to some extent in California, against the military government forced upon the New World by the autocratic powers of Old Spain. The men holding authority under the King of Spain were all too often arrogant tyrants who turned positions of trust to their own personal advantage. Already there had been several abortive uprisings against the authority of Spain in Mexico and in California.

Then came the revolution in Mexico, culminating in 1822 with the complete overthrow of the Spanish-controlled government and the setting up of a new government, making Mexico an independent nation.

With the overthrow of Spanish rule in Mexico came the rather arrogant assumption by the new powers in Mexico that Alta California, the distant province, was a part of the spoils of conquest, to be used to the advantage of the new liberal government of Mexico.

Those earlier grumblings of the dissidents over the Catholic Church controlling so much land in Alta California were turned to advantage by the new faction controlling the government of Mexico. Those in power during the early 1830s, claiming the welfare of the common people as their excuse, confiscated the Church's property in Alta California, and shortly thereafter the vast mission-held ranchos were carved up and dished out as political plums to those who had played their cards right during the years of conflict.

There had been some land grants to private individuals under Spanish rule, but now, under the new government in Mexico, private land grants to those who could curry favor with those in power were made in Alta California, carving up the old mission ranch holdings, ushering in the glamorous Golden Days of the Dons.

In this breaking up of the old mission ranchos, those very same "liberals" who had so bitterly resented Spanish rule completely ignored the rights of the converted Indians living thereon, most of

them born on the ranchos and reared under the paternalistic supervision of the mission padres. The mission Indians were kicked out of
the only homes they knew and left to fend for themselves. Some of
these mission-raised Indios sought employment on the haciendas of
the aristocrats who had acquired their land, working as vaqueros,
shepherds, and day laborers; others simply reverted to their old
roving ways. Under these circumstances, is it any wonder that some
of these displaced persons should turn to pilferage when the opportunity presented itself.

In spite of their unpromising beginnings, those early civilian settlements had increased through the mission years, mostly in the form of
villages in the benign shadow of the old missions. Under the en-
couragement of the new government in Mexico, additional settlers
made the long trek by way of El Camino del Diablo, heading for Alta
California. Some were planning to settle on lands promised them,
others to seek employment on the ranchos of the wealthy or in the
budding industries of the towns.

For the most part, these Sonoreños, as they were called, were of
the working classes, and in starting for the new land they usually took
all their worldly goods with them. The more affluent might come
fairly well equipped, others had scarcely enough supplies for the trip.
Some rode horseback, others walked, leading pack mules or burros.
Family men transported their wives, children, and household goods
in slow-moving carretas drawn by oxen or donkeys.

In theory, these immigrants joined forces and traveled in caravans
numbering up to several hundred persons, counting women and
children, traveling together as a protection against Indian attacks; for
The Devil's Highway crossed through the hunting grounds of the
warlike Apaches and Yaquis, and the Indians not infrequently attacked these poorly guarded travelers. In practice, these caravans
were poorly organized.

Due to the scarcity in the desert of water holes which could accom-
modate a large party, and because of the impatience of the faster
travelers with their laggard companions, these caravans tended to
string out in travel, the vanguard often as much as a week's journey
ahead of the stragglers, with the rest of the party traveling singly or in
small groups in between, camping wherever nightfall overtook them.

Even as these legitimate settlers were heading for Alta California
across El Camino del Diablo, a freebooter fringe of cutthroats was

trailing them, knowing they were vulnerable. Seldom did these caravans have adequate armed support, and knowing this, a band of twenty or so well-mounted and heavily-armed bandits could victimize a whole caravan with little risk to themselves by attacking the scattered groups of travelers separately.

There is little doubt that many of the raids on travelers coming up from Mexico attributed to "wild Indians" were in fact the handiwork of these *cholo* packs who found banditry more to their liking than honest work.

There is a degree of insult in that word *cholo*, whether applied to a man or a dog, for it roughly translates mongrel, and truly many of these packs were mongrels.

In the two centuries just prior to the opening of Alta California, the older settlements of New Spain had developed a class of dissidents with a tradition for banditry. They represented a wide variety of origins: embittered Spaniards who, through reverses of fortune, were forced into a lowered station in life; bastard sons of aristocrats from Indian servants, raised just outside the pale of their legitimate kinsmen and resentful of their subordinate station in life; full-blooded Indians, given a glimpse of the white man's civilization, yet never accepted into that civilization; soldiers who had deserted and must keep on the dodge to avoid court-martial; sailors of various national origins who had jumped ship in western ports to lose their identities among the misfits of the seaport towns; criminals of various national origins who had managed to make their way into Latin America; runaway slaves from the West Indies; misfits and degenerates who found this outcast fringe to their liking; and the ne'er-do-wells who simply preferred the vagabond way of life to the drudgery of hard work.

All these elements went into the melting pot. They lived just outside the pale, an outcast fringe of society; they took women and bred sons to follow their own lawless way of life.

Viewed with suspicion and slurringly referred to as *cholos* by the solid citizens of New Spain, these misfits were constantly being pushed onto the frontier where law-enforcement was lax. Trailing the caravans of settlers, these mongrel packs made their way into Alta California, and a tradition for the California bandido was well-established even before the mission era was over.

During the twenty-five years of Mexico's rule in Alta California, with a migration of settlers coming up from Sonora, and others returning to old homes in Mexico, these cholo packs continued their harassment of travelers, not only on the Sonoran end of the route but along the old mission trail in California as well.

Little was done to curb these bandits, for when soldiers were sent out after them, they simply disbanded and scattered into the back country, later to reform their coyote packs and return to their banditry at some other point along that 2,000-mile route between Mexico City and San Francisco Bay.

Of these bandits of the Mexican years, only a few seem to have been colorful enough to have survived in the folklore of the native Californiano. Perhaps the most notorious of those bandidos whose names did come down through the years was one Domingo Hernandez who, with his gang of cutthroats, harassed travelers along El Camino Real between Ventura and Monterey in the late 1820s and early '30s. Domingo's chief claim to fame seems to have been his grisly collection of trophies taken from his victims. These included a necklace of dried human ears strung on a thong of human hide, and various other articles made of human skin. He is credited with wearing a form-fitting jacket made of human skin, made by skinning the upper torso of one of his victims, then tanning the hide so that the skin of the arms could be utilized as ready-made sleeves for the garment, and with the skin of the neck turned down to form a collar.

*   *   *

The twenty-five years of Mexico's rule in California were far from tranquil ones, and with the passing of over a century and a quarter it is hard now to distinguish between the bona fide *bandido bravo* operating on his own initiative and the riffraff hoodlums sent up from Mexico by the ruling powers there "to put down insurrections" and to collect taxes levied by the government of Mexico.

Ironically, the liberal government of Mexico, in dealing with their own "distant province" Alta California, was using the very same arbitrary tactics which they themselves had so bitterly resented back while Mexico was still under Spanish control.

Governors for Alta California were appointed by the government of Mexico, with little consideration for the opinions of the residents of California, and troops were sent up from Mexico to keep the Californianos in line. Taxes were levied against the Californians, the money going back to Mexico, and the Californianos were forbidden to have trade relations with "foreign powers," restricting the trade with ships putting into California ports, unless those ships had come from Mexico.

In time, in spite of a determined effort on the part of the Mexican government to curb all trade with "foreigners," a black-market trade was developed whereby hides and tallow were traded to English, Dutch, and "American" ships for merchandise brought in by them. And with it all, the Californiano's resentment against Mexico grew, strengthening their determination to throw off Mexico's rule.

The gulf between the "Californians" (those who favored breaking away from Mexico completely) and the "Mexicans" (those who favored keeping California under Mexican rule) widened as the years passed, and there were many confrontations between factions, some of them violent. Perhaps here would be a good place to recount one incident from those troubled years.

The Mexican-appointed governor for California, Manuel Victoria, had engendered considerable resentment among the Californians through this high-handed methods in dealing with them. One of his most bitter opponents was Don Jose Maria Avila, leader of a faction of Californians whose insurrections had proven an embarrassment to Governor Victoria.

Victoria had Avila arrested and imprisoned; and when freed by some of his own faction, Avila set out to avenge the dishonor.

Angry partisans led by "General" Avila intercepted Governor Victoria in Cahuenga Pass, about eight miles west of El Pueblo de Los Angeles, as Victoria and his party were on their way south to San Diego. Here there was an angry confrontation between the two opposing factions.

Lance in hand, hot-headed Jose Avila charged Governor Victoria, wounding him in the side. But before Avila could finish off the wounded governor, Captain Romualdo Pacheco, who was with the governor's party, threw himself between Avila and Victoria and was killed when the thrust meant for Victoria hit him instead.

Though wounded, Governor Victoria drew his own pistol and fired, killing Avila almost instantly, Avila and Pacheco "both falling from their horses nearly at the same moment."

The Mexican faction went on to the Mission San Gabriel, taking the wounded governor with them. Manuel Victoria survived his

wounds, and when able to travel took a ship back to Mexico, re-
signing his office as governor of California.

The Californians took the bodies of the slain Pacheco and Avila
back to Los Angeles, where mutual friends buried the two men side
by side, for both men had been loyal Californians, and Avila's killing
of Pacheco had been accidental.

This tragedy took place on December 5, 1831, at a time when there
was still some division amongst the Californians as to where their
loyalties should be—with the central government of Mexico, or with
the *revolucionarios* who were demanding "home rule" for California.

This was only one among many such incidents between the Californians and the Mexicans during these troubled (for the Californians) and troublesome (for the Mexican government) years of
Mexico's rule in California. However, this incident is noteworthy for
two reasons: one, the near assassination of a Mexico-appointed
governor by *insurrectos*; and the other, the death of Romualdo
Pacheco. For Captain Pacheco, a young soldier assigned to Governor Victoria's staff, left a beautiful young widow, Doña Ramona,
who later married the Scot sea captain, John Wilson, and in her later
years was noted for her efforts to smooth over the discord between
the Americans and the Californianos. And Captain Pacheco left two
small sons, Mariano and Romualdo Pacheco Junior, the latter in
time to become governor of California under the American regime.

Though the avowed policy of Mexico had been to encourage settlers moving into Alta California, the bureauticratic blunders of her
politicos had seriously hampered an orderly growth within that distant province. In twenty-five years under Mexico, though the older
settlements along El Camino Real had increased somewhat in population, the hinterlands were still wilderness, inhabited only by roving
bands of "wild Indians."

During the years of Mexico's control in California, some men of
other nationalities had settled in the province. Some of them—usually
men with California wives—forswore allegiance to their native lands
and became citizens of Mexico. Others remained in Alta California
as aliens, but established places of business on a more or less permanent basis.

From the start, Mexico's policy towards these foreigners was erratic, at times encouraging them to settle in the province and make
investments, for the citizens of Mexico had been slow in moving into

the still sparsely settled land. Then with a change of officials in Mexico there could be a complete reversal of policy, and with it these foreigners often came in for harassment, with arrests and seizure of property an ever-present risk. Thus was bred another element of dissidents.

Resentful over Mexico's autocratic rule, yet aware that the colonies were not strong enough to ward off predatory powers of the Old World should they break away from Mexico, many Californians were of a mind that an alliance with the upstart United States might be the lesser of the evils facing them.

Meanwhile, away across "the great American desert," Texans and Mexicans were fighting over the boundaries of The Lone Star Nation —and good ol' Uncle Sam was playing referee, butting in from time to time to bring law and order.

Without doubt, the Americans in California did play on the resentments of the Californians against the Mexicans in those last troubled years of Mexico's rule in California, using that resentment as a wedge towards the eventual annexation of the province by the United States.

The United States was close to war with Mexico over the borders of Texas when that state was admitted to the union in 1845, when the Americans in California started a little war of their own. It climaxed in June, 1846, when Fremont and his men, along with other Americans, captured Sonoma and raised the Bear Flag. Then a short time later, having learned that the United States had officially declared war with Mexico over Texas boundaries, the Americans in California set out to do a little annexation themselves.

There was sporadic fighting between the Americans and the Mexican troops for some months, with the Mexican faction in California hoping that Mexico would send reinforcements. But Mexico was having problems enough of her own, with General Zachary Taylor and his troops crossing the Rio Grande and pushing deep into Mexico.

Left "an orphan bastard, abandoned by Mother Mexico," California was wide open, vulnerable to any one of the foreign powers which in the past had cast covetous eyes in her direction; and to most of the Californianos, the United States appeared the least obnoxious.

On January 13, 1847, the Treaty of Cahuenga Pass was signed, and California became a protectorate of the United States. The residents of California were to become United States citizens, with their property rights respected. This treaty was signed by Colonel John C. Fremont, representing the United States government, and by General Andeas Pico (a brother to then Governor Pio Pico) representing the Californianos.

It should here be pointed out that this treaty was signed by a representative of the Californians, *not* by a representative of the government of Mexico, hence was a treaty between the United States and the Californians. At this time the United States and Mexico were hard at war on the Texas front, with United States troops already deep into Mexico. On February 22, 1847, General Zachary Taylor and his troops took Buena Vista; on September 14, 1847, Mexico City was taken by General Winfield Scott and his army, bringing the war with Mexico to an end.

On February 2, 1848, the Treaty of Guadalupe-Hidalgo was signed, officially ending the war between the United States and Mexico, setting the boundary of Texas at the Rio Grande; and to top it off, good ol' Uncle Sam paid the powers that be in Mexico $15,000,000 for California, thereby making the transfer of that province "legal." It was a shotgun marriage if there ever was one! Why, the people of California would have had as much right to sell Mexico to some foreign power for $15,000,000 as the government of Mexico had to sell California!

Again an ironic twist of Fate. Just nine days prior to Mexico's sale of California to the United States, an event occurred which was to forever change the complexion of things in California. On January 24, 1848, a small quantity of gold was discovered in the millrace at Sutter's Fort (now Sacramento). At first given little importance, this discovery was in time to have far-reaching effects on the lives of everyone in California.

Had it not been for this discovery of gold, the chances are that the change of allegiance from Mexico to the United States would not have seriously disrupted the lives of the Californianos. For the most part, the British and Americans in California had been on amiable terms with the Spanish-Californians; and the United States' primary interest in acquiring California had been to prevent European powers from getting a foothold on the Pacific Coast—from "coming in the back door." Uncle Sam was having troubles enough at home, what with hot-head factions threatening a civil war.

It took several weeks for word of the gold discovery in California to reach Washington, D.C., and even then the heads of state placed little importance on it. It took nearly a year for word of the gold discovery to trickle around the world, gaining importance as it went, eventually touching off the most loco stampede the world has ever known—The Great Gold Rush of Forty-nine.

*   *   *

During those troubled years of Mexico's control in Alta California, the California bandido flourished. From this distance in time, it is hard to distinguish between the bona fide *insurrecto* and the *bandido*, the patriot and the plunderer, and in many cases the line of demarcation is slim indeed. Always men mask personal ambition behind an espoused cause. Many of those outlaws of an earlier day took their first step outside the law while involved in some form of political revolution.

First there had been the conflict with Mexico, giving the insurrectos some status amongst their peers. Then had come the take-over by a foreign power, giving the rebel a cloak of patriotism. Then had come the discovery of gold, giving the greedy something to grab for. Enter the golden days of the California bandido.

Even before the discovery of gold there had been gangs of bandits harassing the travelers along El Camino Real. Pio Linares and his wolf pack, under the able supervision of Alcalde Jesus Luna, were collecting their toll from the caravans coming up from Sonora. And Solomon Pico and his bully-boys were hard at work along the route between San Diego and Santa Barbara.

The first to hear of the discovery of gold at Sutter's Fort were residents of the older settlements in California, and they were the first to respond to the lure of gold. For the most part, they traveled in small groups, taking with them money to buy supplies in San Jose or at Sutter's Fort; and for the most part, they traveled along El Camino Real. From the start, they were vulnerable to the roving bands of bandits; so from the start, banditry flourished.

Word of the gold discovery was carried south by ships which had been in San Francisco Bay, and by summer men from Mexico and even Central and South America were making their appearance, some coming up across El Camino del Diablo in caravans, others having engaged passage on ships that were headed for Alta California ports.

Ships of various nations came into San Francisco Bay with trade goods, and their sailors, hearing of the discovery of gold, began "jumping ship" and taking off for the mountains, leaving their ships to rot in the bay. Also, American frontiersmen and settlers heading for the Oregon Territory, hearing of the gold in California, changed their routes to Sutter's Fort, and by the latter months of 1848 there was a steadily increasing horde of gold-seekers spreading through the Sierras.

The year 1849 saw the arrival of the first of the Argonauts, those men who had set sail from distant ports expressly to seek the Golden Fleece.

In January, 1847, when the Treaty of Cahuenga Pass was signed, there had been an estimated population of about 20,000 persons in Alta California, not counting the "wild Indians" roving through the back country. The estimated population of California jumped to over 100,000 during the stampede of forty-nine, and in the several years thereafter the increase was about 50,000 a year before the gold fever subsided and the number of new arrivals leveled off.

Men from every country of the world and from all walks of life were among those early gold seekers. Included among them were men who had committed crimes in their own native lands and had had to remove themselves fast to avoid punishment.

There were too many men coming into California, in too short a time and from too wide an origin, for there to be any formal law. The only law that counted was the ancient law of survival.

Although California was officially admitted into the Union as a state in 1850, she was far too remote from "The States" to achieve full statehood. And with a civil war already brewing back in "The States," California could expect no real help from Federal sources in the matter of internal problems. There was only one law left to curb the criminal element—the primitive law of retaliation.

All too often crimes were punished not by due process of law but by a mob under the urging of some hot-head or the influence of liquor. All too often it was the innocent who paid the price for the guilty. In too many instances, law-abiding miners of Latin origin were harassed by miners of other racial orders in retaliation against the depredations of the cholo packs which early had made their way into the mining districts.

As for the California bandido, he was in his element now. Not only were miners on isolated claims vulnerable to robbery and even murder, but also the caravans of men from south of the border returning to their homelands were easy prey. Often these raids on the caravans heading south were quite profitable since the travelers usually carried the gold they had accumulated with them.

Pio Linares and his wolf-pack enlarged their scope, their depredations ranging from San Jose to Los Angeles, overlapping territories infested by other outlaw bands.

It was in this period the name of Solomon Pico emerges from the legendary past, a super-archfiend or a misunderstood hero, depending on who told the story.

Said to have been a kinsman of Pio Pico, the last Mexican governor of California, Solomon Pico engendered much notoriety in those years just following the discovery of gold, and just about every crime known to mankind was ascribed to him. However, from the perspective of the present, one wonders if his alleged kinship to Governor Pico might not have had something to do with his notoriety.

Arrested with certain of his henchmen, Solomon got out on bail, then "skipped the country," leaving his bailsman to explain as best he could.

Solomon's followers scattered, then apparently regrouped under Pancho Daniel and Juan Flores, and they may well have been in cahoots with the Linares gang at the time the latter was being masterminded by Jack Powers. From old reports there would seem to have been an exchange of members between the two gangs when things got too hot in their own bailiwicks.

A Yaqui half-breed named Jesus Castro and his band of cholo followers were chased out of Mexico in the early 1850s, and they came to California, holing up in the Cuyama country, and from that retreat made raids on the old settlements of Santa Barbara and Ventura. They also harassed travelers along El Camino Real and the old inland route known as El Camino Viejo.

This band was eventually cleaned out through vigilante action, with some of the bandits killed. Others scattered, no doubt to join other outlaw bands.

It was about this time that a super archfiend known only as Joaquin made his appearance in the Mother Lode Country, committing atrocities so numerous that it would have taken a dozen ordinary fiends to keep up with him. For three years he scared the living daylights out of honest folks, and the public finally demanded an end to Joaquin.

So the Governor of California organized a Company of Rangers under Captain Harry Love to rid the world of the varmint.

After several weeks of riding through the back country, Harry Love and his Rangers returned with a severed head, purportedly that of Joaquin, and the case was officially closed.

Although the head of "Joaquin" was pickled and put on display, and honest folks breathed easier now that the archfiend had gone where archfiends are expected to go, the outlaw bands continued their depredations, with little chance of being brought to justice. It was too easy to disband and scatter after a raid, then reorganize later. If anything, the bandidos who roved along El Camino Real south of San Jose grew more insolent in their harassment of travelers along this ancient route during the five years following the presumed demise of Joaquin.

Though nominally set up under United States law and court procedure, to all intents and purposes the state south of San Jose was still under the ancient Spanish rule throughout much of the 1850s. The few Americans who had settled in the southern portions of the state were far outnumbered by the Californianos and were powerless to enforce United States law; and the Californianos were resentful over what to them had seemed a double-cross by Uncle Sam and were in no mood to enforce *Americano* law.

In his letters of 1858, Walter Murray says: "I shall now pass over the by-gone times of Solomon Pico and Joaquin Muriata and commence in the fall of 1853, when I first arrived here (in San Luis Obispo)."

Murray goes on to tell of instances in which Spanish-controlled courts released known killers of travelers, and he said, "Scarcely a month has passed without the disappearance of some traveler, or the finding of dead bodies or skeletons on the roads..."

In addition to Pio Linares and his cutthroat band, there were several other gangs operating during this period. Of these, Silvestro Chavez held some notoriety among his fellow countrymen. Said to have been a lieutenant of Joaquin Murrieta during that debonair gentleman's brief period of leadership, Chavez organized a band of his own after Murrieta's disappearance, and for several years harassed travelers along El Camino Viejo, extending his talents to include raids into the mines to the north.

Pancho Daniel and Juan Flores, both of whom claimed to have been lieutenants of Joaquin Murrieta, set about organizing an army of liberation to liberate California from the gringo invasion. And for several years these *insurrectos* gave the settlers of Southern California a bad time.

This band of *insurrectos* was gradually broken up during a two-year period starting with the vigilante hanging of Juan Flores and some of his followers on February 14, 1857. Pancho Daniel himself was later captured, and was hanged in November of 1858.

It was during this period that vigilantes broke up the Linares gang in San Luis Obispo, and vigilante action was taken in Santa Barbara as well to rid the world of "miscreants and malefactors." Among these "miscreants and malefactors" were several Americans whose demise was considered in the public good.

Although various members of three or four independently operating gangs were caught and hanged during this period of vigilante action, temporarily breaking up these more audacious bands of outlaws, those members who had escaped the vigilante dragnets simply went into hiding, to return to their outlawry later with new confederates.

Bandit gangs continued the depredations throughout the Civil War years, unchecked except for vigilante action.

It was during this hectic period of California's gold rush that the names of individual bandits appear in greater numbers, some as arrests of miscreants, some as subjects of vigilante hangings, and some—the fortunate ones—as *bandidos viejos*, to brag complacently to their grandchildren of their youthful prowess back in the years they plied the honorable trade of *el bandido bravo*. For in later years there was little stigma attached to a "reformed bandido." To the native-born Californiano, he was viewed as a hero; and even the Americanos took a tolerant view of the reformed bandidos once the period of their depredations had come to an end, relegating them to a nostalgic niche in the saga of California's rowdy beginnings.

Among the bandidos of the gold rush years whose names have come down in folklore, Joaquin Murrieta, the "veritable Joaquin" of legend and fiction, leads all the rest. Then comes the villainous Manuel Garcia—the "Three-finger Jack" of the Murrieta legend, a man whose sadistic predilections made him a fearsome monster even among his own people.

There were in fact several men of the surname Garcia among those bandidos of the 1850s. Anastacio Garcia, *un hombre muy mucho malo*, is credited with starting the youthful Vasquez on the downward road before he himself was summarily hanged by vigilantes in Monterey. There was also one Jesus Garcia, said to have been a brother of Anastacio, and others of the same surname involved in the banditry of the time. But whether these Garcias were kinsmen or not is hard to say.

Then there was the youthful Jose Antonio Garcia, hanged by the vigilantes in San Luis Obispo in June, 1858, remembered now for a rather pathetic letter he wrote his mother while awaiting execution. The letter has been preserved in the town's archives.

Others named as bandidos of the gold rush years include the brothers Joaquin and Jesus Valenzuela, who were said to have gotten their start down the outlaw trail through participating in "revolutions" down in Mexico before coming up into California.

Other individuals named include: Pancho Daniel, Juan Flores, Silvestro (or Silvestrano) Chavez, Joaquin Venadero, Benedicto Reis, and Felix Higuera, all reputed to have been associates of Joaquin Murrieta at one time. Various members of the Linares gang have been named, including Pio's brother Fernando Linares, and Pio's nephew Miguel Blanco. There was also one Joaquin Lugo, reputedly half-Apache and adept at Apache-style treatment of captives, said to have led a band of his own making forays up into the Mother Lode country.

Among the *paisanos* who had run afoul of gringo law back in those lawless gold rush years were many who have long been forgotten. However, some names did come down through the years, some in the lists of men who were hanged or imprisoned, and others in that vague realm of old-timers' memories.

Captured with Juan Flores in February of 1857 and executed soon thereafter were Juan Cabo (aliases Juan Silva and Juan Sanripa), Francisco (Guerra) Ardillero, Jesus Espinosa, Jose Santos, Diego Navarra, Encarnacion Berryessa, Pedro Lopez, Juan Valenzuela, and three others whose names have been lost with the years—twelve men counting the captain, Juan Flores, who received a separate "trial" by the vigilantes and then was hanged.

Several Americans were hanged as miscreants whose exit was presumed in the public good, in this vigilante cleanup of the 1850s.

Included among these was Thomas King, said to have been a member of Pancho Daniel's band.

Several men thought to be remnants of Jack Powers' band regrouped under Manuel Marquez in the early 1860s, and they gave the settlements of Southern California a bad time until vigilante action broke the band. Those members not caught and hanged scattered and lost themselves in the paisano population.

It was during this period that Indians from the tulares and Utes from the inland deserts were making raids on ranchos and settlements of the south. There were those who said that the Mormons were inciting the Indians to make these raids, pointing out that the Mormon colony near San Bernardino seemed always to be spared when these raids took piace.

One of the Indian leaders, known as Joaquin Jim, was shot and scalped. His scalp was put on display in Pasadena as a "warning to all miscreants."

Old-timers have given many names to the bandidos who were known in Central California in the two decades following the discovery of gold. Some of the bandidos were presumably kinsmen of local families and some of them reformed and in later years followed more prosaic walks of life. There were several Sotos, including a Joaquin, a Jose, and a Miguel; several Blancos, in addition to Miguel Blanco, who was hanged by the vigilantes in 1858; several Martinezes; several Castros; and men of other surnames as well.

There were several Chavezes mentioned, but whether any of these were kinsmen of Silvestrano Chavez or not, I do not know. There were also several of the surname Hernandez, but whether any of these were kinsmen of the notorious Domingo Hernandez of an earlier generation is hard to say.

Some of these bandidos were no doubt men who had been dispossessed through gringo double-dealing and had grievances which to them seemed legitimate; some no doubt were dissidents who hoped to incite a revolution which would take California out of gringo control; many were opportunists who found it easier to acquire gold through holdups rather than through the drudgery of working in the mines; and not a few were outright degenerates who found sadistic pleasure in torturing their victims.

From old-timers have come tales of men who had been skinned alive or burned alive, also of men who had been subjected to grisly mutilations before being finished off. There were recorded instances of men having been roped and dragged to death behind a loping horse. Another "sport" ascribed to these outlaw bands was to take a man, strip him naked and gouge his eyes out, then turn him loose to flounder over rocks and through brush until he died from shock and exposure.

These killings were often charged to "wild Indians," yet many old-timers insisted that more often than not, these brutal torture killings were the handiwork of the cholo packs rather than the usually mild native California Indians.

Although the south-of-the-border bandido did play a big part in the outlawry of those tempestuous years, not all of the crimes of that era were committed by men of that extraction—not by a long shot! Murders, robberies, and the forcible rape of native women by the newcomers were all too common. Nor were these crimes confined to men of any one racial order or national origin. Crimes were committed by Americans, Englishmen, Irishmen, Scotchmen, Frenchmen, Dutchmen, Swedes, "Bohunks," "Sydney Ducks," Greeks, Turks, Arabs, Hindus, and just about any other group that could be named. Even the "lowly Chinamen," themselves all too often the victims of murder and robbery, were not above slitting a few throats to acquire some extra gold.

Bandits continued their depredations throughout the Civil War years, unchecked except for occasional vigilante retaliations. California was too far away to expect Federal assistance, and the rowdy packs roaming through the Mother Lode Country, whether Americans, Mexicans, or foreigners, were little given to law and order.

It was not until The Big War was over and the transcontinental railroad completed (in 1869), linking the West Coast and the Eastern States, that California could be said to have become one of the "united" states. Even then much of Central California was sparsely settled, and for the most part law was lax.

The last of the California bandidos to receive public notice was Tiburcio Vasquez who, it was said, got his first push down the road to outlawry through his youthful association with Anastacio Garcia, reputedly a member of the Murrieta band.

With the hanging of Vasquez in 1875, the romantic phase of *el bandido de California* was ended. However, what was usually referred to as "the Vasquez gang" continued their outlawry in Central

California well into the 1880s before the influx of settlers cramped their way of life.

Throughout the 1890s and on into the early 1900s, the Californianos who found gringo laws irksome for the most part confined their activities to cattle rustling, horse stealing, and petty thefts, thus tapering off the era of the California bandido.

Occasional border incidents during the first two decades of the present century, along with the exploits of Pancho Villa, that swashbuckling brigand, were the last flickerings of a tradition of banditry in the Great Southwest.

   *   *   *

Of all these California bandits, only two have become legends: Joaquin Murrieta and Tiburcio Vasquez. Two men whose actual years of banditry were limited, and whose presumed depredations were certainly overshadowed by the known crimes of other *hombres muy mucho malo*. Why then were these two men singled out to become folk heroes?

Tiburcio Vasquez' life story has been prosaically catalogued through police records of his arrests, trials, convictions, and the prison terms he served. He is best known for that final year of his life, while he was in prison, first awaiting his trial, then, following conviction, awaiting execution. Vasquez was a polite, neatly-groomed little man who begged society's pardon for his many confessed transgressions, yet steadfastly insisted that he had not done the killing for which he was sentenced to be hanged. He was a rather appealing little man who just did not fit into anyone's preconceived notions of what a bold bad bandit should be.

Whereas there are police records to establish indubitably the authenticity of Tiburcio Vasquez, there are no such records on Joaquin Murrieta. At times he has been discounted completely, set aside as but a myth engendered in the fertile brain of a hack newsman, hopeful of a little *dinero* on the side.

Only one concrete bit of evidence was there to carry the legendary Joaquin into immortality: a pickled head floating in a jar of preservative, a pickled head purportedly that of Joaquin. A pickled head which, legend tells us, had a fierce moustache that continued to lengthen as the head floated there in the jar and the years passed. A pickled head which grinned sardonically as the walls of the museum in which it was housed crumbled, then went up in flames, in the Great Earthquake and Fire of 1906 which destroyed so much of the sinful city of St. Francis.

That the Spanish Californians did have legitimate grievances against the gringo usurper goes without question, and that they should produce a folk hero whose exploits against that usurper should be carried on in legend to later generations is but natural. That folk hero was embodied under the name Joaquin Murrieta, the Spanish Robin Hood of the West. But was there ever a flesh-and-blood Joaquin Murrieta? Or was he but a figment of legend-makers' whims?

Historians have argued this point for nigh a century; and the more "historians" entering the argument, the greater the confusion, and the less "history" there is to show in support of the legendary "Joaquin."

Over the past thirty years, so many debunkers have jumped in to debunk the Murrieta myth, tearing the Murrieta legend to shreds, that many reputable historians now doubt the existence of an original Joaquin Murrieta. So perhaps here is a good place to start debunking the debunkers.

Simply because no one can prove a given legend has its base in historic fact does not necessarily prove it to be outright fiction. That no one as yet has been able to prove that a youthful George Washington cut down a cherry tree does not thereby prove that he did not.

Certainly, if Joaquin Murrieta were but a romantic figment of someone's over-active imagination, he had a heck of a lot of people fooled.

Just what is the true life story of Joaquin Murrieta, *el bandido magnifico,* Robin Hood of El Dorado? No one can say for sure today, for too many years have passed since those robust days of the Forty-niners which furnished the background for the Murrieta legend, and too many "historians" as well as outright fiction writers have jumped in and muddied the water as they splashed around in search of Murrieta's "true life story." And perhaps this is as well; for it is doubtful if the real-life Murrieta could ever have been as intriguing as the legendary one.

The provable elements are meager at best. Back in the early 1850s, the depredations of Mexican bandits roving through the Mother Lode Country caused a stir of outrage over the incidents, and somewhere along the line an archfiend known only as "Joaquin" was named as the perpetrator of these dastardly deeds. So to ease the furor caused by this villain, California's Governor Bigler organized a posse of Rangers, under the leadership of one Harry Love, to rid the world of this Joaquin—or was it five Joaquins?

Several weeks of riding through the back country, and Captain Love and his Rangers returned, bringing with them a severed head, purportedly that of Joaquin, and a three-fingered hand, presumed to have been that of "Three-finger Jack." And so the case of Joaquin versus the State of California was officially brought to a close. Or was it?

In 1854 the first "life-story" of Joaquin Murrieta was published under the title *The Life and Adventures of Joaquin Murieta, The Celebrated California Bandit.* The author was John Rollin Ridge. This was a year after Harry Love and his Rangers contributed a human head to prove their claim to the demise of the archfiend known as Joaquin.

In recent years, however, it has become something of a crusade to rip the Ridge book to shreds as nothing but a dime novel, of no historic value at all. So perhaps it is time someone came forward in defense of John Rollin Ridge's Joaquin Murrieta.

IN DEFENSE OF JOHN ROLLIN RIDGE'S JOAQUIN MURRIETA

Was there truly a Joaquin Murrieta who roamed the back country in the gold rush years with a gang of desperados, waylaying unwary travelers and making occasional raids on the mining camps and frontier settlements? Or was this *bandido bravo* but the fictional figment of the inventive mind of one John Rollin Ridge, part-time miner, auditor, recorder, deputy county clerk, poet, and newspaper writer?

In a scholarly way some years back Joseph Henry Jackson, himself a writer and historian of considerable stature, traced much of the Murrieta legend to the book *The Life and Adventures of Joaquin Murieta* by John Rollin Ridge, first published in San Francisco in 1854. Because of the overly melodramatic style of the book, and due to the dearth of contemporary accounts of the life and exploits of one Joaquin Murrieta, Mr. Jackson concluded that in its essence the

Murrieta legend had its birth in what might well be described as a run-of-the-mill penny dreadful.

In 1954, a century after its first publication, the Ridge book was reprinted, together with an introduction by Mr. Jackson in which he sets about exploding "the Murrieta myth."

Since the publication of that long out of print book, together with Mr. Jackson's evaluation of the story, just about every would-be historian and his brother has jumped on this popular bandwagon, ripping the "Joaquin Murrieta myth" to shreds. Such details as the various spellings of the name Murrieta; the fact that the name of Joaquin's lady love has been given variously as Rosita, Rosalisa, Carmela, Carmen, Clarinda, Clarita, Mariana, and other names as well; the various names assigned the hanged brother (or stepbrother); the somewhat nonchalant spelling (or misspelling) of surnames and place names; all these things, along with other seeming discrepancies from one version to another, have been given as "proof" that the Murrieta legend was but fiction, with little if any base in fact.

In truth, most of what has been dished out as "the true life story" of Joaquin Murrieta has indeed been outright fiction. But does that prove that Murrieta, like Santa Claus, never really existed? Did John Rollin Ridge actually invent a mythical hero? Let's look at the other side of the coin.

As to the similarity between John Rollin Ridge's book and the Murrieta legend, it is the old argument as to which came first: the hen that laid the egg; or the egg which hatched out and grew into the hen. Was the Murrieta legend the foundation for the Ridge book? Or did the Ridge book produce the Murrieta legend?

A convincing argument can be advanced for either side. However, it is a hundred years too late for anyone to prove anything now. All anyone can offer at this time is speculation. So, let us speculate.

Suppose that John Rollin Ridge did not invent Joaquin Murrieta as a fictional character. Suppose instead that he heard the arguments that were going on over that pickled head on display and saw the basis for a story in the somewhat composite character these discussions produced. Suppose then that he set about gathering the various accounts and consolidating them into a general story pattern, using his own imagination a bit to emote his characters and give his story life. What then?

Once his story has been stripped of the pompous rhetoric used so often by writers of his generation, Ridge may well have presented a fairly accurate picture of Joaquin Murrieta—or at least, an account based on the campfire discussions of men contemporary to the action. Working on this assumption, let us see what we can come up with:

To start, Ridge's account of Harry Love and his Rangers making a trip into the back country and returning with the assertion that they had killed two bandits, identified as Joaquin Murrieta and Manuel Garcia, seems pretty much in keeping with Captain Love's own version of the incident.

To prove their contention that they had indeed killed the wanted bandits, the Rangers had cut off the heads of both men, and the three-fingered hand of one, then had started back to "civilization" with them. However, the head of the bandit identified as Garcia, having been mangled by the bullet which had killed him, started to turn putrid, so it was thrown away. The other head and the hand were taken forthwith to the nearest saloon and there put into containers and covered with whiskey to preserve them until they could be presented to claim the Governor's reward.

Having served this original purpose, the head and the hand passed into the hands of speculators who put them on display and charged a fee for the privilege of viewing them.

The head, displayed as that of Joaquin Murrieta, eventually was stored in a museum housing frontier relics, and it was presumed to have been destroyed in the San Francisco earthquake of 1906.

This much of the Murrieta saga, at least, is a matter of record.

Did most Californians of that day believe that Murrieta was for real? Or did they recognize him to be but a figment of some story writer's mind?

Back in the spring of 1853, it would have been hard to convince the half-dozen or so *Americanos* in El Pueblo de San Luis Obispo that the arrogant young bandido identified by the native *Californianos* as Joaquin Murrieta was but a figment of fiction when he and his rowdy gang of miscreants rode into town and more or less forcibly took over the Mission gardens as a camp ground. These Americans were so thoroughly convinced of Murrieta's reality that they very prudently holed up in the basement of one of the stores in town and stayed off the streets for two or three days, until Murrieta and his band moved on.

Though no one was injured in this instance, a gambler who blundered into town was robbed of the money he had with him.

An account of this incident is given in the Myron Angel history of San Luis Obispo, published in 1883, thirty years after the incident took place, but soon enough so that people who had been present at the time were still living and would have pointed out any discrepancies in the report, had there been any.

The bandit leader is described as being "symetrically formed, with regular features, an open countenance, but with a gloomy expression."

In his book, Ridge gives an account of Murrieta's stay in San Luis Obispo, as well as an account of a brush with lawmen which this same band had not long after leaving town. Ridge's account is in the main close to the accounts handed down by local old-timers, except that he may have dated the incident a couple of months too early.

Apparently, instead of inventing this incident, Ridge simply made use of someone's word-of-mouth version.

What about the other characters in the Ridge book? Are they all pure fiction?

There is no mystery about Joaquin Valenzuela, and what is known about him would seem to substantiate Ridge's own version of him.

In his letters to the *San Francisco Bulletin* justifying the vigilantes' action in hanging Joaquin Valenzuela, Walter Murray, writing in the summer of 1858, states: "In 1853, he (Valenzuela) was a partner of Joaquin Murietta—the veritable Joaquin." And in another place, Murray says: "When the Harry Love's Ranger Law was passed, this Joaquin Valenzuela, *alias* Ocomorenia, came down to the Tulares, and to Santa Barbara County."

Under the caption "Capture of one of the Five Joaquins," Murray goes on to say, "At the Rancho San Emilio, however, they (the posse) took one Joaquin Valenzuela, alias Joaquin Ocomorenia, who was identified by several persons as one of the five Joaquins, who were mentioned in the Act of 1853, authorizing the raising of Harry Love's company of rangers."

Here, approximately five years after the presumed demise of Murrieta, we find statements by a man who in later years held the position of District Judge, as well as serving a term in the State Legislature—a man hardly likely to be taken in by dime-novel hokum—which would indicate that he and his contemporaries did not consider Joaquin Murrieta a character of fiction.

As for Joaquin Valenzuela and his brother Jesus, they were well known in San Luis Obispo County. Both were well advanced in banditry, having gotten their start, so it has been said, in the "revolutions" down in Mexico before they came into California.

Perhaps here would be a good place to point out that Murray gives the name Ocomorenia as an alias of Joaquin Valenzuela. "The five Joaquins" named by Governor Bigler were: Joaquin Murrieta, Joaquin Valenzuela, Joaquin Carrillo, Joaquin Ocomoreña, and Joaquin Botilleras. Thus it might seem that in hanging Valenzuela, the vigilantes had taken care of two of the "five Joaquins" with one rope.

This would substantiate Ridge's statement that there were but two Joaquins, Murrieta and Valenzuela, the other three names mentioned being but aliases used by one or the other.

There is some indication that Murrieta did use the alias Carrillo, and it would be a logical choice. The Carrillos were an old and influential family in Southern California, quite numerous in the younger generation, and a handsome young caballero presenting himself as one of the Carrillos would have access to the best circles, with little likelihood that his masquerade would be discovered.

Botilleras (or Botellier) has hardly ever been mentioned except as one of the five Joaquins, leaving a strong suggestion that this name was but an occasionally used alias of someone better known under some other name.

That there were two Joaquins might well explain one of the seeming discrepancies in descriptions which have been pointed out as "proof" of the fictional quality of "Joaquin;" that is that in some of the contemporary accounts, *el bandido malo* is described as a personable young man of about twenty years, and in other accounts as a a hard-bitten brigand somewhere in his mid-thirties.

The description of the younger man would seem to fit into the usually accepted concept of Murrieta; while the older man probably was Valenzuela who, it would seem, was within hollerin' distance of forty at the time he was hanged.

What about the other characters as given in the book? Were they real? Or just fictional characters wangled into the story by John Rollin Ridge to give the story more body?

Old-timers of a generation not likely to have been influenced by dime novels told of the bloodthirsty Manuel "Three-finger Jack" Garcia, so it would seem he too was real and not just fictional.

One story tells how Garcia and his wolf-pack captured the two young *Americanos* Fowler and Cowie in 1846, during the conflict between the Californians and the Americans, took them to an out-of-the-way place, put them through a sadistic ritual of torture and mutilation, and then left them to a slow death. This story has come down through the years through sources other than Ridge's book.

Again, it would seem that Ridge simply put down stories which were going around at the time.

Quite possibly Ridge did get some of his characters mixed up or misnamed, and he probably did at times credit Murrieta with acts which in fact had been committed by others. In retrospect, it seems highly improbable that any one man with a following of twenty to thirty men could possibly have committed so many atrocities, over so wide a territory, in so short a time, as the hysteria of the times attributed to "Joaquin;" so logic would say that Joaquin Murrieta and his men were getting the blame for all these crimes even though they were not the only foxes raiding the chicken coop.

In those early years of the gold rush, there were several loosely organized bands of outlaws roving the traveled routes of Central and Southern California, making occasional forays up into the gold fields, then heading south when things got too hot for them. These bands included the ones "captained" by Solomon Pico, Pio Linares, Silvestrano Chavez, Jesus Castro, and Joaquin Lugo, and quite probably other lesser known bands, all operating contemporaneously with Murrieta and his followers. There were also "Californians" who, though they themselves stayed within the law, were not above helping the bandits for a price, giving these men some immunity from the law.

There may have been some grandiose dreams of uniting these various bands into an army of liberation, to liberate Alta California from the gringo usurpers; but these dreams never were realized. There never was any well-planned campaign. Each band acted on the whim of the moment.

Ridge's spelling (or misspelling) of surnames and place names has been cited as "proof" that his book had been carelessly conceived and was of little historic value. Still, the spellings are those which would go with a writer taking down notes from word-of-mouth accounts rather than from written records, like Cantoova (Cantua) and Ornetas (Hornitos). To Californians these place names are recognizable as belonging to the Murrieta legend.

Under frontier conditions, literacy was never high. Words were often spelled by ear. Many family names, both English and Spanish, were subjected to various spellings. Thus the several spellings of the surname Murrieta does not necessarily prove him a figment of fiction. The double "r" is more typically Spanish. The double "t" is an Anglicized variation.

Ridge tells of an American girl Rosalie who was kidnapped and then returned to her people unharmed. This story has been cited as being too theatrical for credence. Nonetheless, stripped of the melodramatic telling, the story is not necessarily out of line. In fact, this story may well have been based on some actual incident.

Mr. Jackson concludes there is too much blood-and-thunder in the Ridge book for authenticity. Nevertheless, the killings as detailed in the book are in line with those lawless times. The incidents told were in all probability based on actual crimes, whether committed by Murrieta and his band or by others. Joaquin Murrieta was not the only *lobo macho* leading a wolf pack in the gold fields of the early 1850s.

Should we discount as pure fiction Ridge's account of the defilement of Rosita? Was there ever any Rosita in Murrieta's life? Was Joaquin's brother—if he ever had a brother—actually hanged as an assumed but unproven horse thief? Did the dastardly gringos horsewhip our hero over some trumped-up charge? Frankly, amigos, I cannot say.

Simply because no one other than John Rollin Ridge recorded these incidents for posterity does not necessarily prove that they did not take place.

All too often the miners treated all Mexican women as if they were among the professional *putas* who swarmed into the towns and mining camps during those early years of the gold stampede. What was even worse, gang rapes of Mexican and Indian women by the wolf-packs of newcomers overrunning the mining districts occurred all too frequently and all too often these degenerates went unpunished.

In those early years of the mines many men were hanged on suspicion of crimes which were later proved to have been committed by someone else. Truly vigilante "justice" was often blind.

Frequently men were stripped to the waist, then flogged severely for some minor offense. After all, it was quicker and cheaper to horsewhip a man than it was to go to the trouble of holding a court trial and then jailing him.

Considering the temper of the times, Ridge's account of Joaquin's mistreatment by a band of ruffians is not out of line with many instances known to have taken place.

In this matter of whether Joaquin Murrieta's grievances can be given credence, or whether they should be brushed off as melodramatic fiction, here is an angle worth considering. During the first fifty years of the Murrieta legend's development, the Americans tended to consider Murrieta just one miscreant of many. They did not make a super-hero of him. It was the Spanish-Californians who passed on in their folklore the tale of the wronged Murrieta—the rape of his sweetheart, the hanging of his brother, and Joaquin's personal humiliation by a flogging.

Now, it is pretty hard to swallow any assumption that the native-born Spanish-speaking *Californianos*, who probably never heard of John Rollin Ridge and his book—and who would not have been able to read the book even if a copy fell into their hands—could have been influenced in their folk tales by a book which had at best a very limited circulation. On the other hand, assuming he was gathering his material from contemporary sources, Ridge would very likely have picked up the Californiano's version of the Murrieta story and incorporated it into his book.

Various detractors of Ridge's book have pointed out the lack of contemporary accounts to substantiate the story. The same could be said of other bandits as well. The day of the press agent for revolutionists had not yet arrived; and as for the newspaper reporters of the day, few had much chance to get first-hand information for their papers.

Editors were loath to play up the lawlessness of the times lest they discourage newcomers who might help to bring law and order to the new land. A long-winded politician or a popular actress would get far more space in a newspaper than any bandit, no matter how annoying his raids might be.

For the most part, it was word-of-mouth accounts rather than written records which kept alive the exploits of the various bandits during those earlier years.

If the true life story of Joaquin Murrieta presents something of a mystery, the circumstances surrounding his death offer an even greater mystery. True, the official version is that he was killed that fateful

July 25, 1853, by Captain Love and his Rangers, who chopped off his head and preserved it in a pickle jar. Yet even as that severed head went on display, there were many who insisted that it was not the head of Joaquin Murrieta.

Joaquin Murrieta, so these skeptics insisted, had been a young man of comparatively light complexion, showing a preponderance of Spanish blood. The head in the pickle jar, on the other hand, would seem to have been that of an older man, more swarthy than Murrieta, with features showing quite strong Indian characteristics.

Some newspapers of the day expressed doubt about the identity of the head in the pickle jar. Some even went so far as to state that the head was that of one Joaquin Valenzuela, who had been with a party of wild-horse runners working in the Gabilan and Diablo Mountains.

The identification of the head as that of Joaquin Valenzuela merits careful scrutiny. After all, Joaquin Valenzuela was one of the names listed on Governor Bigler's warrant; yet when *that* Joaquin Valenzuela was captured five years later, he still had his head on his shoulders. Were there two Joaquin Valenzuelas, one an innocuous *mesteñero*, and the other a bold bad bandido?

There is another possibility—a probability in fact, and one that various old-timers advanced to explain Governor Bigler's seeming ambiguity in naming five Joaquins to be hunted down for the crimes ascribed to one: that is, that Governor Bigler and his advisers assumed that the surnames of the five Joaquins (Murrieta, Valenzuela, Carrillo, Ocomoreño, and Botilleras) were but aliases of the same man, and that if any one of the "five Joaquins" were captured, the archfiend himself would be out of circulation.

It seems highly probable that the man who was killed, and whose head went into that pickle jar, bore a strong resemblance to Valenzuela —*not* to Murrieta—and that he was mistakenly identified as Valenzuela by some member of Harry Love's party. The name Murrieta was apparently substituted somewhat later when the head went on display.

If the Rangers did learn later that they had killed the wrong man, you could hardly expect them to come right out and say, "Beg pardon, folks, we up and killed the wrong man."

If Joaquin Murrieta did not furnish that head in the pickle jar, then what did become of our Joaquin?

Two separate and contradictory versions of Joaquin's last days came down in the folklore of the native Californianos. One version says that Murrieta, recognizing the futility of his cause, simply gathered up his various caches of loot and took off for Mexico, where he bought a rancho and retire into respectable oblivion. There were those among the old-timers who claimed to have seen and recognized Joaquin Murrieta in later years.

However, even as many Spanish-Californians insisted that Murrieta lived to a respectable old age in Mexico, there were others who had a completely different story. Joaquin Murrieta, so they said, had been foully betrayed by certain traitorous associates and had been put to a grisly torture death some weeks prior to Harry Love's raid on the camp of the mesteñeros (or, as some insisted, on the camp of the traitors themselves).

This latter version of the Murrieta story seems to have originated with a certain lady who lived in the Cantua Country for many years, and who in time earned the dubious sobriquet Mariana La Loca, although she steadfastly insisted that she was Mariana Murrieta, the "widow of Joaquin—the veritable Joaquin."

She may, or she may not, have been the Mariana Higuera whose name appears in some of the Murrieta legends.

This lady has been described as having been of sprightly figure, and probably had been quite pretty in her youth. She bore scars on her cheek and breast, said to have been inflicted by the jealous Joaquin when she flirted with some other lover. But, so the story goes, the repentant Joaquin nursed his errant true love back to health and forgave her her indiscretions, then set her up in a small adobe *casa* in Cantua Canyon, that he might bask in her bright company between his raids on the hated gringo usurpers.

For a price, Mariana would give a fairly convincing life story to reporters and tourists interested enough to seek her out. Usually she would tell of Joaquin's beheading at the hands of Harry Love and his Rangers, apparently parroting the usually accepted version the listeners expected to hear. However, in a confidential mood, Mariana would tell fellow countrymen a sharply different account of Joaquin Murrieta's demise. In this story she insisted that he had been double-crossed by traitorous members of his own gang who had caught him off guard and overpowered him, then subjected him to a slow death by mutilations and fire, similar to the torture treatment of captives ascribed to the Apache Indians.

Mariana claimed that she herself found the mutilated body of Joaquin Murrieta, the head still intact, and that she buried the body of her lover near a tree in Cantua Canyon. She was said to have named Manuel Garcia ("Three-finger Jack") as the ringleader in this treachery, and she claimed that she herself had been instrumental in setting Captain Love and his Rangers on the trail of these betrayers.

This tale of "Mariana Murrieta" and her version of the death of Joaquin as told by old-timers of Spanish-Californian descent, unsupported, might seem too farfetched to bear repeating here. Nevertheless, in his book dealing with that latter-day bandido, Tiburcio Vasquez, first published in 1875, George Beers tells of an interview that one of his associates had with this same Mariana Murrieta in which, apparently, she first gave the conventional or "Harry Love" version of Murrieta's death. Then a few snorts of *aguardiente* later, she seems to have reversed herself, telling of her own finding of the mutilated body, head still in place, and of burying it under a tree on the banks of the Cantua.

Mariana described the site of this grave and, upon investigation, a tree with a crude cross cut into its bark, presumably the grave she had spoken of, was located. And, according to Beers, Mariana named one Pedro Venda as the man who had contributed the head for so long on display in the pickle jar.

"Mariana Murrieta" became something of a celebrity in the San Joaquin Valley during the 1880s and 1890s, up to the time of her death in April of 1902, when she was accidentally run over by a train as she was crossing the tracks.

In a little book *Mariana La Loca*, published in 1970 by the Fresno County Historical Society, Dr. Raymund F. Wood tells of Mariana Murrieta's last years in The Big Valley.

Was this Mariana Murrieta who claimed to be "the widow of Joaquin" the Rosita of legend? Or did the ravished Rosita die soon after having been raped by the gringos, as some versions of the story say, leaving Joaquin free to transfer his love to another young lovely? (An old headboard, broken away from the grave it had once marked, was found in recent years, and on it was the epitaph: "Mrs. Joaquin Murrieta. Died in 1852."

Or was Mariana La Loca merely an astute lady who had recognized a profitable racket in this telling of her tales to those willing to make contributions? *Quien sabe, amigos! Quien sabe!*

With a tradition of banditry in California covering well over one hundred years, and with so many *bandido bravos* to choose from, why single out the comparatively unknown Joaquin Murrieta to build into a super-hero?

At most, Murrieta's outlaw career covered less than three years, and he was little known outside his own immediate circle of confederates. There were other California outlaws who were better known than he, outlaws whose careers spanned much longer periods of time, yet they all have faded into obscurity with the passing of the years.

Did John Rollin Ridge, the only contemporary writer who even bothered to try to tell Murrieta's side of the story, invent then, a fictional character for his book? And if so, how did he manage to dupe so many of the Californians who must surely have had enough information to recognize fiction when they read it?

Could a small, hastily compiled, dime-novel-type book actually have had that much influence? By Ridge's own admission, that first edition of 1854 had a very limited circulation. (Few books of that first edition were ever sold, thanks to skulduggery by some people involved in its publication, and only one volume survived to give the original version.)

Some five years later a pirated version of the John Rollin Ridge story was published (author unnamed), and about twenty years later a revised version of the original book was published under Ridge's name. These later editions did receive a much wider distribution. By then, however, the Murrieta legend was well established.

It is hard to see how a penny dreadful could have left such concrete relics as the old adobe building in Cantua Canyon, long a landmark along El Camino Viejo, pointed out by residents of the area as having been built and used by Murrieta and his outlaw band. Built in fortress proportions and equipped with portholes through which men could shoot, this old adobe was no ordinary ranch house.

All in all, when you come right down to it, the theory that the Murrieta legend could have had its origin in a dime novel does seem a bit farfetched.

No, John Rollin Ridge did not invent the Murrieta legend. He was merely the first to try to put down in print a legend in the making. The true source of the legend was that grisly trophy of the hunt, a man's head preserved in a pickle jar—a trophy which was carted around the country and put on display at carnivals over a period of years, exposed to the public as a side-show attraction.

The very gruesomeness of the display was bound to cause specu-
lations, discussions and arguments over whether the man who had
contributed the head had in fact been the elusive bandit known as
Joaquin—and if not, then whose head was it?

With the presumed head of Joaquin Murrieta staring with unseeing
eyes from a pickle jar, people were bound to start asking what manner of man he had been. Had he been the archfiend which hysteria
had for a time painted him? Or perchance had he been a man with
legitimate grievances.

Had Harry Love and his Rangers buried the slain men—or for that
matter, had they left them lying where they fell, members intact—
there would have been no Murrieta legend. Joaquin Murrieta and
"Three-finger Jack" Garcia would simply have passed into that realm
of oblivion which shrouds the lives and crimes of countless other
bandits, men who had their day and then went into the limbo of forgotten men.

What manner of man had Joaquin Murrieta been back in those
years so long ago? No one knows. All anyone can offer now is con-
jecture. Personally, I think we can discount both extremes—the
superman hero and the dastardly archfiend. However, the generally
accepted concept of Murrieta held by most Californians, both Spanish and American, is that he had been an inherently decent young
man who had become embittered over grievances, real or imaginary,
and had set out to avenge those wrongs. This concept seems well
within the realm of probability, if one takes into consideration the
temper of those lawless years.

On this assumption, John Rollin Ridge's Joaquin Murrieta seems
a likely character.

Part III
TIBURCIO VASQUEZ

Tiburcio Vasquez the historic figure, and Tiburcio Vasquez the legend. Immortal—both of them—for as long as people hold an interest in the frontier West of history and legend.

PROLOGUE
VASQUEZ THE HISTORIC FIGURE

Shortly after noontide on a dreary spring day now a full century past (March 19, 1875, to be exact), a hanging took place in the San Jose jail-yard. It was not a very noteworthy event in the frontier West of a century ago. A dapper little man, mustachio neatly trimmed and hair carefully combed, having vowed his innocence of the crimes for which he had been convicted and having begged forgiveness for any and all transgressions which he might have committed, bid a polite farewell to the world which had rejected him, then dropped into eternity. He achieved immortality as two men, Tiburcio Vasquez the historic figure, and Tiburcio Vasquez the legend. Immortal—both of them—for as long as people hold an interest in the frontier West of history and legend.

To some extent Tiburcio Vasquez has been prosaically catalogued in the police files, and the blank spaces in his life story have been filled in from the recollections of his contemporaries, so let's start with these.

Vasquez was born in Monterey, California, somewhere between 1835 and 1840. Even the experts do not always agree. In his *Crimes and Career of Tiburcio Vasquez*, published in 1927, M. F. Hoyle gives Vasquez' birthdate as August 11, 1839, and he says that Vasquez was thirty-five when captured (1874). George Beers, in his *Vasquez and the Hunted Bandits of the San Joaquin*, (1875), gives Vasquez' year of birth as 1838. Others, however, say that the most probable date was August 11, 1835, making Vasquez just under forty when he was hanged. But, does it matter?

Vasquez was born to a respectable middle-class family, of which several generations had been born in California. He was described as having been just under five feet six inches in height, of slender build, dark-haired, but of a lighter complexion than many of his country-men, showing strongly his Castilian blood. He received a better than average education for his time, speaking and writing fluently in both Spanish and English.

History and legend both agree that Vasquez' journey down the outlaw road started in a Monterey cantina, during a brawl in which a local constable was stabbed in the heart—or maybe he was shot. Here again, even the historians cannot agree on just what did happen.

The oafish lawman was drunk and tried to force his unwanted attentions on the lady whom Vasquez, age fifteen (or maybe he was eighteen), was escorting, and in his righteous wrath, Vasquez struck to protect his lady's virtue. *That* is one version of the story.

No! No! Vasquez and another greaser were squabbling over a *puta de la cantina* when the constable stepped in to stop the fight; and in the brawl which followed, the lawman was stabbed by Vasquez (or maybe he was shot, by Vasquez, or by someone else).

Still others insisted that at fifteen (or maybe he was eighteen) Vasquez was probably just an innocent bystander, drawn into the brawl, but not the stabber (or shooter).

The version of this incident given greatest credence by reputable historians is this:

Somewhere back around 1852 (or 1853), Tiburcio Vasquez went to a "fandango house" (a public dance hall) in the company of Anas-tacio Garcia (whose wife was said to have been a first cousin of Vasquez). At the time there were not only other *hijos del pais* (native sons) in the dance hall; there were also men of other nationalities, and somewhere along the line a fight started.

Constable William Hardmount was called in to quell the disturb-ance, and in the subsequent excitement, the lawman was stabbed (or maybe he was shot). In any event, he died. The killer was not identi-fied at the time.

Understandably, the *hijos del pais* present in the dance hall (in-cluding Garcia and Vasquez) prudently removed themselves from the scene of the killing, and none of the witnesses who remained in the dance hall were sure just who had killed Constable Hardmount.

The following day, one Jose Heiguerra (Higuera?), a comrade of Garcia known to have been in the dance hall at the time the lawman was killed, was picked up by vigilantes and hanged without trial.

Though Vasquez was named as a suspect in this killing, it would appear that there was very little evidence against him. However, traveling with Anastacio Garcia, *un hombre muy mucho malo*, Vasquez acquired the miscreant label, and from then on he was often "picked up for questioning" and in general subjected to harassment by law enforcement agencies.

Some months after the killing of Constable Hardmount, Anastacio Garcia was picked up by authorities in Los Angeles and sent back to Monterey to stand trial. However, before he could be brought before a formal court of law, vigilantes took Garcia from jail and hanged him.

Although Vasquez has been named by some authorities as the man who killed Constable Hardmount, Garcia would seem to have been the logical suspect. Anastacio Garcia was "a villain of the deepest dye, a born killer," and no doubt the vigilantes figured his hastened exit from this world of sin was "for the good of society."

Anastacio Garcia was reputed to have been a cousin of Manuel Garcia, the notorious "Three-finger Jack" of the Murrieta legend. Anastacio himself has been linked to the atrocities charged to "Three-finger" before and after their presumed association with Joaquin Murrieta.

Except for the Hardmount incident, history is rather vague as to the earlier years in the life of Tiburcio Vasquez, up to the summer of 1857. Then, on the night of July 15, Vasquez and a compadre "descended upon the corral of one Luis Francisco" and there did steal "one mule of the value of $75, and nine horses of the value of $40 each," and "feloniously did steal, take, and carry away" said property.

Apprehended before the stolen horses could be disposed of, Vasquez was tried in a Los Angeles court and sentenced to five years in prison.

On June 25, 1859, Vasquez escaped from San Quentin in a general jail-break. He was free for nearly two months, during which time he added another charge of horse-thievery to his record.

Picked up in August, and with the added count of horse-stealing against him, Vasquez was sent back to prison, to serve out his original sentence plus an added year for his more recent caper.

On August 13, 1863, Tiburcio Vasquez was released from San Quentin, having served six years. Not too much is known of his activities during the next three and a half years except that he was reportedly associating with "known miscreants and criminals."

In January of 1867, Tiburcio Vasquez was arrested on a charge of cattle rustling, brought to trial, given a four-year sentence, and sent back to San Quentin. He was released June 4, 1870, having served three and a half years of his four-year sentence.

It was during the next four years that Tiburcio Vasquez was to make his bid for immortality as a bandit chief. And it is here that it is hardest to separate historic facts from legend, and legend from outright fiction.

Without doubt, Tiburcio Vasquez did pick up a following of men not averse to working outside the law, and among those men were some hardened criminals. During those four years of Vasquez' freedom, there were unprovoked killings charged to "the Vasquez gang," but whether Vasquez himself had any part in these killings is not certain.

For the most part, those incidents in which Vasquez himself was known to have taken a part would seem to indicate a perverse whim to humiliate someone he held a grudge against, rather than a blood lust. During holdups the victims were robbed, then left hog-tied. Some of the robberies promised no possibility of a large haul, but still could have been disastrous for Vasquez had he been taken captive.

The insolence and frequency of the raids ascribed to Vasquez and his brigands were vexing enough to bring forth a general outcry from the public. Then on August 26, 1873, an incident that was to change the whole course of events took place.

It started as a routine holdup. The target was Snyder's Store in Tres Pinos, a small settlement in the Diablo Mountains. However, unlike in other holdups known to have been the handiwork of Vasquez and his henchmen, this time one of the outlaws got trigger-happy and killed three men, innocent bystanders who were unarmed. Two of them—Bernal Berhuri, a sheepherder, and George Redford, a teamster—panicked and ran; they were shot down before they could reach shelter. The third man, Leander Davidson, proprietor of the village hotel, was shot down as he attempted to shut the front door of his establishment.

The bandits ransacked the settlement, then took off with their loot; and by the time neighboring settlements could be notified and a posse formed, the bandits were long gone, lost in the wilderness of the Diablos or the Gabilans.

Because of the public outrage over this senseless killing of unarmed men, Governor Newton Booth offered a reward of $1,000 for the capture of Tiburcio Vasquez, a reward which was raised progressively over the following months, eventually to reach the sum of $8,000 before Vasquez was finally captured nearly nine months later.

If Vasquez were hoping to win friends and influence people, he was going at it the hard way. Throughout the fall and winter following the Tres Pinos raid, other robberies took place, many of them bearing the stamp of the Vasquez band.

On December 26, 1873, the little San Joaquin Valley settlement of Kingston was overrun by the outlaw band and sacked. In less than ten minutes over thirty-five men had been tied up and robbed by the outlaws.

On February 25, 1874, Vasquez and a pal, one Cleovaro Chavez, held up the stage station at Coyote Holes, northeast of Los Angeles, then robbed the stage as it drove in. Again the victims were left hog-tied.

The public raised such an outcry over these misdeeds and a series of lesser ones that Governor Booth felt it expedient to have a hunt organized specifically to run the wolf to his lair; and for Tiburcio Vasquez, time was running out.

On May 14, 1874, Vasquez and a youthful recruit, one Librado Corona, were captured while eating a noon meal in Greek George's roadhouse near Los Angeles. Shortly thereafter, Vasquez was transferred to San Jose to await trial in the Tres Pinos killings.

The trial of Tiburcio Vasquez was held in San Jose in early January, 1875. The verdict: Murder in the first degree. The sentence: Death by hanging.

Appeals were made to the State Supreme Court, and to the newly installed Governor Ramualdo Pacheco, but both of these appeals for clemency were turned down.

On March 19, 1875, two months after his conviction Tiburcio Vasquez was hanged.

The following comments are in no way meant to question the integrity of those involved in the trial, or the legality of the trial itself. And taking into consideration the temper of the times, no other outcome would likely have been possible.

Vasquez was tried specifically for having fired the shot which killed Leander Davidson as he was attempting to close the front door of his hotel.

Understandably, the residents of Tres Pinos were confused in trying to reconstruct the rapid turn of events leading up to the robbery,
the robbery itself, the killings, and the acts of the various members of
the bandit gang during the time they were in the little settlement.
(Some of the residents of the town were hog-tied in the back of
Snyder's Store when the killings took place, hence they were not eye-
witnesses.)

Tiburcio Vasquez was the big bad wolf as far as the public at large
was concerned, and he and his wolf-pack were getting the blame for
all the crimes committed in Central and Southern California; hence
Vasquez himself was a natural to be identified as the actual killer.
There were witnesses whose integrity could not be questioned who
insisted that Vasquez himself had done the killings charged to him.

However, included among those witnesses naming Vasquez as the
actual killer was Abdon Leiva, a former member of the Vasquez
band, a man who himself had taken a dominant role in the Tres Pinos
robberies. He had surrendered when cornered by the lawmen, then
turned state's evidence against his former associates in return for
immunity for himself. His testimony during the trial would seem to
have been given undue credence.

When put on the stand, Vasquez insisted that he had never killed
anyone "from the day he was born," and he named Abdon Leiva and
one Romulo Gonzales, another member of the band, as the ones who
had done the actual killings during the raid on Tres Pinos.

Now a sidelight on the trial: Judge Belden's speech of instructions
to the jurors just before they were sent out to make their final verdict.
It makes for interesting reading.

Judge Belden bore down heavily on that aspect of the law which
says that if a murder takes place while a felony is in progress, all
participants in that felony are equally guilty of murder, regardless of
who did the actual killing.

The following paragraph is a quotation from Judge Belden's rather
lengthy speech of instruction to the jurors, most of which is in the
same vein, emphasizing this one aspect of the law.

It is not necessary for the prosecution to show that the defendant fired the
fatal shot, or by whom it was fired. It is sufficient if it was fired by one of the
members of the party there associated together for, and actually engaged in
robbery, and that it was fired in furtherance of the common purpose to
commit this robbery, that in such a case all of the persons thus associated in

the robbery, are equally accountable for the homicide, and all thus associating and acting, are guilty of murder in the first degree.

It was as if Judge Belden himself, having heard the evidence doubted that Vasquez would be convicted, yet felt that a first degree murder conviction was necessary "for the good of society."

Having received these instructions from the presiding judge, the jury had little choice but to bring in a verdict of murder in the first degree, regardless of whether they felt that Vasquez had or had not fired the fatal shot. After all, three unarmed men *had* been killed during that robbery in Tres Pinos, in which, by his own admission, Vasquez had taken part.

So Tiburcio Vasquez was hanged; and in December of that same year, Abdon Leiva was released from prison and allowed to return to his native Chile. And officially the case was closed.

The facts known about Tiburcio Vasquez do not reveal him as a particularly bloodthirsty bandit, as bandits go. The killings attributed to him by legend (and sometimes "history") may well have been committed by someone else. This would seem to have happened in the killing of Constable Hardmount, for which the "logical suspect" was Anastacio Garcia.

Vasquez' three prior convictions—five years for horse-stealing, an added year for his jail-break, and four years for cattle rustling—were for non-violent crimes. Counting the ten months he spent in prison following his final arrest, up to the time of his execution, he was in prison and hence out of circulation for more than ten years of his adult life. In fact, from the time he was arrested on that first charge of horse-stealing in July of 1857 to the day of his death in March, 1875, Vasquez had less than seven and a half years of freedom in which to acquire his reputation as *un bandido notorio*. For the rest of that nearly eighteen years he was behind bars.

As with Joaquin Murrieta, it was the element of overkill that spawned the legendary figure. Besides, there were those who did believe that Vasquez had told the truth—that Leiva, who had bought his own freedom by turning state's evidence against his old comrades, had done the killing for which Vasquez was hanged.

Had Vasquez simply been given a prison sentence, there would have been no legend. He would have gone back to San Quentin as just another lawbreaker, a three-time loser serving his sentence. He would have been forgotten long before he had any chance for parole.

It was the grim finality of the hanging, plus some people's belief that he had told the truth, which kept Vasquez alive in the fireside discussions, eventually to grow into a legend, and in time to become a folk hero.

TIBURCIO VASQUEZ, THE LEGENDARY HERO

The legends in which Tiburcio Vasquez figures are many and varied. Some no doubt have roots in real incidents; others are completely imaginary. It is hard to winnow true legend from outright fiction where notorious characters are concerned. The stories which follow are authentic in that they were garnered from the fireside yarns of old-timers rather than from the flood of "true life-stories of bandit leader Tiburcio Vasquez" which have accumulated over the years since Vasquez' death.

For the most part the tales in the folklore surrounding Vasquez are not tales of gory carnage. Rather, they are stories of lightsome loves; of wry misadventures; and of foxy maneuvers in which our hero outwits the accursed gringo lawmen.

I realize that students of Tiburcio Vasquez the historic figure are going to view some of these yarns with a jaundiced eye. They will snort derisively and point out various probable discrepancies in some of the stories. Nonetheless, to all carping critics, I say: To Heck with you! Here we are dealing with Tiburcio Vasquez the legendary hero, *not* with Tiburcio Vasquez the historic figure. Vasquez the legend is far more colorful, more human, and more full of life than Vasquez the historic figure could ever be. So why not let Vasquez the hero of folk tales have his day?

Tiburcio Vasquez, the bandit leader? Legend (supported by recorded instances) pictures him a man of whimsical moods, a man less bloodthirsty than his detractors would have painted him. The Spanish-Californians had seen an alien race take over, completely disrupting their way of life within the span of one generation. It was easy for them to transpose their own resentments and frustrations to the grievances Vasquez had presumably suffered, to see in his rebel deeds their own rebellious impulses, and to make of him a true folk hero.

At times both history and legend have painted the Vasquez gang as bloodthirsty and rapacious, citing instances of their senseless killing of innocent people, wanton destruction of property during raids, and brutal rapes of defenseless women. Certainly some gang members were brutal degenerates who held no scruples against any crime or offense, but there is some question as to whether Vasquez himself was a party to these atrocities.

There were instances in which certain ladies did return from the outlaws' mountain retreats with tearful stories of having been kidnapped and forced to submit to the bandits' lustful pleasures. Were these ladies truly kidnap victims? Or were they merely light-headed dames who had willingly gone away with free-spending paramours and then, when ardor cooled and their gallants deserted them, concocted the kidnap stories to protect tarnished reputations? *Quien sabe, amigos! Quien sabe!*

Tiburcio the Gallant, the lover of women? Oddly, this rather pompous little man did seem to have a strong magnetic appeal to women. While in jail—in Los Angeles, recovering from superficial wounds he had received at the time of his capture, and later in San Jose, awaiting his trial—Vasquez received many messages of sympathy, as well as confections and flowers, from women he scarcely knew. Some of these women even came to the prison to offer their sympathy in person—much to the annoyance of those in authority who tried their best to discourage such unseemly attention to such a "black-hearted scoundrel."

Many of these women knew Vasquez only from hearsay; others, perhaps, had met him at one time or another and had been charmed by his gallantry in parlor or ballroom. Surprisingly, most of them were respectable women, sincere in their belief that Vasquez was the victim of prejudice and racial persecution.

Legend (and to some extent history) says that this romantic Don Juan of the Gabilans had many *dulcianas*, scattered from San Jose to San Diego, and that he was forever pressed for time, spreading his gallantries over a wide territory, lest in pleasuring one lovely he lose another.

Legend (and history) says that unsympathetic lawmen, upon learning of these pleasurable dalliances, would set ambushes at the abodes of these lovelies, and only the instinctive cunning of our hero prevented his ignoble capture and incarceration.

Of a truth, sooner or later Vasquez' Casanova complex was bound to produce complications. So here is as good a place as any to recall one instance, considered fully authentic, which did have a profound influence on Vasquez' destiny. And for this series the story might well be entitled:

THE INFERNAL TRIANGLE

It was during the winter of 1871-72 that Tiburcio Vasquez became acquainted with Abdon Leiva, a Chilean who had a small ranch near the New Idria quicksilver mines and who had earned a fair living for his family by shoeing horses for the company operating the mines.

Becoming enamoured with Leiva's voluptuous and apparently not unresponsive wife Rosaria, Vasquez persuaded the unsuspecting and unreluctant blacksmith to move his wife and children into the Cantua Canyon country, and soon Leiva took his place as one of the outlaw band.

During the two years that Leiva was with the gang, he entered wholeheartedly into all their illegal activities. He was both resourceful and cunning, and in those two years he advanced himself to an influential place as one of Vasquez' most trusted lieutenants. He is said to have taken an active part in that raid on Firebaugh's Ferry in the San Joaquin Valley, among others.

Leiva was apparently instrumental in planning and carrying out the robbery at Tres Pinos, in which the bandits killed three men. Shortly thereafter, while the outlaws were hiding during the manhunt brought on by these unprovoked killings, Leiva returned to camp unexpectedly to find the virile Vasquez and the ravishing Rosaria in what was, by Vasquez' own candid admission, "an act of flagrant dereliction."

The cuckolded Leiva and the derelict Vasquez patched up their disagreement in the interests of escaping the dragnet of lawmen already closing in on their hideaway.

The unprovoked and senseless killing of men who had offered no resistance in that Tres Pinos robbery had triggered a state-wide manhunt for the bandits responsible, and in time they were traced to their hideout in the mountains. This forced a quick breaking up of the gang and a wide scattering to avoid being tracked down too easily. In this enforced scattering, Vasquez took the fair Rosaria with him, leaving the self-preserving husband to go in the other direction.

Vasquez kept Rosaria with him for a while; but when she got too big with child for fast traveling, he most ungallantly deserted her, leaving her to get out of the mountains as best she could.

Rosaria had a miscarriage because of the hardships she faced in the mountains. When she finally reached civilization, she had a most heart-rending story to tell—that she had been kidnapped at gunpoint by *el capitan de los bandidos*, taken to the mountains where Vasquez forcibly had his will of her, and then abandoned, to find her way out of the mountains alone.

FOOTNOTE: Both of the Leivas appeared as witnesses for the prosecution at Vasquez' trial, and without doubt the testimony of the cuckolded Leiva and the vindictive Rosaria weighed heavily against Vasquez.

Some historians have tended to present Abdon Leiva as a simple but inherently law-abiding man who had been "seduced into a life of crime by a false friend who coveted his wife." However, it is hard to build up too much sympathy for any man who would relinquish a legitimate though monotonous livelihood and remove his family to an environment where their only associates were outlaws. Also, Leiva's own record over those two years with the outlaw band would indicate a man with few scruples, and a man who could hold a dominant place with his fellows. In fact, it seems not improbable that Leiva harbored ambitions to supersede Vasquez and to install himself as the big he-wolf of the pack.

In sharp contrast to this earthy saga of the infernal triangle, which seems to have been fully documented, there is the fey narrative of Vasquez' youthful first-love, lost to him forever through the girl's uncompromising sire; and since this girl's name is usually given as Anita, let us for this series call the story:

THE ANITA LEGEND

Tiburcio Vasquez, age about seventeen, fell deeply in love with the lovely Anita, daughter of a Californiano of prideful birth. Alas for true love! The girl's sire, knowing of Tiburcio's wayward ways, forbade the young lovers to meet and ordered Vasquez never again to darken the doorways of his hacienda.

And so, in true Romeo and Juliet tradition, Tiburcio and Anita eloped, and without churchly ceremony took up their abode in a mountian hideaway.

Again, alas for true love! The vengeful father discovered this idyllic retreat, descended upon it with a contingent of underlings, shot at the retreating Tiburcio, wounding him, and then took the weeping Anita home, to be placed in a convent for the rest of her life.

By the time the young Tiburcio could ride again, his one true love had been lost to him forever; and in his grief and anger, he turned wholeheartedly to a life of crime.

FOOTNOTE: This legend of the lovely Anita, Vasquez' one true love, lost to him forever, has come down in the folklore of the Spanish-Californians, and it would seem to merit its own place in the Vasquez legends. A version of this story was picked up by George Beers and incorporated into his book on Vasquez' life. However, because of its length and melodramatic telling, many historians now discount the story completely as but a bit of fiction written by Beers himself.

Obviously, Beers did use his own imagination quite freely to be able to stretch Anita's abduction out through five chapters in his book; but that fact alone does not rule out some such incident's actually happening in Vasquez' youth, an incident already growing fuzzy in the memories of those from whom Beers got his story some twenty-odd years later.

Since this legend has come down in the folk stories of the Californianos, it would seem logical to assume that Beers got his story from the *hijos del pais,* rather than they from him.

The lovely Anita and the voluptuous Rosaria were not the only loves in the life of our hero—not by a long-shot they weren't!

The tales of Tiburcio the Gallant Lover are legion, and if only one-tenth of them were true, our hero must have been amazingly virile! No desert was too sun-scorched and dry, no mountain range too rugged and steep, nor its jagged passes too impassable, for our hero. No flood-swollen river was too dangerous to cross, no threat of the accursed gringo lawman, nor any fear of an irate husband's wrath, could dissuade our hero from seeking out his current love when the desire moved him.

And so, let us continue this little series of stories with one in which we find Tiburcio in bed with a woman.

TIBURCIO IN BED WITH A WOMAN

Hard-pressed by a party of lawmen, Tiburcio Vasquez took refuge in the home of a compatriot. Alas! The resolute lawmen, having trailed our hero to this very door, demanded immediate entrance under threat of complete annihilation should the head of the house refuse to open the door.

The host's wife, having recently given birth and so confined to her bed, seems to have been a lady with rare presence of mind. Flinging back the quilts of her bed, she motioned for Tiburcio to crawl in at her feet and curl up there, then drew the covering back over the bandido as well as over her own lower body.

The husband then opened the door, and with profuse apologies to the lawman that he should have found the door latched, he invited the sheriff to enter his home.

With calm dignity, the lady motioned that the baby wa sleeping— please do not disturb the little dear!

As the sheriff searched the room, the lady continued to prattle on, speaking of the fine infant she held in her arms. She so charmed the lawman with her Madonna-like innocence that he failed to notice the odd-shaped hump in the quilts around her feet.

With embarrassed apologies for having intruded into their home, the sheriff departed the *casa* of these Californianos. He returned to the courtyard, mounted, then motioned his men to follow.

The men of the posse rode away, muttering with disgust at the escape of a quarry they had been so sure was within their grasp, nonplussed as to how the bandit chief could have eluded them, disappearing as though into thin air.

FOOTNOTE: In one version or another, this tale from the past has oft been repeated, has even come down through the years in print. Possibly the story was based on some actual incident in the adventuresome career of our hero. Then again, it may be just one of those yarns too good to let die.

However, if this tale is not melodramatic enough, how about the one which follows? A tale of a fair lady, and a narrow escape for our hero. A tale which might be entitled Tiburcio the Gallant.

TIBURCIO THE GALLANT

Tiburcio the Gallant, the romantic lover of ladies fair, was attending a *baile* (dance) in the home of a fellow Californian, and all was serene. It was a most joyous occasion, with rich food, fine wines, and lovely ladies—a brief glimpse of heaven for any man who perforce must ride the outlaw trail.

Gracefully waltzing with a beauteous young lady, Tiburcio had not a fear nor a worry in the world; for here in *la casa graciosa* of his friendly host, he was among friends, compadres, fellow countrymen. The loathsome gringo lawmen? Well, there was a certain place reputed to have an over-warm climate...As far as Tiburcio was concerned, the accursed gringos could go there and take their places with El Diablo!

The possibility that these obnoxious gringo lawmen could break in on this festive occasion? Well, *that* possibility never once entered Tiburcio's mind.

What was that? A hush fell over the merry throng. A dread whisper was passed from one set of lips to another, swept like a grim echo throughout the hushed room. The gringo lawmen blocked all the windows and exits, and the gringo sheriff was entering the door.

Tiburcio Vasquez the intrepid highwayman, a wanted outlaw with a price on his head, was trapped—trapped like a mouse in a half-empty barrel of frijoles!

Once again a woman's rare presence of mind saved our hero from ignoble capture. With a dexterous twist of her wrist, the lovely lady (his partner in the interrupted waltz) heisted the hoops of her voluminous skirt and motioned for our hero to pop under. She dropped the hooped skirt back in place, covering Tiburcio as he crouched there behind her knees.

With her arms uncompromisingly folded across her shapely bosom, her feet staunchly planted right there in the middle of the dance floor, the lady faced the sheriff with a cold disdainful stare. Her whole demeanor bespoke her frank disgust at this boorish interruption of the dance in progress. Her manner implied that no one but a lowborn gringo would be guilty of such a serious breach of common courtesy.

The discomfited sheriff made his search of the house, then left the premises in disgust. He had been so sure that here at last the notorious bandit had finally been cornered; his informant had been positive that he had seen Vasquez enter the house, and no one had seen him leave.

FOOTNOTE: As the Spanish-Californians saw it, the lady was not the least bit disgraced by having done this most unconventional deed. In fact, in later years, several women were said to claim the distinction of having been the heroine of the hoop skirts.

As with most tales related by word of mouth rather than the printed page, this story from out of the past has been handed down in several versions. Some accounts say the incident took place in an Indian village, and the woman with the voluminous skirts was an Indian woman whom Vasquez had befriended. Some versions describe the setting as an elegant mansion belonging to aristocrats and the hoop-skirted heroine as a "fine lady" of impeccable reputation who acted out of loyalty to a valiant compatriot. Still others, however, say the setting was a public dance hall and the heroine a lady of the night. Some have even linked her with another widespread legend, that of the deceitful Delilah who eventually betrayed Vasquez into the hands of the gringos.

As for this Delilah, some have painted her as a woman without conscience who, for a price, arranged Vasquez' capture. Others more charitable, have explained that the lady suffered from moon-madness. They laid her misfortune on her great-grandmother, saying that in her dotage *la vieja* absentmindedly placed the sleeping infant near an open window, and the full moon shining through the window worked its magic spell as it shone on the head of the babe, marking her infant brain with moon-madness. Therefore, on the three days and nights of the full moon, she had no control over her impulses.

These stories did in fact have wide circulation and went into print in one version or another.

In her book *The Salinas, Upside Down River* (published in 1945), Anne B. Fisher tells how, when the sheriff rode into the Indian encampment looking for him, Vasquez hid under the skirts of an Indian woman whom he had previously befriended. Mrs. Fisher also tells how Vasquez had been given refuge under the bedcoverings of a woman with a newborn babe. She also reiterates the oft-repeated statement that Vasquez had been betrayed by his lady-love, who arranged his capture for the gringos' gold.

Mrs. Fisher undoubtedly got her Vasquez stories from her interviews with old-time residents of the Salinas Valley, at a period when many of "the older generation" were still living.

In his book *California Vaquero* (published in 1953), Arnold R. Rojas tells how the hoop-skirted lady furnished a safe hiding place for our hero when the gringo shriff invaded the dance hall.

Mr. Rojas gives the lady's name as Teresa and says she was the consort of Greek George, the camel driver in whose house Vasquez was captured that fateful May 14, 1874.

Others have recounted these tales, some in print even, in one version or another. But—Aw Heck! Why completely destroy the image of Tiburcio the Invincible Lover!

Let us now contemplate a more heroic legend, a story of wanted men and a raging river.

WANTED MEN AND A RAGING RIVER

Jim McFall, wanted by the law on a little matter of "borrowing" horses without first getting the owners' consent, had reached a flood-swollen river and there drew rein; it was the season of heavy rainfall, and already many of the streams were considered impassable.

Jim paused on the brink. Across the river there would be safety; for the lawmen did not want him badly enough to risk their own lives in the roiling water. But was the crossing possible for any man? If Jim rode into that raging river, might not he be likely to drown?

At this crucial moment a man garbed as a true caballero rode up astride a fine grey horse. The elegant stranger paused a few seconds on the bank to estimate the current. Then, with a nonchalant "vamos" and a beckoning wave of his hand, he spurred his not-too-willing horse into the turbulent water.

Jim McFall took heart, feeling that if another man could make the river crossing, he himself could. Anyhow, drowning would be preferable to stretching a rope! So Jim spurred his own definitely unwilling mount in behind the horse of the stranger, now swimming against the swift current.

Out in midstream, one horse went down in the raging torrent, but the rider freed himself from the floundering animal. The other man, realizing that his own horse could not swim against the current as long as he was burdened with a man on his back, slipped from the saddle and reached forth a helping hand to the man whose horse had gone down. Then both men grabbed the tail of the swimming horse, that he might pull them to safety.

Fighting the current, both men and the horse reached the bank safely. However, looking back as he climbed the bank, the horse saw the bedraggled creatures hanging to his tail. He spooked and bolted, leaving both men on solid ground but afoot.

Undaunted by this misfortune, the intrepid stranger motioned for Jim to follow, and in time they came to the home of a Californiano, a friend of the stranger. Here both men were given dry clothing and food, and were made welcome to stay the night.

In the morning, the friendly paisano loaned each man a fresh horse, and each prepared to go his own way. As the debonair stranger was bidding Jim McFall *adios*, he introduced himself and told his destination. Only then did Jim McFall learn the name of the valiant caballero, and the reason he had braved the raging river.

The stranger was none other than the famed bandido, Tiburcio Vasquez, a man with a price already on his head. The reason for his haste? Not, as one might suspect, a vengeful posse on his trail, determined to bring his eventful outlaw career to an ignoble end. Hell, no!

The romantic Tiburcio had received an ardent epistle from a lovelorn lady admirer, and he had been speeding to join his *dulciana* lest a protracted delay in reaching her should cool her ardour!

FOOTNOTE: In one version or another, this story of Tiburcio Vasquez braving the rain-swollen river to keep an appointment with his current love has had a fairly wide circulation, in print and through the fireside yarns of an earlier generation.

Arnold R. Rojas relates this incident in his book *California Vaquero*. I came across this book after writing a rough first draft of these Vasquez stories some years back. Mr. Rojas was an old-time vaquero of the Kern and San Luis Obispo counties area. Since he apparently knew Jim McFall personally and got his story first-hand, I somewhat retailored this yarn to more closely follow Mr. Rojas' account. For this may well have been an actual incident and not just a tall tale.

The same thing may be true of the story which follows: the tale of The Purloined Horses.

THE PURLOINED HORSES

While encamped in the La Panza Mountains one day, Tiburcio Vasquez and certain members of his gang discussed a little business venture. They would collect for themselves a goodly band of horses, taking a few head from one ranch and a few head from another, but not too many from any one source lest the loss be noticed too soon. Then, when they had accumulated a sizable herd, they would drive the horses down into Mexico and sell them, thereby collecting a goodly profit from their proposed enterprise.

It seemed an almost foolproof venture. Almost, but not quite.

Unfortunately an argument developed between El Capitan Vasquez and one of his lieutenants over just how this enterprise was to be conducted; and in this conflict of wills, most of the men involved took sides against Vasquez.

In a petulant rage, El Capitan Vasquez strode away from the bickering pack, saying that those who were with him could follow him, and those who were against him could go—you can guess where!

Only two men were loyal to their captain, and they followed him when he rode away from the camp.

The outlaws who had remained with the rebel lieutenant went about their proposed venture. In time they had collected a worthwhile herd of horses in a box canyon with sufficient water and grass to sustain the horses until the men were ready to drive them on to Mexico. They had to wait for an opportune time because these stolen horses had to be driven past the older settlements of the Southland, without detection by the accursed gringo lawmen.

While these insubordinates were gathering their herd of stolen horses, Vasquez and his two faithful followers were watching the recalcitrant band from their own camp hidden farther back in the hills.

When Vasquez was satisfied that the accumulated herd of horses was large enough to merit taking, he and his two compadres slipped down to the canyon to scout out the situation. They found a rope barrier had been placed across the mouth of the canyon to keep the horses from straying, and a guard had been stationed not far away.

Two gentle horses were wearing bells, a fact noted by Vasquez; so he and his two compadres slipped in amongst the grazing horses, removed the bells, unloosed the rope barrier, then silently drove the horses down the canyon.

Vasquez and one of his companions started out, driving the herd of horses southward. The other outlaw remained behind to circumvent their adversaries through a ruse which Vasquez himself had devised.

The man who remained behind replaced the rope barrier and tied the bells to the rope. Then from time to time he gave the rope a slight tug, causing the bells to tinkle as if on the necks of slowly grazing horses.

Sitting comfortably by his campfire, the guard was thus reassured by the sound of the bells; hence he failed to go check on the herd as he had been instructed to do.

With the first hint of dawn, the bell-ringer mounted his own horse and rode away to rejoin his compadres and their purloined horses, by now well on their way to Mexico and, hopefully, a profitable sale there.

Back in their own camp, the outlaws arose and ate a leisurely breakfast, unaware of the loss of their stolen herd.

When at last the outlaws went to the box canyon and found their horses gone, Vasquez and company were far, far away. And even worse than losing their stolen horses, the outlaws found that their saddle horses had also been taken, leaving them on foot until such a time as they could reach a settlement where they might borrow or steal other horses.

FOOTNOTE: This wry tale of Vasquez and his compadres hijacking the stolen horses from his insubordinate gang has come down through the years in various versions.

In his *California Vaquero* series, Arnold R. Rojas tells several of the Vasquez stories, including this one. Mr. Rojas also gives an old account of how Vasquez and his band picked up a trail herd of three hundred mules from ranches along the Coast and drove them inland, then south, to sell in Baja California.

In that first half-century following his hanging, Vasquez remained very much alive in the memories of old-time residents of Central California; for this was "Vasquez country," and the exploits of El Bandido Bravo were still the subjects of fireside tales. Even as the numerous raids attributed to Vasquez and his men were favorite topics, so also were his insolent taunts directed against the men of the law. It was sort of like tying a knot in the ol' Devil's tail.

LIKE TYING A KNOT IN THE OL' DEVIL'S TAIL

Glumly the Sheriff of Monterey County indicated to his men that they might as well make camp for the night. There was grass aplenty for the horses in the meadow below the spring, and water for both horses and men, and Gilroy, the nearest town, was still a good twenty-five miles away.

Grumbling disgustedly that while their horses would have plenty to eat and drink, they themselves would have to make out on hardtack biscuits and dried jerky, the men of the posse unsaddled their horses and hobbled them before turning them loose in the meadow below the spring chosen as an overnight camp.

There was considerable muttering that if they had not wasted so blankety-blank much time swinging 'round by that blankety-blank New Idria Mines they could have made it into Gilroy in plenty of time for a restaurant-cooked supper!

"Quit your damn bellyaching!" the Sheriff snapped. "If you loco yahoos had reached a town, you'd of swizzled so damn much swill you wouldn't be worth your salt tomorrow."

The Sheriff himself wasn't in a particularly happy mood. When he had organized his posse three days back, he had had such big hopes of bringing the brigand Vasquez back to Monterey with him. But everything had gone sour!

Three days of combing the Gabilans and the Diablo Mountains, and what did he have besides a pack of saddle-weary galoots grumbling about having been dragged out into nowhere on a crazy wild-goose chase! Three days of scouting out every possible place a band of men on the dodge might logically use as a hideout, and still nary a sign of Vasquez and his coyote pack anywhere!

It had all started back ten days ago when a posse of lawmen from Kern County, following a raid on one of their own scattered settlements, had chased the Vasquez gang up into the Tehachapi Mountains and there lost their trail. So, in disgust over losing their quarry, the Kern County posse turned back and returned home.

Logically, it seemed the gang would make their way southward towards Ventura or Los Angeles, split up and find a hiding place there among the paisano population, lie low until the pursuit died down, and then go back to their annoying raids once more.

Then our friend the Sheriff of Monterey had gotten what seemed, at the time, a very hot lead. From someone he considered a reliable underground source had come word that the wily Vasquez had once again pulled a daring maneuver: he had not done the logical thing, seeking refuge in the southland; instead he had doubled back with his men and even now was hiding in his old stomping grounds in the rugged La Cañada de Cantua, in the Diablo Mountains of Central California.

To head the posse which at long last captured the notorious bandit chief! Truly *that* would be a brilliant feather in the cap of any aspiring lawman!

Quietly the Sheriff of Monterey made his plans, first gathering his most trusted deputies without giving the public any advance notice of his intentions. Then, before dawn, the Sheriff and his men started out from Monterey for a trip into the rugged Cantua country, which was under the jurisdiction of Monterey County at the time of our story, although in later years it became the southeastern tip of San Benito County.

They rode doggedly through the mountains for three days, but nowhere did the posse find hide, hoof, horn, nor hair of the wanted bandits. There was nary a sign that anyone had camped at any of the known springs, nor any signs that horses had been tethered in any of the swales and meadows they had passed through.

The posse had even swung round by the New Idria Mines, hoping to gain some information there.

The foreman of the New Idria Mines had been most cooperative— maybe too cooperative! He had blandly assured the Sheriff that he himself would question the men working at the mines to see if anyone had seen any suspicious characters hanging around the district. In fact he had accompanied the Sheriff as the latter made a tour of the mines trying to question the paisanos working there.

Nobody, it would seem, had seen anyone in the least resembling Vasquez, or any of his followers, anywhere at all during recent weeks.

The Sheriff had expected the paisanos to have sympathy for Vasquez and his followers, but as to the foreman...something strange was going on!

Just how come the New Idria Mines, of all the quicksilver mines in Central California, had suffered no robberies—even though it sat right there next door to La Cañada de Cantua, for so many years a favorite hangout for the outlaw bands!

If *that* weren't proof enough, then top it off with that holdup of the stage some months back!

In reporting the holdup, the driver of the stage had said that when Vasquez first confronted the stage and ordered the passengers to debark, he had been his most insolent self; then as the mines foreman and his lady stepped down from the stage, the bandit chief had seemed startled.

Vasquez had tipped his hat and said that gallantry prevented his robbing a stage in which so lovely a lady was riding. Motioning his men to follow, the bandit chief had ridden away, the stage and the passengers alike unrobbed.

Well! Gallantry had never prevented these Robin Hoods of the Gabilans from taking rings and brooches from lady passengers on other stages in the past!

So what! It was all water under the bridge now! That lead which at the time had seemed so reliable had probably had its origin in cantina gossip, as had so many seemingly reliable leads in the past.

The Sheriff himself was an experienced tracker; and if anyone had camped in the Cantua country within recent weeks, he should have seen some signs of their presence.

No doubt, Vasquez and his men had in fact gone south, as common sense would dictate.

It was but the luck of the game! grumbled our friend the Sheriff of Monterey as he and his men prepared their camp for the night.

Come morning, the Sheriff and his deputies re-brewed the stale "dregs" in the coffee pot, ate the last of their jerky and hardtack, then went to the meadow below their campsite to retrieve their hobbled horses.

The horses were gone—and a bit of cross-tracking told the whole wry story.

Taking advantage of the subdued light of a waning moon, someone had sneaked into the meadow in the wee small hours of the day, and these miscreants had loosened the hobbles and led the posse's horses away. Not a horse to be seen!

Cussing fluently, the Sheriff and his deputies set out on that twenty-five-mile hike to Gilroy, the nearest settlement—a most inglorious turn of events.

There was no doubt in anyone's mind just who the perpetrators of this dastardly crime had been, though it had been a most foolhardy bit of bravado on the part of the bandits.

Had Vasquez and his men been in need of horses, they could have stolen horses of equal value elsewhere, and with a lot less risk. Obviously, this stealing of the lawmen's horses had been a taunt directed at lawmen in general—like tying a knot in the ol' Devil's tail.

Having accomplished this feat, the knot-tyer would gain the plaudits of his admirers. But most certainly, such a knot tied in the Devil's tail wasn't likely to improve the Ol' Boy's dispostion at all!

FOOTNOTE: The story of Vasquez and his merry men stealing the lawmen's horses, leaving them to walk home, has come down through the years in various versions. It may well have had its base in some actual incident. The same can probably be said of the story which follows, another story of a long walk home.

THE LONG WALK HOME

"Amigo, you will unbuckle your gun belt and drop it to the ground!" The man holding the rifle spoke sharply. "I warn you! Make no mistake, amigo! I, the Great Tiburcio, shoot my traitorous friends!"

So rudely brought back to present realities from the pleasant land of daydreams, Dan Clark reined his mount to a halt as he stared unbelievingly at the elegant apparition which had appeared as if by magic from behind a point of rocks along the trail.

Looking into the cold unrelenting eyes of the flashily-dressed horseman who held the rifle leveled at his chest, Dan knew this was no whimsical prank to be laughed off, then forgotten.

Mechanically, Dan Clark unbuckled his gun belt and let it drop to the ground.

"What—why—friend Tiburcio, why do you hold your rifle on me?" Dan stuttered his disbelief. In the past he had been—or thought he was—on friendly terms with Tiburcio Vasquez and his men. "Is this not carrying a jest too far?"

Dan Clark, owner of a small ranch in the mountains, had given meals to Vasquez and those of his men who had chanced to pass his ranch. In fact, Vasquez himself had upon occasion eaten supper with Dan, then shared his bunk for the night; and Dan had never felt there should be any animosity between them.

With no great worldly wealth to tempt the bandits, Dan had never worried about these contacts with the outlaws, and he had found Vasquez to be an amiable and entertaining guest.

"It is no jest, amigo!" Tiburcio made answer, a gleam of whimsical malice in his eyes. "You, friend Dan, need a lesson, and you shall get a lesson!"

"What—what have I done?" Dan was still bewildered by this seemingly unprovoked change in the manner of a man whom he thought he knew quite well.

"Can you, friend Dan, deny that you have spoken of my comings and goings to men of the law?" The outlaw's eyes grew hard. "The truth! Do you deny it?"

Dan looked away. He could not deny the accusation. He had spoken of those overnight stays of Vasquez and some of his men, but only in answer to direct questions by the sheriff.

Dan Clark was by nature a law-abiding fellow, and he had been unable to lie to the sheriff. He had not wanted to "squeal" on Vasquez or his men, and in answering the questions he had avoided saying anything which might betray their whereabouts at the times of the questionings.

"You will dismount, friend Dan!" The man with the gun gave the order curtly. "You will refrain from any attempt to retrieve your gun!"

Dan was a rugged fellow, standing a good six feet in height. He could usually hold his own in rough-and-tumble fighting and was not in the habit of taking orders from anyone. He had an edge over the bandit in both height and weight, but that rifle leveled at his heart was a great equalizer.

Still spluttering that this was no way to treat a friend, Dan Clark did as he was told.

"You will take off your boots and socks!" Tiburcio ordered curtly.

Bewildered, Dan seated himself and removed his boots and socks.

"Take this cord, False Friend! Tie your ankles!" Tiburcio tossed a cord to Dan who resentfully complied with the order. This was carrying a joke too far! Too damn far!

"A most slovenly knot! Retie it!" Tiburcio spoke sharply. "Do not try my patience, friend!"

Still muttering about jokes being carried too far, Dan retied the knot.

With the lithesome grace of *el leon del monte*, Vasquez swung from the saddle.

In spite of his hobbles, Dan scrambled to his feet, only to be pushed unceremoniously back to the ground.

Vasquez straddled the prostrate and by now thoroughly angry young rancher and quickly bound his wrists behing his back. Then Vasquez emptied Dan's pockets and viewed the contents, the most interesting to the bandit being a purse containing about seventy dollars.

"This I shall give to the poor!" Vasquez stuck the purse in his own pocket, then laughed uproariously. "I, Tiburcio, am very poor!"

Other items which Vasquez found of interest were a watch with Dan's initials on the back, a signet ring, a pocket knife, and a few odds and ends which Dan happened to have in his pockets. "These I shall keep to remember a friend by—a friend whom I used to love! A false friend, but a friend nonetheless." Vasquez pocketed the trinkets, adding "I am a most sentimental man!"

The watch, the money, and all the other items taken, combined, might have been worth two hundred dollars—certainly a small looting by Vasquez' usual standards. But to Dan, striving to make a go on a small unproductive ranch, it was a considerable loss. And the watch, though of only moderate cash value, held for Dan a sentimental worth, for it had been a gift from his folks back east on his twenty-first birthday.

But pride would not let Dan beg; and in glum silence he awaited further developments.

Vasquez cut a rawhide thong from Dan's saddle, and with it he tied Dan's boots together, then draped them across the saddle horn where already he had hung Dan's gun belt, with the pistol still in its holster. Then he added Dan's sombrero, held by the thong Dan had used as a chin-strap to hold the hat in place during windy weather.

"Your horse will I lead down the trail for a distance, then turn him loose, to return to your ranchito," Tiburcio explained. "Tiburcio is no common thief! You will find your horse and saddle after your long walk home!"

Vasquez mounted his own fine grey horse, then picked up the reins of Dan's buckskin. "Struggle valiantly against the cords which bind thee, friend Dan," he said. "If you struggle hard enough, in time you should free yourself."

With a mocking salute, Vasquez rode away, taking with him Dan's horse, gun, and boots.

In time Dan Clark did free himself, then gingerly set out on that twenty-odd mile trek to his ranch far back in the mountains. There was little chance of anyone from whom Dan might seek aid coming along that remote wilderness trail.

Now, to a man properly shod and used to hiking, a twenty-mile hike may seem a small matter. But Dan, like most of his breed, was constitutionally opposed to walking under any circumstances if he could possibly avoid it. He would have considered that twenty-mile hike a killing experience shod in riding boots, and now he was being forced to make it barefoot.

Several years had elapsed since Dan's barefoot-boy days, and his feet had lost their calluses. They were soft-skinned and tender, and soon became bloody and sore from the sun-heated earth, the rocks, the brush snags, and the cockleburs. So, after an hour of slow painful hobbling along the rock-strewn trail, Dan set about to improve the situation.

His coat was gone because the day had been warm and the coat had been tied behind the cantle; however, he did have on his vest. He took this vest and ripped it down the middle seam in the back. Then, with strings made by tearing strips from his shirt, he fashioned rude sandals which eased the pain of walking to some extent.

Dan trudged slowly on. The sandals were hard to keep on, and he had to pause from time to time to replace the ties that were constantly wearing through. In time his shirt was gone, all used up in making these tie replacements.

Evening came on, then night; and with the coming of darkness, Dan was forced to stop. He could not see what lay in the trail, and already his feet were too bruised and sore to risk further injury.

Now Dan wished for his coat—for his vest even—for as night came on, the mountain air turned cold and, clad only in his britches and underwear, he was soon chilled to the bone.

In time it was daylight again, and Dan started walking, stiff and sore from his night in the cold—and mad clean through!

The sun came up, and as the day progressed the air began to warm. At first the warmth was a pleasant relief from the early morning chill; then it increased to a heat the tired footsore Dan found almost unbearable.

In time the last of the shirt strips wore away completely; so Dan was forced to use first his undershirt and then his underdrawers as bindings for his sandals.

By now he was going on sheer willpower, but it never entered his mind to give in to fatigue and despair.

Doggedly he trudge on in the glaring heat of a day turned unseasonably hot. His head ached from the heat, and his bare shoulders and back were badly sunburned. The temptation to find a shady spot and give up the struggle was strong. But his was a stubborn nature, and so he trudged on.

In time Dan Clark came to the mountain meadow where he had cleared land for his house, barn, and corrals—the place he called home. And there, waiting patiently at the stable door, was his buckskin horse, still saddled. And still slung across the saddle horn were Dan's boots, his sombrero, and his gun belt, the pistol still in its holster, all waiting for him at the end of his long walk home.

Truly might it be said that Tiburcio Vasquez was no common thief! His methods of evening a score should be proof of that!

FOOTNOTE: Dan Clark is of course a fictional character, created to give life to an old legend. If I remember correctly, it was Johnnie McGovern who told the story of the young rancher who was made to walk home barefoot by Vasquez as a punishment for having "talked too much." Johnnie gave it as one of the Vasquez stories going the rounds in his own early years.

There have been other versions of this story, and it may well have been based on some true incident. Like so many of the Vasquez stories, it would indicate a man somewhat vindictive at times, yet lacking the bloodlust shown in the deeds of many of the outlaws.

Another facet in the complex nature of the man is given in the following story of the mysterious stranger.

THE MYSTERIOUS STRANGER

All throughout the forenoon, the young woman went about her routine tasks in a happy mood, mindful of the table, of The Book there on the table, and of that which was within The Book. Not only was there The Word within The Book—and truly the young woman did place a simple, childlike faith in The Word—but now there was something else equally important to her in it—$500 in greenbacks.

The girl, and the young woman was little more than a girl, saw nothing sacrilegious in using The Book as a repository for money. It had been her faith in The Word contained in The Book that had given her courage to leave the comfort and security of her parents' home back east and come West with her young husband, to a homestead out here in this unsettled land. And it had been faith in The Word and in the rightness of things which had borne her up in these first struggling years in their new home, years in which setbacks had taken their meager savings, forcing them to go deeply into debt.

However, things were looking brighter now for the girl. Her husband had sold a bunch of cattle, the first increase from their small herd, and the money the cattle had brought should take care of their most pressing needs, as well as clear off some of their indebtedness.

She would feel safer when her husband got home and could take the money into town and put it in the bank. However, he had had this chance for a couple of weeks' work at wages, and *that* money too was important. For it had been money thus taken in at odd jobs, spliced in with his own work put into the homestead, which had kept the family in food and clothing during the five years they had lived on their little ranch in the mountains.

And, after all, nobody knew of that $500 there in The Book on the table.

With two young children under foot and a nine-month-old baby in his crib, and with all the household and barnyard chores which frontier women took for granted, the young woman found that the forenoon had slipped by rather quickly. She was preparing the noonday meal for herself and her children when a "Halloo!" from outside took her to the door.

"Madam, may I speak to the man of the house?" The stranger spoke in English, though his costume and appearnace bespoke him a Spanish Californian.

The girl hesitated, not wishing to divulge that she was alone. But lying would be useless if the man were in fact one of the outlaws known to be roving through the back country, and it would be rude if the stranger were here on legitimate business. She replied, "My husband will not be home until late this evening."

"I am sorry to find that your husband is not home." The stranger spoke courteously. Then, looking towards the noontide sun, he hinted, "I have ridden far, and there are no places serving meals hereabouts."

Again the young woman hesitated. But she was not one to see anyone go away hungry at mealtime. "Señor, unsaddle your horse, then come in and join me for dinner."

"Gracias, Señora! You are most kind! I am indeed hungry, for I have had coffee only for breakfast, and nothing since." The stranger's smile was pleasant and his manner polite. He added, "However, my horse will stand better if I leave him saddled."

The stranger rode around to the back of the cabin, and there he tied his horse conveniently close to the rear door, still saddled, ready for an immediate getaway should a hasty departure prove needful. This fact the girl noticed, but did not comment on.

From force of habit, acquired early on the frontier, the girl took note of the horse, a fine silver-grey gelding, spirited and powerfully built, and of the saddle and other trappings, all of which were enlivened with much hand-wrought silver.

The stranger himself was noteworthy. Though slightly under medium height and of slender build, there was a panther-ish strength and self-assurance about him. His clothing was also worthy of note: carefully tailored, and far too elaborate and expensive to be that of any working vaquero from one of the local ranches.

Could this self-assured stranger be—?

A vague dread assailed the girl. The name of Tiburcio Vasquez was a household word in the Central California of the early 1870s, and the deeds ascribed to the notorious bandit leader, as well as his bitter hatred of all gringos, were well-known to everyone.

As a member of the hated gringo race, the young woman knew she might well have a reason to worry should the mysterious stranger indeed prove to be the famed bandit leader.

The manner of the stranger was respectful as he entered the cabin, and he took the chair offered him with a polite "Gracias, Señora!"

The children, a girl two years old and a boy not yet four, sidled bashfully up to the stranger, and he spoke to them affably. Surely this gentlemanly caballero could not be the bloodthirsty bandit of the grim stories going the rounds. So thought the young woman as she finished preparing dinner, then set the meal on the table.

At the hostess' request, the stranger took his place at the head of the table, then did justice to the meal, for he was indeed hungry.

When at last the guest was through eating, he pushed his chair back, with a polite "Gracias, Señora! A most satisfying repast!"

Then his manner changed. "You have guessed my identity! Have you not?"

The young woman nodded, unsure of the safest answer.

"The fame of the Great Tiburcio Vasquez echoes the length and breadth of all California!" the stranger boasted. "The gringo tyrants have learned to their sorrow that Vasquez is not a man to trifle with, nor to be ignored!"

The courtly caballero was gone, and in his place was the arrogant brigand. Vasquez went on, "Your husband has recently sold some cattle, and the money has not yet been deposited in the bank, hence it must be here in this house! Do not lie to me! I have ways of knowing these things!"

With a sinking heart, the girl realized that transactions such as the sale of cattle could not be kept secret. She said nothing, but the stricken look in her eyes told the outlaw that his guess had been accurate.

"Get that money! Or you and your children will suffer!" Vasquez spoke harshly, and the girl, remembering the bloodcurdling tales which were circulating about the notorious bandit chief, made no effort to hold out further against him. Instead, she went to the table, opened The Book, and leafed through it until the five one-hundred-dollar bills were in her hand.

"This is all the money that we have. To lose it will mean that we lose our home." The girl did not beg, simply stated a fact, as she handed the money to the outlaw.

Tiburcio Vasquez, hardened bandit with a price on his head, looked at the money in his hand, then at the woebegone face of the woman. "Thy need is perhaps greater than mine, Señora. You shall keep the money," Vasquez said as he returned the money to her.

With a gentle touch of his hand, Tiburcio Vasquez bid a farewell to each of the toddlers and to the sleeping babe in his crib. The brazen brigand was gone, and the courtly cavalier had returned, as he addressed the young mother: "They are fine children, Madam, and thou art a most worthy wife. Thy husband is a most fortunate man and truly do I envy him his good fortune!"

Then an impish gleam came into the eyes of Vasquez as he added, "Do not feel sorry for me, Señora! Sorry for me in my keen disappointment in leaving without your money! The Great Tiburcio shall replenish his empty purse in short order, but elsewhere, not here!"

With a boyish laugh the outlaw turned, then strode out the back door to his horse, and having mounted, he saluted the girl with a grandiose sweep of his sombrero.

"Adios, Señora! Muchas gracias! Your kind hospitality will I long remember!" And with that, he touched spur to his horse and rode away.

FOOTNOTE: Like the preceding story, this is a somewhat fictional build-up to give life to one of the old stories handed down through the years. This tale of Vasquez taking money from a young woman and then returning it to her came by way of what would seem a reliable source, and it may well have been based on an actual incident.

History records Tiburcio Vasquez as a ruthless, embittered, self-indulgent man. And yet there seems to have been dormant in his complex nature some inherent quality of decency and honor.

This is only one of many such stories in which he displayed impulses of generosity and compassion. In similar vein is the story which follows, a story of bread cast upon the waters.

BREAD CAST UPON THE WATERS

For Tiburcio Vasquez, *El Bandido*, the future looked grim indeed. It would seem La Señora Buena Fortuna had turned her back on him completely and had relinquished him to her evil sister, Madama Mala Fortuna, who even now was leading him onto dangerous ground where he might well end his devil-may-care career swinging at the end of the gringo vigilantes' rope.

It had all started with that holdup of the stage up near San Juan Bautista—a routine bit of business surely! Usually the Vasquez gang holdups were carried off smoothly, and without undue risk, but this time Madama Mala Fortuna had entered the picture and dealt her hand.

A party of vigilantes, out on another holdup case, chanced to meet the stage shortly after it was robbed. Hearing of the robbery from the irate victims, the posse took off in quick pursuit of the bandits. With a hot trail to follow, they overtook the too-confident brigands as they were taking their noontide siesta in the shelter of a grove of trees some fifteen miles from the scene of the holdup.

In the shootout which followed, some men on both sides of the fray were wounded, and several of the outlaws were taken captive by the vigilantes.

The bandits who managed to escape that first barrage scattered, some getting to their still-saddled horses tethered back in the brush; but others, not so fortunate, were forced to take off on foot through the dense chaparral, to lie low until the posse left the scene, or risk almost certain capture should they be sighted.

Vasquez himself had managed to retrieve his own horse and escape, but not completely unscathed. A bullet from one of the men of the posse had grazed his ribs, leaving a wound that was painful, though not in itself serious. If neglected, however, this wound could cause complications.

Traveling south and avoiding the more traveled roads, Vasquez managed to keep ahead of the posse, but could not escape them completely, for having learned from some of the bandits taken captive that Vasquez himself had taken a certain trail, they had picked up his tracks early, and were following him doggedly. And even worse, Vasquez was now in country unfamiliar to him and, try as he might, he could not give his pursuers the slip as he had done so often in the past.

Then Mala Fortuna dealt him her most telling doublecross, for Vasquez' horse, already weary from the long chase, had gone lame. Knowing that the vigilantes, still doggedly on the trail, would in time overtake him, Vasquez could see only one chance of escape.

Choosing a rocky creek bottom where tracks would not betray him, Vasquez dismounted. The loot from that last holdup was stashed away in his saddlebags and, not wanting to give up this booty, he removed the saddlebags from his horse, then pulled the bridle from his horses's head, draping it over the saddle horn. With a quick lash across the rump with his quirt, he started the weary horse on his way.

Hopefully, the horse would keep going south, leaving a clear trail for the posse to follow. This should give Vasquez a little time to double back on foot, and with luck he might be able to find a hiding place before the vigilantes discovered that they had been duped.

Unwilling to give up the loot, Vasquez sought out a hollow tree where he cached the saddlebags, to be recovered at some future date.

For Tiburcio El Bandido the future was looking progressively grimmer. After three days of ducking around through the brush like an oversized conejo-rabbit, Vasquez still had not been able to give his pursurers the slip completely.

Several times in the three days since he had abandoned his lame horse, Vasquez had been uncomfortably close to the human bloodhounds who so persistently dogged his trail, though he tried to cover his tracks. Cut off from escape routes by the men of the posse, and still in unfamiliar country, he had no way of contacting sympathetic fellow countrymen who might have aided him. And even worse, those riding-boot footprints he had to leave when crossing soft ground were a dead giveaway to his pursuers.

Though Vasquez had his pistol with him, he dared not fire at game, knowing that a pistol shot might be heard and bring his pursuers upon him; nor could he build a fire, for the smoke would give his position away. Roots and berries would have to be his fare for the time being. And to compound his troubles, that gunshot wound along his ribs had become infected and could bring on blood poisoning, if not treated soon.

Yes, it would seem that La Señora Buena Fortuna had completely deserted Tiburcio Vasquez, the dauntless bandido.

In the heat of midsummer, wending his way up across the rocks of a canyon already beginning to run short of water, Vasquez was in desperate straits. True, by working deeper into the rugged Sierra Santa Lucia, and by covering his trail as best he could as he traveled, he had so far managed to keep out of the clutches of the vigilantes, who were still doggedly combing the lower reaches of the mountains for him. However, that same posse effectively cut off any chance for him to seek out friends who might aid him; and that wound on his side, at first little more than skin-deep, was by now, after seven days, badly infected. Unless it were treated soon, it would be only a matter of time before he would succumb, like some wounded beast of the wild, leaving his bones in the wilderness far from the haunts of men.

Resolutely Vasquez refused even to consider surrender to the posse, knowing that if he did, a vigilante hanging would probably be his fate. Better to die alone in the wilderness than to dance at the end of a lynch-mob's rope!

Preoccupied with finding a firm footing up across the water-smoothed rocks of the nearly dry creekbed, Vasquez at first gave little heed to the mournful plaint of a dove, even though the call was repeated several times. But when the call of the dove gave way to the strident Who! Who! Who! of an owl, the fugitive froze in his tracks.

Respectable owls did their "who-whoing" at night, not in broad daylight! And here the sun was close to its zenith!

Looking in the direction from whence came that insistent "who-who," Vasquez espied an Indian woman, standing partially hidden in the brush some distance up a side canyon.

Aware that she had caught the man's attention, the woman beckoned, then disappeared up the draw with its thickets that could furnish easy concealment.

Vasquez changed his course, taking the side canyon, and when he reached the spot where he had last seen the woman, he paused, nonplussed since no one was in sight.

Again that "who-who-who!" of the owl, this time much farther up the draw, so Vasquez proceeded, always getting some sign of any change in direction from the woman, although she continued to keep some distance ahead of him.

Once when the willows along the watercourse gave way to an open meadow, Vasquez could see that several women, all carrying baskets, were traveling up the draw ahead of him. All, it would seem, were carefully camouflaging their trail; yet apparently they were willing enough that he should follow them.

As for Vasquez himself, he had no desire to have the vigilantes pick up his trail, so he too was careful to leave no sign of his passing.

In time the trail entered a narrow gorge. Then a drying waterfall, seemingly impassable, blocked further travel up the canyon floor. Here the women left the watercourse and began to climb up the steep wall of the canyon, using a series of ledges and fissures in the rock wall which would have proven a hopeless maze to anyone unfamiliar with the trail.

Climbing carefully to avoid losing his own footing, Vasquez followed the women up the cliff front, then out onto a ledge which offered a passage above the waterfall. Eventually this trail led out of the narrows and into a small upland meadow, and in this isolated glade was a native village, with people going about their daily chores.

The houses were but crude huts, made of poles covered with brush and animal hides. Apparently this was a summer camp only, the residents returning to the lower reaches of the mountains before winter set in.

It was not a large band inhabiting the village, perhaps twenty-five adult Indians, and about as many children. All seemed friendly.

The men approached diffidently, each man in turn proferring his hand with a polite, "Buenos dias, Señor Vasquez," indicating they recognized their guest and wanted to show friendly intentions.

Vasquez surmised that the Indians had seen him in his wanderings earlier, had wanted to offer aid to him, but had been hesitant about bringing a white man into their remote mountain retreat lest they lose this hideaway to the alien usurpers who had already taken from them their ancient lands along the rivers.

The woman who had first signaled for Vasquez to follow apparently held a place of authority in the clan; and quite probably the final decision as to whether or not to offer aid to Vasquez had been left to her discretion. She was a woman of advanced age, and apparently was a *curandera* or medicine woman, for she remarked about the clotted blood staining Vasquez' shirt, then set about brewing some herbs.

Having brewed her potions, the old woman gave Vasquez a bowl of pungent tea to drink, then ordered him to remove his shirt that she might poultice the festering wound on his side, by now a foul-smelling sloughing sore.

Meanwhile, the other women of the village had been preparing the food, roast venison augmented with roots and berries, for this was summertime, when Nature was bountiful.

Having shared in this primitive repast with the friendly Indians, Vasquez addressed the medicine woman in her own native Salinan dialect: "Venerable grandmother, why hast thou risked bringing me, an alien, here into your secret mountain sanctuary?"

With gentle dignity, the venerable lady replied: "As a child, I was a neophyte of the good padres at the Mission San Antonio, and one axiom that I remember from those years is: Bread cast upon the waters will return to the giver tenfold. Though in poverty ourselves, we try to give aid to others even less fortunate." She paused, then went on, "There is another reason also. Two winters ago, we were camped near La Cañada de Cantua, in a time of near famine, when game was scarce and work for the men non-existent. We were reduced to a diet of acorns and grubs dug from rotted wood. Then thou, Señor Vasquez, saw our plight, and thou ordered thy men to bring us provender. All winter long, at least twice a week, a wagon would stop at our village, with a side of beef and sacks of corn meal and frijoles."

Again the woman paused. Then she added, "God wouldst have been displeased, Señor Vasquez, had we not come to thine aid."

Bread cast upon the waters. It had been but an impulse of the moment, that order to his men to furnish provisions to the Indians camped not far from his own camp in the Cantua country. Certainly it had been no great drain on Vasquez' own resources, since the beef butchered had been rustled from Salinas Valley ranchers and the corn meal and frijoles had been pilfered from poorly guarded warehouses in towns up and down the Long Valley.

For Tiburcio Vasquez, it might truly be said that this bread cast upon the waters had returned tenfold—and then some! For Tiburcio El Bandido knew that it had been his own life which had been given back to him when the Indians had decided to come to his aid.

FOOTNOTE: Various versions of this tale, some in print, have come down through the years—how Tiburcio Vasquez, hard-pressed by a posse and seriously wounded, had been given sanctuary in a mountain retreat by friendly Indians whom he had previously befriended. This may well be one of the Vasquez legends based on an actual incident.

EPILOGUE

Back in the early 1920s, an old-time Californiano of Spanish descent stopped for a few days at the old homeplace at La Panza, to look over old scenes and to discuss the La Panza Mines, active in an earlier day.

This man, Hernando Chavez by name, and my uncles Will and Othor Still, got to swapping yarns about the early days, and the Vasquez gang, once well-known in the La Panza area, came into the conversation.

Señor Chavez had a number of anecdotes on the early-day outlaws of Central California, including several tales based on the life and exploits of Tiburcio Vasquez himself.

It was from Hernando Chavez that I first heard the story of Vasquez hiding under the lady's skirts (a version in which the heroine of the hoop skirts was a lady of the gentility who acted through a feeling of patriotic duty). From him also came the story of the lovely Anita, Vasquez' first lost love, as well as versions of the stories of the purloined horses and of the sheriff's posse who lost their mounts to the wily bandido. Señor Chavez also contributed a most entertaining

version of Vasquez' betrayal by a conniving female. That story went
something like this:

Luciana, the lovely light of Tiburcio's life, was tempted by the
gold of the villainous gringo lawmen, and for a price she agreed to
lay a trap for our hero. Luciana was to set a lamp on the stand in
front of the window of her boudoir to signify that Vasquez had entered her house. Then, when he entered her bedroom, she was to
close the curtains of the bedroom window, but was to leave a small
crack in the draperies, that the lawmen might peek through. Thus
they could time their entry with precision.

Lying in wait, the heartless lawmen saw the signals, and at the
crucial moment forced entry, capturing our hero in a most com-
promising position, quite incapable at that moment of either de-
fending himself or escaping.

Others have also told how a deceitful Delilah betrayed the amorous
Tiburcio by setting a trap baited with her own ample charms, leaving
Vasquez vulnerable to an easy capture by the ruthless men of the
law. The names of this double-dealing lady have been given, and they
are legion: Luciana, Luisa, Jacinta, Modesta, Mariana, Juanita,
Rosamunda, Rosabella, and others.

Some have pictured this lady as a she-Judas who willingly sold
her lover for a price; others, more charitable, have said she was *poco
loco en la cabeza.*

Acutally, this story—that Vasquez was betrayed by a false lover
who, for a price, aided the authorities in his capture—is perhaps
the most widely spread of all the Vasquez legends, not only in the
folk tales of the Spanish Californians, but also in many books and
articles on the bandit leader which have been compiled throughout
the years. Unfortunately, as charmingly romantic as this story is, it
hardly squares with the report by the men of the posse who made the
capture.

George Beers, a newspaper reporter who was with Undersheriff
Albert Johnston and his posse at the time Tiburcio was captured,
gave these details:

Tiburcio Vasquez was not arrested at night in a romantic moment
in a lady's boudoir. He was arrested at noon in the roadhouse of one
Greek George, who catered to the needs of wanted men. There were
no betrayng signals. The possemen, having kept the roadhouse under
surveillance for several days, recognized Vasquez' grey horse tethered

at the back of the building and, not wanting to risk the escape of their quarry, they commandeered a lumber wagon that was being driven towards the inn.

This wagon was owned by a paisano known to both Greek George and Vasquez as a man they could trust. This unwilling driver was forced at gun-point to let the possemen hide themselves in the bottom of his wagon, then to drive up into the yard of the inn, as was his habit in the past.

Greek George's wife, a Spanish-Californian, was busy serving the noon meal to Vasquez, young Corona, and her own children. She saw the wagon approaching, but since she recognized the driver, she did not give the alarm. Once in the yard, the lawmen quickly surrounded the house, cutting off escape for the two fugitives inside.

Vasquez leaped out a back bedroom window and made a beeline for his tethered horse out back, but a shot from George Beers' gun clipped him in the shoulder, and a charge of buckshot from the double-barreled shotgun of Deputy Frank Hartley caught him in the backside.

Painfully though not fatally wounded, our hero surrendered without further ado, an inglorious finale to a most colorful career.

It was but a routine arrest—so said Reporter George Beers, who was present and should know.

Vasquez himself had inadvertently tightened the noose when, a month earlier, he and some of his henchmen descended upon the ranch house of one Alexander Repetto, a prosperous Italian sheepman, intending to rob him.

Vasquez was disappointed that the sheepman did not have any large amount of cash on hand. Threatening to kill him if he refused, Vasquez forced Repetto to make out a check for $800, then send his nephew into Los Angeles to cash the check. Vasquez held the old man hostage in his own home while the youth was gone.

Although the nephew tried to carry out his instructions and did cash the check without disclosing his reasons, an observant bank official suspected something amiss and notified the authorities. A posse formed and set out for Repetto's ranch.

Meanwhile the youth had given the money to the outlaws, who had released their hostage and left the premises. However, as they were making their getaway, they robbed three travelers they chanced to meet along the road.

Although the outlaws did escape the posse on this occasion, this
little caper was to cost Vasquez his freedom, for it had pointed his
whereabouts in the Los Angeles area. Forthwith a closer surveillance
was placed on all who might be sympathetic, and in time Vasquez
and his band were located as having a camp in the *monte*, not far
from Greek George's tavern.

To be perfectly honest with you, I have given both versions of the
capture of Tiburcio Vasquez, the great bandit leader. Take your
pick of these version, amigos, take your pick! Me, I like Señor Chavez'
version best; while it may not be the correct version, it seems a shame
to discard it, so why not preserve it as a part of the Vasquez saga?

Actually, there does seem to be some historic basis for the legend
that it was Tiburcio's romantic escapades which brought about his
eventual downfall. However, it would appear that his betrayer was
not a deceitful Delilah, but a cuckolded husband.

As detailed earlier, Vasquez had been having a pleasant little affair with Rosaria, the voluptuous wife of Abdon Leiva, one of his
lieutenants. Aware at last of the two-timing, and smarting under the
sly taunts of his amused companions, Leiva could do nothing openly;
he knew his own position in the gang could not withstand an open
break with the gang's chosen leader. However, this affront to his
masculine ego may well have been a deciding factor when the dragnet
of the law closed in on Leiva and he surrendered.

The authorities did not admit publicly that Abdon Leiva was the
informant. However, it seems almost certain that he did buy immunity for himself for his own part in the Tres Pinos robbery and
the murders of three unarmed men, by giving the locations of Vasquez' probable hideouts and the names of persons likely to harbor
the outlaws.

Certainly, Leiva's testimony—along with Rosaria's own spiteful
tale of having been kidnapped at gunpoint, forced to go with Vasquez
into the mountains, and there forcibly raped—did weigh heavily
against Vasquez at the time of his trial.

The strategy of the law enforcement agencies during Vasquez' last
months of freedom would seem to bear out an assumption that someone within Vasquez' own circle of acquaintances had given information on his habits. For many months there was surveillance of persons
thought likely to harbor the bandit chief, and the lawmen crowded
in, pushing him out of old haunts, until at last he was cornered in

the *monte* (brush country) in the La Brea district, about ten miles east of Los Angeles, as the town was a century ago.

In addition, Leiva and Rosaria were put on the stand by the prosecution as witnesses against Vasquez. Having testified against his former chief, Leiva was released from prison on December 3, 1875, and allowed to return to his native Chile—on the face of it, almost proof positive that some deal had been made.

There appeared to be no indication of monkey business between Vasquez and Greek George's wife. Greek George, a native of Smyrna, was brought to the United States with that shipment of camels in the 1850s, operated a roadhouse in the La Brea district, and was suspcted of catering to such Californianos as happened to be on the outs with the law.

At the time of his capture, Vasquez and certain members of his band were camped in the brush country back of Greek George's inn. They had formed the habit of riding in for stove-cooked meals, coming in groups of two or three at a time to avoid the suspicion that a larger band of men riding together would cause.

On the forenoon of the day that Vasquez was captured, Greek George had gone into Los Angeles to do a little scouting for Vasquez, but he had been picked up and detained by the lawmen lest he give an alarm.

Now, back to the deceitful Delilah: Here we have an excellent example of a legend in the making. Take that incident (fully authentic) of Vasquez and the two-timing Rosaria being caught by the cuckolded husband "in an act of flagrant dereliction," then overlap this story onto the incident (equally authentic) of the bandit leader being arrested in Greek George's house while Greek George himself was absent and his wife was at home, then add to this the damaging testimony of the vindictive Rosaria at Vasquez' trial, then allow the exact details of these incidents to grow hazy in the minds of people with the passage of time. The result: Elements taken from three different incidents, all fused into one story—the legend of the deceitful Delilah.

And now, before closing this series on the life and loves of Tiburcio El Bandido, a thought-provoking sidelight: It has been said that Vasquez, imprisoned and awaiting trial, admitted to certain acquaintances that though he had never been married officially, he had in fact over the years begat several offspring, at that time scattered out over the state. However, said Vasquez, not the least bit repentant, since it was now too late to rectify matters, it would be more chivalrous *not* to identify these heirs, or their mothers.

In the summer of 1879, when my grandfather, Dr. Thomas C. Still, moved with his family into the La Panza Mines, there was a family living in the neighborhood who went by the name of Vasquez, and it was common gossip among the neighbors that the children in this family were in fact the offspring of Tiburcio Vasquez, left fatherless when the bandit leader was hanged some four years earlier.

This family grew up, each went his own way, and in time they were forgotten. Were these children truly the sons and daughters of Tiburcio Vasquez the outlaw? Or had this identification been based on a misconception because they had the same surname as the bandit leader and lived in the district he was known to have frequented during his lifetime?

If indeed these were the sons and daughters of Vasquez, did their mother keep this knowledge from them? Or did they know and keep the secret forever locked in the backs of their minds, fearful lest the relationship be made public?

Part IV
THE VASQUEZ GANG

Some comments on known associates of Tiburcio Vasquez, during his lifetime and in the years following his death, and other outlaws of the 1870s and 1880s.

THE VASQUEZ GANG

Tiburcio Vasquez the bandit leader must have had a following, else how could he have been a leader? This much at least everyone agrees on. Who, when, where, what, and how many? Amigos, here is where we hit a snag. Was Tiburcio Vasquez a revolutionary general with a large well-organized army of "freedom fighters," as some have portrayed him? Or was he but a punk gangster with a small ragtag following of minor cutthroats whose exploits have been blown all out of proportion by a fatuous following in later years, as some of the later debunkers insist? Here even the experts can't agree; and probably the truth lies somewhere between.

Serious historians have tended to be cautious—too cautious perhaps—in recognizing men claiming to have been members of the Vasquez band, other than those who can be neatly catalogued through police records. However, only a few of the gang were ever arrested and brought to trial, and those who did escape the dragnet of the law were never fully identified.

Considerable space has been given to Vasquez' youthful association with Anastacio Garcia, who may have been a kinsman by marriage, and whose cutthroat career ended abruptly when the vigilantes hanged him. However, history is vague as to who else might have been compadres of Vasquez during those years before his first arrest on a horse-stealing charge, which sent him to San Quentin in August of 1857.

In the three and a half years following Vasquez' release from San Quentin in August of 1863, his closest compadres (so history tells us) were "the human wildcat" Juan Soto and the gentlemanly Tomas Redondo, alias Procopio, alias Tomas Murrieta, said to have been a nephew of Joaquin Murrieta. Unfortunately, this warm friendship was interrupted when Vasquez was sent back to San Quentin in January of 1867, on a charge of cattle rustling. The friendship was renewed upon Vasquez' release in June of 1870, only to be cut short when Juan Soto was killed in January of 1871 in a gunfight with Sheriff Morse. Shortly thereafter, the dignified Procopio was sent back to San Quentin for grand larceny. History is rather vague about Vasquez' other friends in those earlier years and in prison.

It is the last four years of freedom for this Robin Hood of the Gabilans (or should I have said robbin' hood?) that produces the greatest controversy. Some have portrayed Vasquez as the organizer of a band of "revolutionists" with roots in Old Mexico, and this school of thought even went so far as to say that "history might well have been changed had not Vasquez been betrayed into the hands of his enemies." However, others insist just as positively that Vasquez was but a small-time racketeer, with a nondescript following of cheap hoodlums and little organization behind the band.

Old-timers (both Californians and Americans) who were close enough to the scene to have formed opinions of their own have said that in the last four years of Vasquez' own freedom, his followers consisted of two groups. There were perhaps twenty to thirty "lieutenants," men close enough to belong to the inner circle of confederates, and who in one way or another took part in at least some of the raids ascribed to Vasquez. There was also an outer fringe of "compadres," acquaintances who were willing, for a price, to furnish aid, sanctuary, supplies, and information to Vasquez and his men, but who probably were not privy to the plans of the gang.

Even "history" gets a little confused as to who and how many men took part in certain of the raids attributed to Vasquez and his band. Some of the old newspaper accounts say that as many as thirty men took part in some of these raids, but later historians tend to discount such reports as exaggerations. It would seem that for the most part Vasquez limited his "crew" to between five and ten men, a number large enough to insure "cooperation" from his victims, yet not so large a band as to hamper a quick getaway.

When Vasquez was arrested in Greek George's house in 1874, his second in command was a Mexican named Cleovaro Chavez. He was with Vasquez during the Repetto extortion caper and the holdup of three travelers that same evening, but he escaped the dragnet, going into the New Mexico Territory. Later he was captured in Arizona,

and his head was cut off and brought back to California for identification, then turned over to a museum to be put on display like that
of the presumed Murrieta. At least this is one version of Cleovaro's
exit.

In the winter of 1873-74, an army deserter named Charles Weeks
was picked up and returned to his base camp for courtmartial, and
there he signed a confession that while A.W.O.L. he had joined the
Vasquez band, and had taken part in some of the raids charged to
them. Weeks named another American, George Russell, a man
named Gibson, and a Negro, Arthur Lee, as having been with the
Vasquez band the fall before. This statement might bear out some of
the witnesses who claimed that there had been "white men and
Negroes" taking part in some of the raids, in the company of a "band
of Mexicans."

In later years, there were many men who claimed that in their own
vigorous youth they had been members of Vasquez' band—had
ridden with the valorous Tiburcio on some of his raids. But as one
old-timer, a Spanish-Californian, put it: "It is hard to separate the
claims of those who did verily serve under such illustrious men as
the noble Murrieta and the estimable Vasquez from the idle bragging
of insignificant men who were seeking a little reflected glory by riding
the tail of a comet."

                    *   *   *

In the fall of 1867, when my grandfather, Dr. Thomas C. Still,
brought his family into El Pueblo de San Luis Obispo, that town
was still more "Spanish" than it was "American," and at that time
most of the "back country" was uninhabited wilderness.

The U.S. Census for 1870 gives the total population for the whole
of San Luis Obispo County as 4,700 persons, most of them living in
the settlements along El Camino Real, on the coast, and along the
Salinas River.

Back in the San Luis of the late 1860s, the vigilante hanging of
seven men of the old Linares Gang a decade earlier was still a live
topic of conversation, and with the outlaw gangs more insolent and
crime on the increase, the honest citizens were in constant fear that
the lawless element would once again get control, as they had back
when the infamous Jack Powers was masterminding the renegades.
There were mutterings that the only good bandit was a dead bandit.

In August of 1869, a feud of long standing between two American settlers, Michael Ruick and N. C. Gilbert, ended in a shootout in which Gilbert shot and killed Ruick and Ruick's wife. However, since there had been aggravation on the part of Ruick as well as Gilbert, the jury returned a verdict of second-degree murder, and Gilbert was sentenced to eleven years in prison.

In June of 1870, a man named Zenobio Valenzuela was shot and killed on the street in San Luis Obispo, and a young boy on the street was seriously wounded by a stray bullet. Yet, although the killing took place in broad daylight, with other people on the street at the time, the witnesses suddenly developed poor eyesight when questioned by the authorities, and the killer (or killers) in this gangland type killing of Valenzuela were never apprehended.

In January of 1871, an old man living in an outlying district was shot in the back in his cabin while he was cooking a meal. A short time later, one Vicente Arias was picked up with various articles, including a saddle, which had belonged to the victim. Under pressure, Arias confessed to the murder, was put on trial, and sentenced to life in prison.

In August of 1871, the body of a San Luis Obispo County rancher, Francisco Guerra, was found lying in the road, a bullet in the back. Apparently Don Francisco had started out for town, but had been ambushed and shot for whatever money he might have been carrying on his person at the time.

Bodies of unidentified travelers once again were being found along El Camino Real, and once again there was talk of reorganizing the Vigilantes to bring the miscreants and malefactors under control. Under these circumstances, the honest citizens of the sparsely settled and inadequately policed settlements of Central California were justifiably worried, for they were vulnerable to robbery and extortion, and legal recourse was almost nonexistent.

Then along came Tiburcio Vasquez and his Merry Men, cutting their high-jinks and getting their names in all the papers. Is it any wonder that Vasquez and his band should get the credit for all the crimes that were being committed?

Tiburcio Vasquez was no stranger in San Luis Obispo County, and men known to have been members of his gang were well known, some of them with kin or close friends in the town or in outlying districts. In fact, one of Vasquez' better kept secrets was a hideout which he used upon occasion. This retreat was situated along the San Juan River, on the eastern watershed of the La Panza Mountains.

In the early 1870s, at the time Vasquez and his band were on the loose, there was a scattering of Spanish-Californians living along the San Juan, on the outskirts of the La Panza Ranch which at that time was owned by Jones and Schoenfeld.

A few of these settlers were homesteading; most were simply squatters. Some worked as vaqueros on the La Panza Ranch; some eked out meager livelihoods from a few cows, goats, pigs, and chickens, along with a small fenced-in garden plot. Others made their livelihood from means not likely to have met with society's approval. Of these paisanos along the San Juan, there were kinsmen and compadres of men known to have been associated with Vasquez, men willing to aid the outlaws when the need arose.

A man named Nuñez had a saloon in one of the tributaries of the San Juan, and legend credits him as having been the "front man" for Vasquez and his band when they chanced to be within the district, gathering information for them, and furnishing supplies as needed. Also, Vasquez and his men did have an open-air camp in a side draw not far from Nuñez' saloon, and it was said that in inclement weather the outlaws sought shelter with friendly paisanos or availed themselves of vacant houses and barns.

In the spring of 1878, about three years after the colorful career of the estimable Tiburcio had been brought to so untimely an end, gold was discovered about two miles up the canyon from Vasquez' old camp along the San Juan. Within the next year this discovery brought an estimated six hundred or more men into these La Panza Mountains, some looking to take gold out of the ground, others to take the gold from the miners, or for reasons of their own to lose themselves in a crowd.

Because of their previous familiarity with the area, plus the fact that a large percentage of the prospectors coming into the La Panza Mines were native-born Californianos or more recent arrivals from Mexico and thus likely to prove friendly, some members of the old Vasquez band still on the loose found the confusion of the gold fever a good cover-up for their own extralegal activities. It was a known fact that outlaw bands committing robberies in older settlements of the Salinas and San Joaquin Valleys, and even as far south as Ventura and Los Angeles, would seek escape in the La Panza Mountains, since it was easy to disguise their own identities among the throng of newcomers.

Once they had reached the mines district, men wanted by the law had little trouble in evading the lawmen. If an officer had a warrant for one of these bandidos, he got no cooperation at all from most of the *hijos del pais*; and unless that officer knew the wanted man personally, he stood a good chance of having the miscreant in the very group he was talking with, with no one present divulging that man's identity.

Because some of those seeking refuge in the La Panza Mines were known to have been associates of Tiburcio Vasquez during his heyday, those outlaws rendezvousing in the La Panza Mountains were usually referred to simply as The Vasquez Gang on an assumption of previous ties, even though the Great Tiburcio had long since died.

At this late date, it is impossible to differentiate between men who had actually been associates of Vasquez during his lifetime and those who were simply "riding the tail of a comet." And so, for this chapter and the series of yarns which follows, the term "the Vasquez Gang" is used in its broader sense, and readers are asked not to get too technical in weighing the historical merits of the stories.

Just who were these men making up "the Vasquez Gang"? Among those history has named as members of Vasquez' band, his most trusted cohort seems to have been a personable young Mexican named Cleovaro Chavez. He was with Vasquez in most of the raids in which Vasquez himself was known to have taken part. Then, of course, there was Abdon Leiva, whose saga was detailed earlier.

A Frenchman named August DeBert and another Frenchman nicknamed Horbada (Jorobado - hunchback) were with the band during some of the earlier raids. Unfortunately for him, Horbada talked too much when drinking. A skeleton believed to have been his was found in a cave, and it was assumed that some member of the gang had "shut him up."

Teodoro Moreno, said to have been a cousin of Vasquez, was a member of the band and took part in most of the raids, including Firebaugh's Ferry and Tres Pinos. Moreno was captured in November of 1873, tried, and sentenced to prison.

Romulo Gonzales, a "bloodthirsty full-blood Indian," was recruited early in 1871 and was with the band on most of the raids. Vasquez named him, along with Leiva, to do the actual killing at Tres

Pinos. A posse later picked up Gonzales, but they failed to recognize him and released him.

Fernando Asero, suspected of having taken part in the Tres Pinos raid, escaped the dragnet, but he committed a later murder and was captured, tried and hanged.

Narciso Rodriguez and Francisco Barcenas were early recruits (1871) and took part in some of the first raids attributed to Vasquez. Rodriguez, however, was soon picked up by the authorities. He was tried and sentenced to prison, where he drank poison alcohol and died.

Manuel Rojos and Jose Garcia are said to have taken part in raids with Vasquez, and others have been identified as associates of Vasquez in his last four years of freedom.

The gang was forced to break up as they fled "justice" after the Tres Pinos murders, so Vasquez enlisted several new recruits. Among these were: Ysidro Padillo, who had been a suspect in the brutal murder of an Italian family near Tulare; Blas Bicuna, whose reputation as a killer was well known; T. Monteres; G. Gomez; and the youthful Librado Corona.

Charles Weeks, the army deserter, named the following members of Vasquez' band: Pancho Centur, Chicito Tedra, Romano Jesus, Jose Santescus, Moreno, and a dark Mexican called Antonio.

Among those men who have in the past been named as "compadres" of Vasquez (men who furnished him aid) were: "Greek George" Caralambo, known also as George Allen; one Chico Lopez and one Joaquin Castro, both having furnished sanctuary during those last months that Vasquez was in hiding; Anselmo Herrera, whose son at one time held considerable fame in the boxing world; Nuñez, the saloon-keeper of Vasquez Canyon who, it is said, aided Vasquez in those last months; Juan Castile, known also as John Castrel, a rancher who furnished shelter for the outlaws; and Trinidad Salvador, a rancher whose pretty daughter found favor with the outlaws. And there were others.

Old-timers of San Luis Obispo County, speaking from their own memories, identified a number of men reputed to have been associates of Vasquez, and who themselves figured in the outlawry in central California during the decade after Vasquez' capture. Prominent among these miscreants were: Pascual Benadero, Francisco Valenzuela, Federico Gonzales, Librado Corona, Narciso Asuña, "Mike"

Soto, Reginaldo Santos, Joe Valenzuela, and Cholo Castro, all reputed to have been associates of Vasquez during his years of outlawry. It was said that these men tried to reorganize the outlaw band in the decade following Vasquez' capture, each hoping to become the big he-wolf of the pack.

Pascual Benadero (Venadero), it is said, turned his talents elsewhere after Vasquez was captured, becoming a paid hatchet-man for certain ranchers who wanted obnoxious squatters removed from their holdings. Also, Benadero was suspected of being responsible for the unexplained disappearances of several men considered troublesome by certain local politicians who swung considerable power and were not averse to hiring someone to bushwhack too-persistent opponents.

Reginaldo (Renaldo) Santos may not have been an actual member of the Vasquez band during the time Tiburcio headed it, but he did make his appearance on the Central California scene shortly after Vasquez' time. He recruited some of Vasquez' followers and used the old sanctuaries in the La Panza Mountains, and in the Gabilans and Diablos to the north. Although Santos and his band centered their activities south of the Tehachapis, for the most part, he and his followers take their place in "The Vasquez Gang" legends.

It was said that Santos himself met an untimely end in some dispute among his own men, killed by subordinates who resented his harsh discipline.

Several men who were in and around the La Panza Mines during the gold excitement were named as having been members of "The Vasquez Gang" of the late 1870s. They included: Anselmo Herrera (some said he died while in the mines and was buried in the little graveyard there), Teodoro Monteras, Juan Lopez, Juan Montaña, Romano Garza, Jorge Gomez, Chico Castro (said to have been a brother to Cholo), Joaquin Castro, Joe Soto, Jesus Sedillo, Chili Martinez, Pancho Blanco, Jose Reales, Santos Reis, Rubin Ruiz, Indio Cordero, and several Garcias, numerous Valenzuelas, and others as well, men who may have developed only a little blindness where their fellow countrymen were concerned, yet may not have crossed the line themselves. Then there was "Joaquin Murrieta" of the Seventies, but more on him later.

These men who roved the outlaw trails of Central California met various fates. Some ended their wayward careers prematurely, at the

ends of vigilantes' ropes, in shoot-outs with lawmen, or in feuds
within their own factions; some found their youthful exuberance
cooling behind prison bars; and some (the lucky ones) lived to a ripe
old age without ever having been brought to account for their youthful waywardness. And, no doubt, some of those self-named as early-
day bandits were but "insignificant men riding the tail of a comet."

It appears that the Valenzuelas were a numerous and salty clan,
to judge by the frequency with which their name crops up in the folklore of the old-time Californians.

First there was Old Man Valenzuela, who ran a tough clip-joint
up in the Mother Lode country in the days of the forty-niners, while
his wife (if indeed the lady were a wife) helped out by being the
madam of a fancy-house stocked with pretty wenches brought up
from Mexico to "pleasure" the miners. Meanwhile, their sons helled
around the mining camps, getting into trouble.

Having made their fortune, this estimable couple removed themselves from the iniquitous mining camps and came down into the
Salinas Valley to retire into respectable oblivion. So said various
old-timers who claimed to have known the couple, either up in the
gold country or in later years.

As to those hell-raising sons, it was said that some of them were
killed in barroom brawls. The others in time joined the outlaw fringe
of society, and history has lost track of them.

There was the notorious Joaquin Valenzuela, of the Murrieta
legend, and Joaquin's equally infamous brother Jesus, who escaped
the vigilante dragnet in 1858, as detailed in an earlier chapter. Then
there was the Juan Valenzuela who was hanged in 1857 as a member
of the Flores gang.

In the years of the gold excitement in the La Panza district, several
Valenzuelas were identified as members of outlaw bands. These include Francisco, Fernando, Joe (Jose? Joaquin?), Jesse (Jesus?), and
one Freddie (Federico?). As to whether these latter-day delinquents
were kindred of the earlier ones—*Quien sabe, amigos! Quien sabe!*

There was also Zenobio Valenzuela, who was killed in San Luis
Obispo in what appeared a gangland reprisal. Whether or not he was
kin to the outlaws, I do not know.

In fairness, it should be pointed out that not all the Valenzuelas
living in Central California in those frontier years were outlaws.
There were Valenzuelas (some with given names identical or similar

to those of the outlaws) who were honest law-abiding men earning legitimate livelihoods on small farms and ranches, or working as vaqueros and horse-breakers on the larger ranches. These men should not be confused with the bandits.

Apparently several different Valenzuelas came up into California from Mexico in those early years, and some brought their families with them. They may not have been close kin at all. The 1870 census of San Luis Obispo County lists five separate families of Valenzuelas, each with an origin in Old Mexico. As to the previously mentioned bandidos of the same name, understandably they were not on hand to be counted when the census taker was making his rounds.

A similar situation exists with the name Garcia. History records the cutthroat Manuel Garcia ("Three-finger Jack") and his equally bloodthirsty kinsman, Anastacio Garcia, whose exploits have been detailed earlier. There was also Jose Antonio Garcia, a misguided youth hanged as a member of the Linares Gang in 1858, and several Garcias said to belong to the Vasquez Gang during the 1870s. These included a Joe Garcia and his brother Jesus, known to have been in the La Panza Mines for a time.

However, there were several prominent law-abiding citizens with the surname Garcia living in San Luis Obispo County in this same period. These included Don Ynocente Garcia, whose ranch holdings in time became the settlement of Pozo; Don Julian Garcia, a staunch defender of law and order and a highly respected resident of the county; and Don Jesus Garcia, one of the early settlers on the Carrisa Plains, who developed an extensive cattle ranch there in the early decades of the present century. The integrity of these men was never questioned.

There were other cases where outlaws and honest citizens had similar or identical names, causing embarrassment and confusion as the stories were retold with their characters not precisely identified. After all, the surname of a reputable family made a convenient alias when a man was on the dodge, and most of the outlaws had several aliases.

And now, back to that provocative miscreant Joaquin Murrieta, who has the aggravating habit of popping up at the most unorthodox times, when presumably he had already been laid to a circumspect rest.

Among the old-timers of Central California were several who

insisted that back in the lusty seventies they had seen a man identified to them by others (presumably in the know) as Joaquin Murrieta. Some of these insisted that this man was the veritable Joaquin himself, in person, having returned to California following an extended sojourn in Mexico. Others, not so positive, qualified their statements by saying "a man identified as Joaquin Murrieta," though not necessarily THE Joaquin Murrieta of legend. Also, the name Joaquin Murrieta appears with disconcerting regularity in the folklore surrounding the Vasquez Gang and other outlaws of the 1870s, from far too many sources to be discounted completely.

Among the Spanish-Californians whose own memories would encompass the 1870s were several who said there were *two* Joaquin Murrietas, the *bandido bravo* of the 1850s, and a younger man who appeared on the California scene in the 1870s. Some have identified this younger Joaquin as a cousin or nephew of the legendary Joaquin. Some have said this later Joaquin was a son.

There was a legend among the Spanish-Californians that back in his precocious youth—before leaving for Alta California with Rosita, his one true love—Joaquin Murrieta begat a little *bastardo* from an Indian servant girl on his father's hacienda. This unwed mother (so the story goes) named her little son Joaquin for his father, and the boy grew to manhood in Mexico under the stigma of illegitimacy, yet using the surname of his sire.

Having reached man's estate, this junior Joaquin took a *pasear* up into Alta California, to view for himself the scenes of his sire's glorious deeds, even perchance to emulate them. Then he returned to Old Mexico, where this son of *el bandido bravo* spent a circumspect old age. So sayeth this legend.

Historically, Tomas Redondo, bosom pal of Vasquez, did in fact claim to have been a nephew of the "veritable Joaquin," and upon occasion he used the surname Murrieta as an alias (see George Beers' account of Redondo, written in 1875). However, Tomas Redondo was better known by the nickname Procopio, and besides, he was behind prison bars, hence out of circulation, at the time this resurrected Joaquin appeared on the California scene.

This Joaquin Murrieta of the 1870s has appeared far too often in the folklore of the people, and even in print, to be discounted completely as only a figment of someone's overactive imagination. It is probable that a man using the name was in the area in the 1870s.

Was this second Joaquin Murrieta a kinsman of the legendary Joaquin—perhaps a nephew or cousin, or Joaquin's own bastard son? Or was this other Murrieta a man who chanced to have a name similar to the outlaw of an earlier day? (Contrary to what some of the debunkers have implied, the surname Murrieta is not a figment of Rollin Ridge's inventive mind. Murrieta is an old and respected surname south of the border.)

Or was this Joaquin Murrieta of the seventies but an alias of some man with no real claim to it, an insignificant man getting a little reflected glory by riding the tail of a comet?

Quien sabe, amigos! Quien Sabe!

*   *   *

You say, kind reader, too much space is being given to the Spanish-California *bandido*, in contrast to that given his counterpart, the American bandit of the gold rush years, and how come?

Amigos, this series of stories is written from the perspective of the Salinas Valley and its environs, the section of the state which was one of the last strongholds of the Californianos' resistance to the gringo takeover, hence a natural sanctuary for the California bandido seeking escape from the law for crimes committed elsewhere.

True, we of Central California do have a scattering of American badmen we can brag of. There was of course the crafty Jack Powers, whose double-dealing career has been mentioned in an earlier chapter, a villain of the deepest dye and well worthy of a niche in the annals of local crime. (Or was Powers himself but another victim of those lawless years? A man framed into infamy and used as a scapegoat by opposing factions, themselves warring for power? History is somewhat divided on this score.)

Then there are the James brothers, Frank and Jesse, whose uncle, Drury W. James, owned the historic La Panza Ranch back in the 1860s—they did spend a year in California, most of it with their uncle in San Luis Obispo County. But Drury James was a respected and influential citizen of the community who would not have countenanced any delinquency on the part of his nephews. Also, this was before the James brothers were fully launched in their outlaw career, and it would seem they were on their good behavior while in San Luis Obispo County.

The same can be said for the notorious Dalton Brothers, who had

kinfolks in the Estrella district in eastern San Luis Obispo County
and who were known to have tarried with their kin here upon occasion. But seemingly the Daltons kept out of mischief while here, and
their sojourn attracted little attention at the time.

Then there was that mixed-up Merry Andrew who for a time lived
a Jekyll-Hyde life, alternating between being the respectable businessman Harry Little and the devil-may-care highwayman Dick
Fellows, a bold bad bandit whose wry misadventures shouldn't have
happened to even a bold bad bandit.

There was also that latter-day pair of train robbers, Sontag and
Evans, whose exploits for a time held the public spotlight over in
the San Joaquin Valley. And there were other miscreants and malefactors of other than Mexican origin who upon occasion wandered
through the Salinas Valley, some even meeting an inglorious end
swinging at the end of the vigilantes' ropes, as happened to that
roving gambler Rafe Jackson.

For the most part, however, the American outlaws of the gold rush
years turned their talents towards working the boom towns and
mining camps of the Mother Lode country—after all, that was where
the "big money" was. There were Black Bart, Rattlesnake Dick,
Reel-foot Williams, and all the others who plagued the mining camps
and held up stages back in those roisterous frontier years. But theirs
is a separate story. It was the California bandido who dominated
the folk tales of the Salinas Valley; so this series will deal largely
with him.

*   *   *

My grandfather, Dr. Thomas C. Still, moved with his family into
the La Panza Mines in the summer of 1879, about one year after the
discovery of gold in what was then known as The Vasquez Canyon
(with the old Vasquez camp about one mile down the canyon from
Grandpa's mining claim), while the excitement over the discovery of
gold was still strong, and while an outlaw element held a dominant
place among the throng of prospectors milling through the La Panza
Mountains.

There were at least three saloons in Vasquez Canyon to supply the
needs of the miners; and as the only doctor available, Grandpa was
called upon quite often to patch up the losers of whiskey-inspired
altercations in which somebody had been knifed or shot. This, along

with doctoring such prosaic ailments as broken limbs, pneumonia, ruptured appendixes, and dysentery, as well as birthing the babies for the families living along Vasquez Canyon, gave him a good chance to become acquainted with the *hijos del pais*—and that would include some men wanted by the law at the time but lying low, anonymous as strangers roaming the mountains.

For the most part, Dr. Still remained on amicable terms with the native Californians; hence he was in a position to know something of their true stories.

Wherever there is the promise of gold, a lawless element is sure to appear. In those first years of the La Panza Mines, miners were strong-armed into giving over accumulations of gold dust; sluice boxes were robbed; and occasionally some prospector in an out-of-the-way canyon would disappear without adequate explanation.

In this period, there was some outlawry in other parts of San Luis Obispo County. Occasionally the stage crossing the Cuesta Grade between Santa Margarita and San Luis Obispo was held up, strong boxes taken, and the passengers robbed of whatever of value they might have on their persons. Also, upon occasion, some store owner or saloon keeper was accosted by a pack of ruffians and forced to turn over any money he might have on hand. However, for the most part, the outlawry was committed outside San Luis Obispo County; afterwards the outlaws would return to the La Panza Mountains, to hole up until the hunt died down, for the time being losing their identities among the throng of strangers who were legitimate prospectors.

During the first five years of excitement over the mines, lawmen from other counties often came into the La Panza Mountains, looking for men wanted for crimes committed within their jurisdictions; the county seat in San Luis Obispo was off across the Cuesta and not easily contacted by a posse pursuing a fugitive from the Salinas or San Joaquin valleys. Occasionally a wanted man was picked up, but more often than not, once in the brush-covered mountains, the fugitive was safe.

These mountains were also a sanctuary for outlaws from south of the Tehachapi Mountains. Following some raid in the southern part of the state, the bandits would come up by way of the Tejon Pass or the Cuyama country, thence to the La Panza Mountains.

One day my uncle Will Still was riding through the back range looking for strayed cattle when he heard gunshots in the distance. He rode out onto a point where he could look down across the San Juan River valley, and saw a band of between fifteen and twenty men racing their horses at break-neck speed up along the river flats. Perhaps a half-mile behind them was another band of men in hot pursuit. Shots were exchanged, but there was too great a distance for accurate firing.

That evening, a thoroughly disgruntled posse returned by way of the Still family home, where they stopped for supper. They had lost their quarry when, reaching the rugged Bear Trap country, the wanted men scattered, disappearing into the brush-covered slopes and canyons. The posse was from Kern County and had been pursuing a band of renegades who had held up a stage carrying a considerable amount of money being sent to a bank in Bakersfield. This money was never recovered.

Although the Vigilantes who had acted so forcefully in breaking up the old Linares Gang in San Luis Obispo in 1858 had disbanded soon thereafter, there had been some impromptu justice during those lawless years when a civil war was going on back east, usually spur-of-the-moment mobs who dispersed once the lynching or flogging had been accomplished. Then, along in the mid-seventies, came the Coon-dogs.

The self-named Coon-dogs had been formed as a vigilante group to combat a gang of "cattle-russellers and hawss-thieves" who had begun to make serious inroads in the herds owned by inland ranches in the seventies. As originally formed, these vigilantes were comprised of several of the local ranch owners and ranch foremen from eastern San Luis Obispo County and from Kern County, together with a pack of hot-headed young fellows working as ranch hands on involved ranches. These Coon-dogs operated for a period of about fifteen years.

In later years Frank Fotheringham, foreman on the La Panza and Carrisa during the years these ranches were owned by Jones and Schoenfeld, used to tell of one incident in which he himself took part.

A band of renegades had gathered up a sizable herd of horses from local ranches and started south with them, intending to drive them on to Mexico for sale. The Coon-dogs quickly formed a posse and set out in pursuit, overtaking the horse thieves somewhere in the wilderness country just south of the Tehachapis, and there recovered the stolen horses. Frank was wont to end his narrative with an oblique remark about "horse-thieves who would steal no more horses!"

Although the avowed purpose of these vigilantes had been to promote law and order, in time the Coon-dogs lost sight of their high-minded purpose and degenerated into a lawless pack, as is too often the case with outside-the-law law enforcement. The pressures of the organization were turned away from curbing outlawry, and certain of the ranchers turned the activities of the vigilantes toward their own personal gain. It became a rowdy hell-raising lark for the young fellows who were usually involved in the enforcing.

Many of the old-timers felt that often the burning of squatters' homes, and even some of the killings ascribed to the outlaws, had in fact been perpetrated by the Coon-dogs themselves as a means of ousting unwanted settlers.

In the wake of the mines excitement, a raunchy pack of ne'er-do-wells drifted into the La Panza district. Made up of a duke's mixture of Americans, Mexicans, and foreigners, this unwholesome pack was suspected in thefts of livestock and petty thefts from ranches and homes in Salinas Valley towns, the thieves hieing themselves back to the mountains when things got too hot for them elsewhere.

The general feeling on the part of those living in the area was that this rowdy pack of miscreants was being masterminded by one Ed Clark, a congenital trouble-maker who had a talent for egging the ruffians into various exploits without himself getting involved deeply enough so that legal action could be taken against him.

Ed Clark, so the story goes, found himself in a penniless old age, and so he had to spend his last days in a county hospital where he got religion after it was too late to do him any good.

Those who had followed Ed Clark in time drifted away—if they hadn't already ended up in some hidden grave through the actions of the Coon-dogs, who used this band of misfits as an excuse to continue their activities through the 1880s, before they finally disbanded.

It was in 1882 that Dr. Still moved his family to a new location, about one mile north of the old mining claim in Vasquez Canyon, to be along the new road which had recently been put across the mountains, linking the San Joaquin Valley with the towns of the Coast. Here a rambling frame house was to serve for many years not only as the family home, but also as the La Panza Post Office and Store and as an inn where travelers could get meals and a bed for the night and overnight forage for their horses.

For the most part, the Still family remained on friendly terms with the Spanish-Californians, and among those who would stop for a meal, or for a bed for the night, were certain men who in their youth had been members of outlaw bands. Some of these men had served out a prison sentence or a "hitch on the chain gang." It was from these reformed bandidos, as well as from others of their countrymen who, though themselves law-abiding, had in the past had contacts with men of the old Vasquez Gang, that some of the following stories originally came.

Time has a way of blurring detail, and in collecting these stories I ran into a confusing mixture of garbled information as to who, when and where; yet all of these stories are based on actual incidents.

And so, let us start this series of Tales of the Vasquez Gang with a rather grim story of a man who was literally roasted to death in his own cabin.

Part V

TALES OF THE VASQUEZ GANG

Although presented in story form, these tales are not fiction. Each is based on an actual incident.

ROASTED TO DEATH IN HIS OWN CABIN

In those years before the old Mexican land grant known as the Huer-Huero Rancho was subdivided into small farms, there was an old trail heading eastward from Santa Margarita, out through the Las Pilitas country, then on through the Huer-Huero towards the Estrella River. This route was known to old-timers as The Old Outlaw Trail.

One fork of this trail curved by way of the Camate country, going southward along the San Juan, by way of the La Panza, then up through the Carrisa, on into the Cuyama country, eventually reaching the southland, Ventura and Los Angeles, which in those years was largely comprised of native Californianos and newer settlers from south of the border. The other fork of this trail went eastward, into the San Joaquin Valley, then on to the mining camps of the Sierras. And both these forks of the Old Outlaw Trail were used most frequently by men who for reasons of their own chose to avoid the easier and more direct routes across country.

It was back in those lawless years that Wesley Scriver took up a homestead some ten to fifteen miles east of Santa Margarita, his cabin not far from this trail of dubious reputation. One day, while in town, Scriver remarked that he had seen indications that this trail was being used on moonlit nights to drive cattle and horses eastward. Presumably this was livestock stolen from ranches along the Coast, and presumably the thieves were heading for the mines country in the Sierras, where such livestock could be sold without too many questions asked.

When Scriver returned to his homestead that evening, he found an unsigned note tacked to his cabin door, warning that gents with big mouths might live longer elsewhere.

Scriver was not a man to scare easily. He showed the note to various neighbors and he took the note with him the next time in went in to

San Luis Obispo, showing it to various persons there. However, he did not move away from his homestead; and though he was watchful, keeping a loaded gun close at hand, he went about his farm work much as usual. Later developments were to prove his caution not enough.

Some weeks after the warning note had been posted, a neighbor riding by found Scriver's cabin had been burned to the ground, and Scriver's charred body was found in the cabin. That warning note had been no idle threat.

There were those among the old-timers of the Santa Margarita area who said that from the position of Scriver's body, and the condition of the cabin, it would seem that the murderers had blocked all the exits while Scriver was asleep, then had piled tindery-dry brush all around the cabin, possibly even using coal-oil or some other inflammable material, and had then touched fire to the tinder.

Awakened by the flames, Scriver had made a desperate but futile attempt to force the door open, but without success. He had literally been roasted to death in his own cabin.

FOOTNOTE: This story from out of the long ago is fully authentic. Mention of this incident of the homesteader who refused to be run off his land, and of his charred body being found in his burned cabin later, has appeared in several of the histories of San Luis Obispo County.

In many ways this case bears a strong resemblance to an earlier incident, that of Jack Gilkey, who was killed on the Camate by members of the Linares Gang, for knowing too much.

There were in fact a number of cases within San Luis Obispo County, and neighboring Kern County, back in those lawless years, in which men living in remote areas were found dead, or such men disappeared under suspicious circumstances. It was believed these men might inadvertently have been witness to some illegal act, and they had been killed to keep them from telling about it.

And now for another tale from the long ago, a tale which might be given the title The Mail Must Go Through.

THE MAIL MUST GO THROUGH

To Joe Arana, back in that winter of 1880, there was nothing note-worthy about the trip. It was just another trip of many in the weekly routine of carrying the mail between the San Joaquin Valley settlement of Bakersfield and the Coast town of San Luis Obispo.

With a sure-footed horse under him, and the mail bag tied securely behind the cantle, Arana had no particular problems other than those of any cross-country traveler in the days when roads were almost non-existent. Certainly he had no premonition of danger as he crossed the rain-sodden Carrisa Plains, then started down through the rugged canyon which would eventually bring him to the rain-swollen San Juan River.

For some way this trail curved along the side of a spur, high above the watercourse, a narrow trail where the footing was treacherous at best, and Joe was giving more attention to the trail than to the surroundings. He was taken by surprise when a man stepped from behind some rocks, ordering curtly in Spanish, "Stop! Or I'll shoot!"

Hardly had the bandit spoken before Joe Arana jabbed spurs to his horse. Ducking low, he plunged off the trail, down the steep brush-covered slope of the canyon side.

Taken by surprise that anyone would risk that dangerous descent, the holdup man fired, but his bullet went wild.

From positions behind the rocks, other outlaws fired; but they too had been taken by surprise that anyone would risk the slope, and by the time they reacted, Arana was disappearing down the canyon, out of range for accurate shooting.

The outlaws made a run for their own horses, hidden some distance farther along the trail, then took off in pursuit of the mail carrier, by now a considerble distance down the canyon.

Racing the outlaws to the river, Joe Arana spurred his horse into the swirling current, for there was no time to look for a shallow ford to cross. His horse swam the river safely, then climbed the bank to the open river flats beyond. Taking off in a fast lope, Arana headed for the post office of La Panza.

Reaching the river, the bandits drew rein. They had no stomach to risk the roiling water. And so, cursing their disappearing quarry, they turned back.

Having reached the La Panza Post Office, Joe Arana changed into dry garments, and since it was getting well into the evening, he spent the night there.

In the morning, having procured a fresh horse, Arana continued his journey, an additional forty-odd miles, to San Luis Obispo, and there made his report of the attempted holdup.

Arana named one Federico Gonzales as his assailant. This man was reputed to have been one of Tiburcio Vasquez' lieutenants. Following the capture of Vasquez, Gonzales organized a band of his own, but even prior to this attempted holdup, he had been wanted by the law for various crimes.

As an aftermath of his experience, Joe Arana suffered a severe bout with pneumonia, brought on by that plunge into the river and then the ride to the post office through wintery winds in wet garments. Nonetheless, to Arana, these were but minor inconveniences. For might he not, even now, be lying dead out there on the trail?

Some of those bullets had passed mighty close over the head of Joe Arana as he raced down the canyon.

FOOTNOTE: This story of the attempted holdup of Joe Arana came from Don Jose Blanco, a native Californiano, who in his own youth was a close associate of certain men reputed to have been members of the old Vasquez Gang at one time, hence he had heard many of the stories involving the outlaws of the 1870s. He had known the Arana brothers who for several years carried the mail across country on horseback, and he got his story of this holdup from one of them.

And now for a grim tale involving that pack of self-appointed upholders of law-and-order known as

THE COON-DOGS

To the young man making camp at Demicio Spring, on the old Chimeneas range, the future held great promise. Was not he, Miguel Lugo, now a man of substance? Did he not now own a fine band of horses? And was not this wealth the result of his own hard work and sagacious trading?

Hard work and good judgment, and the future would hold great prosperity for young Miguel Lugo!

With admirable ambition, the youth had painstakingly saved his hard-earned dollars that he might one day be a property owner.

Chopping wood through the winter, joining the sheep-shearing crew in the spring, then herding sheep during the summer, he had accumulated what to him was a small fortune, and this he had invested in horses. Three years working thus and putting the money he had earned into horses, and his herd had increased to twenty head.

In this fall of 1879, the grass in Vasquez Canyon was sparse, for the cattle of the larger ranches had overgrazed the native grasses throughout the spring and summer. So, with winter coming on, Miguel Lugo was taking his horses to fresh range in the Tehachapi Mountains.

Miguel planned to herd his horses in the mountains during the winter months, then in the spring bring them back to the La Panza area and turn them loose, to graze where they chose, then seek for himself another sheep-shearing job.

The horses should be safe from theft; for did they not carry the brand of Miguel's stepfather? Miguel had no brand of his own. That would come later.

Having hobbled the more venturesome of his band that they not stray too far during the night, Miguel paused to admire his property.

Several were colts which in time would be broke, then sold. The rest were mares and fillies, some with spring colts by their side, colts which three years from now could be broke for sale, adding even more profits to Miguel's investment. And in the spring, several of the mares would have additional colts, more profit for later years.

Pascual Benadero, Miguel's stepfather, had had two unused horses over his immediate needs, and he was short of pasturage for them, so he had asked Miguel to take these two surplus horses along. This Miguel had cheerfully done. For did he not owe his stepfather that much respect?

Miguel Lugo went about his morning chores in a leisurely manner; he saw no real hurry in breaking camp. Let the horses feed for another hour and they would drive that much better. Their bellies would be full, and they would be less likely to scatter in the driving.

Miguel could hear the bell on the old lead mare tinkling some distance down the draw, and the rest of the herd should be in the general vicinity of the old bell-mare. Thus reassured that all was well, the youth went on with his chores of breaking camp.

Tejon, Miguel's saddle horse, tethered near camp, became restless, raised his head, snorted and looked down the draw as though sensing something out of the ordinary.

Miguel looked in the direction Tejon indicated, but he could see nothing. Then a rider came into view from around a bend, followed by other riders.

There appeared to be about twenty men in the party, and Miguel wondered what emergency could have brought them so early in the morning. They must have ridden much of the night, for Demicio Spring was remote from any of the ranch headquarters.

As the riders drew near, Miguel recognized his stepfather Pascual Benadero in the lead, and this fact added to his perplexity. Benadero had said nothing yesterday of any such trip when he asked Miguel to take his two horses along.

Miguel's perplexity turned into consternation when his own pleasant "Buenos dias, padre" brought forth a blasphemous tirade from his stepfather.

Often foulmouthed and ill-tempered, Pascual Benadero was not too well liked by most men of the country, but now, for some reason, he seemed in charge of the assembled group of grim-faced men. He swore as he pointed an accusing finger at Miguel, then roared, "There! That is the bastard who stole my horses! You yourselves saw my brand on those horses down the arroyo!"

"I looked them hawsses over real careful," one of the older men remarked to his companions. "They got Benadero's brand—all 'cept two what's got brands I don't rec'nize."

"We caught us a hawss-thief red-handed!" someone else bellowed. "Caught with the goods in his possession!"

"String the bastard up!" yelped another member of the Coon-dog pack. "String the bastard up!"

"Here's a rope to do the job with!" The feisty youth who had been the first to speak of a hanging hopped down from his own mount and picked up Miguel's reata—the reata which Miguel himself had so painstakingly made from rawhide the winter before. "Hanging is the only cure for a hawss-thief!"

"Learn other jaspers not to take hawsses what don't belong to 'em!" someone else put in. "Hang 'm!"

With a sinking heart, Miguel recognized his peril, but all chance for escape was cut off by that somber band of men surrounding him.

"Padre, what is the meaning of this?" Miguel addressed his stepfather in Spanish. "Two of those horses you sent by me yesterday, saying they would be better for a few months feeding in the mountains. The rest of that band are mine! Paid for with money I have myself earned!"

For answer, Pascual Benadero spat contemptuously into the face of the boy, then heaped upon him many vile names.

Several of the younger rowdies jumped down from their mounts and grabbed the still bewildered youth roughly, then tied his hands securely behind his back.

The feisty one placed the noose of the reata around Miguel's neck, then gave the rope a jerk. "Jest a taste o' the stranglin' choke o' the rope yuh'll git jest as soon's us'n all c'n git you to a tree!"

"I am innocent," the youth pled of his captors. "I have stolen no horses! These horses are mine!"

"They all are innocent!" one of the older Coon-dogs remarked sneeringly. "Ketch 'em with the stolen hawsses right in their possession! Still, they're innocent!"

"Innercent! Jest like a new-borned babe!" the feisty youth drawled, and the pack laughed.

One of the younger Coon-dogs saddled Tejon, Miguel's own saddle horse. Then rough hands grabbed the boy and threw him up onto the saddle. Then Tejon was led into a creekwash where a branch of a large tree overhung the steep bank. The end of the reata was thrown over this branch, then tied to the trunk of the tree, the noose still in place around Miguel's neck.

Tejon was led from under the tree, and Miguel was left there, hanging in mid-air, strangling, gasping for the breath that the tightening noose denied him, kicking and trembling, swinging 'round and 'round and 'round, suspended there by the hanging rope, under the limb of the tree.

Some of the Coon-dogs laughed derisively, but one of the band could not stomach the sight of a man strangling to death slowly. Turning away, he muttered, "Somebody put the varmint out-uv his mizzry! Don't let the critter suffer that-a-way!"

Emboldened by this remark from one of the vigilantes, Benadero stepped forward and pulled the pearl-handled pistol from his belt— Miguel's own pistol which had been lying in its holster near his bedroll, and which Benadero had picked up and put into his own belt while the Coon-dogs were preparing for the lynching.

Taking deliberate aim, Benadero riddled the youth's body with six shots from the pistol as the boy swung there under the tree limb.

The body of Miguel Lugo flinched in the final struggle for life, then hung lifeless and still.

Pascual Benadero walked over to where the body of his stepson was hanging and went through his pockets, taking the youth's wallet, watch, jackknife, and other personal effects. Then, to compound this infamy, Benadero unbuckled the belt which Miguel had been wearing and jerked it from the body, for the belt had a fine silver buckle which Miguel had acquired in a trade. And if this were not sacrilege enough, Benadero then jerked the boy's boots from his feet as he swung there, for the boots were new and were expensive.

By now, the Coon-dogs were mounted and riding away. Leave the horse-thief hang there for the buzzards to strip! A hanging carcass would serve as a warning to other galoots inclined to take that which belonged not to them! Hanging was the only cure for a horse-thief!

The grazing horses, satisfied for the time being, began coming back to the spring for a drink of water. Benadero caught Miguel's pack-horse and put the camp equipment on him, then headed the bell-mare back towards the La Panza country. The rest of the band would trail along, following the mare, with Benadero, leading the still-saddled Tejon, bringing up the stragglers.

No one would question Benadero's claim to the horses, for did they not have Benadero's own brand on them? Who was there to say these were not Benadero's own horses now that his stepson was dead?

*   *   *

Beneath a giant oak known throughout the land as the Mancilla Tree, there in Vasquez Canyon, stood the house of Mancilla, with its tule-thatched roof and its walls of rough logs chinked with dried mud. The floors were of hard-packed earth, floor lumber being hard to come by so far back in the wilderness in this year of 1879.

Though the back rooms of this primitive house must still serve as living quarters for Don Valentin Mancilla and his good wife Maria, the front room had been converted into a combined saloon and general store, that the Mancillas might earn a livelihood. And with the prospectors now swarming through the hills since the discovery of gold had received such wide publicity, the Mancillas had added a dance pavillion, built from lumber hauled the long way around, coming by ship to the seaport near San Luis Obispo.

This house under the Mancilla Tree in Vasquez Canyon was the hub of social life in the La Panza Mines in 1879. The miners came to the house of Mancilla to buy needed supplies, to lounge and to swap yarns, and perchance to warm their blood with Don Valentin's strong whiskey. And to this house of Mancilla came also the womenfolk of the families living thereabouts, to gossip among themselves as they bought supplies for their families.

The woman standing at the counter in Mancilla's store looked sad, her face careworn and haggard, for she had slept little the night before. Carefully, la Señora de Benadero made her purchases, paying for each item as she decided upon what seemed the greater bargain, checking her balance of coin each time before making the next purchase. She had little spending money, for her husband gave her only a meager allowance with which to buy food. Yet, his anger was fierce should his table be stinted when he came home for a meal.

As the wife of Pascual Benadero, one-time lieutenant in the outlaw band of the notorious Tiburcio Vasquez, life for the woman had not been easy. Harsh-spoken and at times brutal, Benadero was not an easy man for any woman to live with. However, with the patient resignation of her race, she had accepted the abuse she was constantly subjected to as but the lot of women, to be borne with stoic silence.

The vague fears of Señora de Benadero came now from a far different source—from some words let slip by her husband the afternoon before, as he was about to leave the house on some unexplained mission. Somehow, Señora de Benadero had sensed that her husband's trip was to have something to do with her son Miguel, and the glint in her husband's eyes boded ill for the boy.

Why should Benadero hate his stepson so fiercely? the mother asked herself. Miguel had always been as dutiful towards his stepfather as any flesh-and-blood son, had always shown his stepfather a filial respect and obedience. Even now, practically a grown man and earning his own way in life, Miguel still gave his stepfather a son's obedience.

For Señora de Benadero, the day had dragged by slowly, and with evening coming on and still no word from either her husband or her son, her dread increased. There had been some veiled remarks on the part of men outside the store which she had overheard as she passed them coming into the store, remarks that the Coon-dogs had been out the night before. And knowing that this vigilante pack all too often took the law into their own hands, she was worried lest Miguel were involved.

The front door swung open. A burly, florid-faced man—Benadero himself—came into Mancillas' store and strode over to where the woman was standing by the counter. Contemptuously, he tossed a pair of handmade boots onto the counter in front of the woman; then with a brutal laugh he turned and walked away, twirling a pearl-handled pistol as he left the room.

Around the man's waist was a new belt, a belt with a silver buckle—a belt and buckle the woman had seen her son wearing the last time he was home, just before he left, driving his horses down Vasquez Canyon just yesterday morning.

With a moan of anguish, the woman picked up the boots and pressed them to her bosom. Then she left the store, carrying the boots, her purchases of food forgotten, still on the counter there in the house of Mancilla.

*   *   *

Three years had passed by since the lynching of young Miguel Lugo by the Coon-dogs. Three years which had made great changes in the life of Pascual Benadero—in Benadero himself who, through those danger-filled years of life as a bandido, had never feared God, man, or the Devil, but who, in the years since his betrayal of his stepson, had developed a mortal dread of the Devil.

Satan's leering face now was always before Benadero; the clank of chains in the hands of Satan's demon underlings rang constantly in his ears—chains with which those devil-inspired demons would in due time bind him, chains with which those demons would drag him off to the never-ending tortures of Hell.

And always, behind the malevolent face of El Diablo, there was another face, bewildered, accusing: the face of Miguel Lugo, Benadero's murdered stepson.

Back at the time of the vigilante lynching, Pascual Benadero had been a robust man, in the prime of life; yet, in the ensuing three years, he had wasted away to a gaunt shell of his former self. Nevertheless, in spite of his strange malady, during his seizures Benadero had developed what seemed almost superhuman strength. It took several men to hold him down on his bed when one of these seizures was upon him. When he was rational his strength left him and he became docile.

However, even when rational, it was as though demons stalked him, giving him no peace of mind.

From the beginning of Benadero's weird demon-haunted illness, his wife had patiently ministered to him—in spite of her own heartbreak over the death of her son. But without the kind aid of neighbors she could never have coped with her husband's strange illness.

Dr. Still was called upon, but there appeared no physical ailment— nothing that the medical diagnosis of the time could explain. The sickness was a guilt-bedeviled conscience which in time drove the man beyond human resistance—a demon-harried soul, fearful of Hell's fires.

Beyond giving the guilt-tortured man a sedative, there was nothing that the medical resources of the time could offer to ease the situation.

Pascual Benadero was having one of his bad days, and his wife had called in several of the men working claims not far from the Benadero home, for during his recent seizures Benadero had become even more violent than in the past. It was feared that in his demon-racked frenzy he might injure himself or some other person.

In time the spasms subsided and Benadero sank back on his pallet as one dead, though a feeling for his pulse disclosed that life had not yet left him.

The neighbors relaxed. Surely now for a time the haunted man would lie quietly, his seizure over for the time being.

A frenzied shriek rent the air. Stark naked, the madman leaped from his bed and ran out of the house. He raced down the canyon, screaming in mortal terror, his anguished yells echoing from the canyon walls.

Recovering from the first shock of surprise, the men who had been attending Benadero gave chase, and in time they overtook the madman. Grabbing him, they held fast, though it took the strength of several men to overpower him. Then, with a sense of horror, they saw that it was a corpse that they were holding there within their grasp.

It was a dead man who had leaped up from his sickbed and had run screaming down the canyon. A dead man whom in time they had captured and held fast. Or so it seemed to the men holding the corpse of Pascual Benadero.

Pascual Benadero was buried in the little graveyard in Vasquez Canyon. Others of the outlaw band had also been buried there through the years. Some had died of natural causes, some from the violence of their way of life. And beside these graves of lawless men were other graves, the graves of young children. For at best, life in those early years was harsh, and the ailments that could cause death in the very young were many.

FOOTNOTE: This story is based on a well-known incident of the early days, the lynching of the boy Miguel Lugo by the Coon-dogs at the instigation of the boy's own stepfather, who had deliberately framed evidence against the youth, then taken an active part in the hanging.

The basic facts in the case have never been in dispute. Miguel Lugo had driven his horses as far as what was then known as Demicio Spring, on the unfenced back range of the historic Chineneas Ranch, on the Carrisa Plains. This place has been marked on Forest Service maps as Dead Man's Flat, and for many years the grave itself could be located.

The motive for Benadero's perfidy is not clear now, nearly a century later, though various explanations have been offered for one. Some old-timers have suggested that Benadero may have had some trouble in the past with the boy's real father and therefore harbored a churlish dislike for the son.

Then there is the obvious motive of greed; for with the youth out of the way, and with the horses bearing Benadero's own brand, no one was likely to question his claim to them.

Two other possible motives have also been suggested. One was that Benadero himself had been stealing horses and had come under suspicion, and that he hoped to shift suspicion from himself to the boy by sending a pair of stolen horses with him, then joining the posse hunting the boy down. There was also the suggestion that Benadero might have had a far more involved plan, a plan which if successful could have proved quite lucrative.

For some time prior to the lynching, Benadero had been trying to join the vigilante group known as the Coon-dogs, but they had turned him down. He had been a known associate of various members of the gang of "horse-thieves and miscreants" which the Coon-dogs had vowed to clean out, and the vigilantes were skeptical of his sudden interest in law and order, feeling that he might well be trying for an inside position whereby he could play both sides against the middle.

Even before the lynching incident, rumor had named Benadero as the hatchet man hired by certain men from the respectable segment of society who found it expedient to hire a professional killer to dispose of some troublesome person.

Benadero may have thought that the sacrifice of his stepson could gain him admission into this inner sanctum of lawless law-enforcement; and with this acceptance he could work as a paid gunman, working to rid the range of squatters and horse-thieves.

An odd sequel to the lynching of Miguel Lugo was that within a period of about three years from the date of the lynching, the three men who had been ringleaders in the affair had themselves met violent deaths. Besides Benadero, with his demon-driven demise, two others also had succumbed to the demon curse. One man had been dragged to death by the horse he was breaking. The other man, while loading cattle at one of the freight yards, slipped and fell between the moving cattle cars and was so badly mangled by the wheels that he died in agony before he could be gotten to a hospital.

As for the younger members of the Coon-dogs, most of them straightened out with the passing years, several of them becoming prominent in county affairs. And so, since so many years have elapsed since the lynching of the hapless youth, there seems little point in naming names here.

The incident of Benadero entering Mancillas' store with some of the boy's personal possessions, including his boots, belt, and pistol, and of his tossing the boots on the counter in front of his wife (the boy's own mother) is not fiction. By chance, my grandmother happened to be in the store at the time and witnessed the incident.

Benadero's demon-haunted death is not fiction, either; most of the accounts of the incident as handed down by old-timers of the area have stressed this phase of the story.

At the time of this incident my grandparents were living but a short distance from the Benadero home and knew both Benadero and his wife quite well. As with others living in eastern San Luis Obispo County, my grandparents in time learned of the lynching and had their suspicions as to who had done it. These suspicions were in time confirmed by things Benadero would say while in his delirium. But by then too much time had elapsed since the lynching for any legal action to be taken. After all, how much weight would the ravings of a madman have in a court of law? Most certainly the lynchers would not testify against themselves; and the lynchee was no longer around to tell his side of the story.

As for Benadero himself, most of the folks of the area felt that Unseen Powers were dishing out retribution, and they were of no mind to butt in.

In presenting this story, I have drawn on the recollections of my uncle Mentley Still, adding some details as supplied by Don Jose Blanco, whose version of the incident is quite close to that of my uncle.

THE COURT-MARTIAL

The darkness of the November night was only partially relieved by the faint light cast by a waning moon. The stars looked down on the sleeping camp, cold and unsympathetic. And for Juan Mateo, the world of living mortals would soon come to a dismal end.

Sleep there could not be on this fateful night for young Juan, bound hand and foot, awaiting his own execution. His wrists tied behind his back made reclining uncomfortable, and even when he rolled over, belly down, to ease his cramping arms, he found it hard to relax. When a man is facing eternity, there is no time to be wasted in sleep.

Juan Mateo twisted his body around and managed to resume a sitting position, even though the thongs which bound his wrists and ankles cut into the flesh, causing him added pain. Dully, he reveiwed in his mind the events which had led up to his present predicament.

Less than eight months back Juan Mateo, just turning seventeen, had joined the band of *revolucionarios* captained by Reginaldo Santos, whose exploits were beginning to draw attention in the southland.

Nurtured through adolescence on tales of the derring-do of the gallant Tiburcio Vasquez—the saints rest his soul!—and his own mind filled with romantic dreams of a bandido's adventuresome life, the youth had felt himself to be quite an adult when older men accepted him as a member of the outlaw band. Then had come the night of his undoing.

Placed on duty as a sentry one night, he had panicked and run away at the unexpected approach of a party of lawmen, leaving without first warning his comrades. Taken by surprise, the outlaws had been ingloriously routed; even worse, two men had been killed by the lawmen, and another taken captive and hanged.

Following this fiasco, Juan Mateo had returned to his own people in Los Angeles. But his reprieve had been short-lived. Two grim-faced men from the outlaw band had hunted him down and brought him back to this camp in Vasquez Canyon, in the shadow of the La Panza Mountains, long a haven for men of the outlaw bands.

A court-martial had been held, with El Capitan Santos presiding. The trial had been short. Juan Mateo had been accused of his crime and had been asked what defense he had for his cowardice.

What defense could Juan Mateo give for having deserted his post in a time of emergency? He could think of no defense; had he not, when the moment of crisis was upon him, panicked and runaway?

Sadly, Juan had said at the time of his court-martial that he had no defense. He had been a coward.

El Capitan Santos had given the sentence: On the morrow, as the sun rose above the ridge to the east, Juan Mateo was to be shot, that other members of the gang should take warning. Death was to be the price should fear outweigh duty!

A faint touch of frost was in the air, and by sunup the frost would be thick on the ground, but Juan hardly noticed the cold, scarcely giving heed to the flickering campfire which from time to time was given added fuel by the outlaw left on guard. Yet, in a way, Juan Mateo was aware that it was no longer summer, though the chill was in his soul laid bare. How quickly the summer had fled, leaving winter only a short time away.

It had been springtime when Juan Mateo had joined the outlaw band, and the first surging of young manhood's hot blood had been coursing through his veins, making the adventure seem courageous and fine—a knight going forth to do battle in a righteous cause. But there would be no more springtimes for young Juan, and soon his stalwart young body would be moldering in the cold winter ground.

Once during the night Juan had called out to Alfredo, then on guard, for the demand of nature was upon him and he had to find relief and, bound wrists and ankles, he was powerless to aid himself.

Alfredo was sympathetic and had aided him as best as he could, that he not be forced to suffer even greater discomfort than that which the bonds already caused him. But Alfredo had not unbound him, not even for so short a moment. Should a guard let a prisoner escape, that man himself would face the firing squad.

The grey light of early dawn saw the camp awake and preparing for that which was to come. Silently breakfast was prepared and eaten by the somber men of the outlaw band. Juan Mateo's hands were loosened that he might eat a last meal before his execution, but he could not stomach food. He did drink a cup of strong coffee which seemed to bring warmth to his blood, and for this he was thankful.

The evening before, lots had been drawn to decide the executioners. Having eaten breakfast, the six men assigned to the firing squad looked to their rifles that all should be in readiness when time came for the execution.

Once again Juan Mateo's wrists were bound securely behind his back, then the thongs on his ankles were loosened. Two of his erstwhile comrades helped him to his feet, steadying him as he was led to the place of execution, for his bonds had cut off circulation and the muscles of his legs were cramping.

Gallantly the condemned youth tried to face these, his own last moments on earth, with courage. Should he not die as a man should die? That his footsteps faltered—was that not caused by the numbness in his ankles where the thongs had cut into them during the night? That his eyes smarted and there was moisture in them—was that not from the frosty air?

Juan Mateo was placed with his back against a giant oak tree, that its venerable strength might support him as the bullets drove in. His comrades than stepped back from the line of fire to await the moment of execution.

Placing his feet firmly, his legs apart that he might not falter and slump to the ground before the bullets hit his body, Juan Mateo faced death valiantly, his head held high, his shoulders back. In his eyes was the stricken look of a wild forest creature faced with death.

Juan Mateo looked towards his executioners who, so short a time back, had been his comrades, then turned his gaze to the distant ridge to the east, the ridge that marked the western border of the Carrisa Plains. The glow of the still-hidden sun warmed the autumn sky... brought with the glow of promised warmth a warning also... a foreboding of that which was to come.

Juan Mateo could not take his eyes from that distant ridge. For when the sun topped that ridge... topped that ridge...

Even as the first edge of the rising sun met Juan Mateo's sight, six shots rang out—six bullets entered his chest. With a sigh that was half a sob, the youth lurched. Then his knees buckled under him and he sank slowly to the ground.

The body of Juan Mateo twitched for a short moment, then lay still.

For Juan Mateo, life had ended, and he was not yet eighteen.

FOOTNOTE: This story of the young recruit in one of the outlaw bands who had been court-martialed and shot as a warning to other members of the band—reminding them that failure to hold a post would not be tolerated—came by way of Don Felipe Pacheco, a descendant of one of the early-day Salinas Valley families, as a story that he himself had heard in his youth.

The name of this youth has been lost with the passing of time; so, that he be not nameless, I have given him the name Juan Mateo for this story. However, Don Felipe did say the boy was with the band captained by Reginaldo Santos.

Now for another tale from the long-ago involving that renegade band under Captain Santos, a tale of a courageous young man, and of a ricocheted bullet.

THE RICOCHETED BULLET

Trusting their horses to keep to the trail, the men of the posse slumped wearily in their saddles. Saddle sore and disgusted, their minds on the comforts of home, they gave little heed to their surroundings. It had been a long, grueling chase, but the outlaws had given them the slip and now the lawmen were cutting across country on their way home. By now the bandits would be many miles gone, and good riddance! Let some other posse pick up their trail when they surfaced somewhere to the north!

Rounding a bend in the trail, the posse-men were startled to see a group of horsemen approaching from a side canyon. The whine of bullets brought the lawmen to instant action—they ducked for the nearest cover.

Of a truth, the outlaws had met as great a surprise as had the men of the law. The bandits had led their pursuers on a long wild-goose chase, then foxlike, they had doubled back, feeling safe from further pursuit. Would not the posse, having lost the trail in the mountains, then take the easiest route home, circling by way of one of the better trails?

It had never occurred to the renegades that the lawmen, having given up the chase, would cut across country through rough terrain on their way back to the southland.

After the first wild exchange of shots in which no one was injured, the bandits took off, amid a scattering of lead. The posse-men, by now over their first shock of surprise, raced after the bandits, hot on their trail.

The outlaws scattered, taking off through the rugged brush-covered canyons, for this ground was familiar to the bandits, but not to their pursuers.

Scattered as the outlaws were in their flight, the men of the posse knew it would be fruitless to try to track them down. Disgusted over this second escape of their quarry, the lawmen returned to the trail to resume their trip home. Unhappy though they were that the bandits had again given them the slip, they still had much to be thankful for. For had the bandits seen the lawmen first, the latter might well have been drawn into a fatal ambush.

Having again outwitted the lawmen, the bandits made their way to a previously appointed place of rendezvous in the La Panza Mountains. Arriving singly or in small groups, the early comers awaited the coming of their comrades, and in time all made their appearance.

There had been no fatalities, and only one man had been injured. In that last wild exchange of bullets, Romano Garza had been wounded.

Romano, the dauntless—the debonair. Always had Romano Garza seemed to lead a charmed life. His daring exploits and his unquestioned courage had earned him a place of respect among his peers. Had not Romano shown great courage when, as a youth of eighteen, he had ridden in several raids captained by the Great Tiburcio himself?

In the five years since the estimable Vasquez had been captured—sold out by one of his own lieutenants—Romano had achieved recognition as a soldier in General Reginaldo Santos' army of *insurrectos*. And though Romano had often placed himself in positions of extreme danger, not once throughout those years as a *revolutionario de California* had he been injured. Now, in a skirmish hardly important enough to be mentioned, his luck had gone bad.

He was brash, even boastful at times, yet he had always seemed to live up to his boasting. Had he not proven his skill and his valour many times over? Had he not always done his part—often more than was required of him? Had he not taken an active part in most of the raids the *insurrectos* had made in the southland?

Daring, strong of body, a skilled horseman, Romano had earned the respect of his fellows. Proud of his own vital manhood and his virile young body—*un hombre muy mucho macho*—Romano was like a young mesteño stallion in his arrogant self-confidence. Was not his body young, supple and strong! Was not he, Romano, a man!

Taller than most men of his race, trim and well-built, darkly handsome, Romano Garza was the offspring of a Spanish grandee and a Yaqui maidservant, and in the turbulent soul of the young man both bloods pridefully demanded recognition. Vain of his own good looks, Romano dressed expensively and well. Should not a man of pride clothe himself with distinction?

Quick in a fight, yet a loyal friend, Romano's feuds and friendships were many.

Careless with money, Romano's share of the loot was usually quickly spent, first on himself, then on the girls of the cantinas where he found much enjoyment in times of prosperity. Romano's sweethearts of the moment were many, and unfortunately, all too often he forgot completely his young wife Miguela and their two little sons down in Ventura, leaving Miguela to fend for herself and the children by working as a waitress.

A spirited horse, a good saddle and gear, and his guns—these things were important to Romano. These and the excitement of his profession, and the pleasures of the moment—these were the things that were important to Romano; let the future take care of itself!

At the age of eighteen, Romano had turned his back on his own people, and on the vaquero's life that should have been his, and with bright dreams of the romantic adventuresome life of an *insurrecto*, he had joined the notorious band of outlaws captained by the Great Tiburcio Vasquez himself; for six years Romano had followed the outlaw trail. Now, stunned by the shock of his injury and in great pain, Romano Garza was finding that the adventuresome life of *un bandido* had lost most of its glamour.

As he rode into the little flat in what, in later years, would be called the Beartrap Canyon, and up to the temporary camp of his compañeros, Romano's swarthy face was grey from the pain of his injury, and he clung desperately to the horn of his saddle.

Apprised of Romano's injury, his companions were sympathetic. Nonetheless, under the circumstances, to call on a doctor would be out of the question. Juan Montaña, who in the past had been Romano's closest compadre, dressed the wound as best he could, but in this remote camp there was little to work with. And Juan sat by the side of his friend all night, for sleep could not come to Romano.

In the morning, the members of the band held a brief conference, then decided to make camp for a few days longer. After all, it was good strategy to hole up for a time, and this out-of-the-way canyon was as good a place as any. For this was the year of the gold rush into the La Panza district, and should anyone come upon their camp, they could claim they were prospectors, arousing little suspicion. Even if lawmen should be alerted, there was little chance of arrest, for they had all been wearing masks during the holdup of the liquor store down near Ventura, and there was little chance any of the band could be recognized.

Five days went by, and though Juan had done what he could for Romano, dressing the wound each day, matters had worsened for Romano. The sweat and dirt of his own body, along with shreds of clothing carried by the flattened bullet into the wound, had left it infected. Instead of healing, the wound had become a swollen, festering sore, causing him great pain. It was all too apparent that blood poisoning had already set in.

To compound Romano's troubles, his companions, at first sympathetic, had become restless and were blaming him for the delay. All were anxious to leave the La Panza Mountains and be on their way to the northern Gabilans.

Reginaldo Santos, the acknowledged leader of the outlaw band, was a man little given to concern over the misfortunes of others. Bluntly Santos had given Romano an ultimatum: Submit to the crude surgery which seemed his only hope for recovery, or the band would simply go their way, leaving him to his fate.

To the pain-racked frightened young man, the ultimatum was a harsh one; yet a decision had to be made, and without procrastination. Reluctantly, Romano agreed to submit to the surgery, for it seemed his only chance for survival.

To old Fernando fell the task of treatment. Through the years Fernando had developed much skill in the treatment of ills in both horses and men. And did not men and horses have much in common?

The preparation was simple; there was nought in the way of surgical instruments except Fernando's knife.

At the sight of Fernando whetting his knife, dread overcame Romano's resolve, and he would have escaped had not his companions forced his submission.

Fernando gave little heed to the dread in the soul of the young man now his patient. Horse or man—did it matter! Callous of any sympathy towards his patient, Fernando set about his task, impersonally but with considerable skill, acquired through years of combining some degree of training as a veterinarian with the emergency treatment of men who could not seek the skills of a qualified doctor.

The rough surgery was soon accomplished, though of anesthetics and antiseptics there were none. Not even the long shot of whiskey to substitute for anesthesia was available, for the last of the whiskey had been drunk during the days of waiting. Crude though the operation had been, it had been the only chance Romano had for life—and he knew it. He had seen other men die of blood poisoning, and their deaths had not been easy ones.

On the faces of the onlookers was respect as well as pity; had not Romano faced his ordeal with courage? Unspoken in the minds of all was the realization that the surgery might have come too late to prevent blood poisoning, the all too common aftermath of seemingly nonfatal wounds which became infected.

Eager to be on their way north, the outlaws saddled their horses and rode away, leaving Juan to care for Romano until he too was able to ride—or until Death claimed him. And truly there was no gain in their staying longer; there was nothing now that could be done except what Juan would do.

*   *   *

Restlessly Romano Garza paced the slopes of his mountain retreat, struggling within his own mind for a fresh evaluation of his life—past, present, and future.

His wound had long since healed, for his was a hardy, healthy young animal body, capable of withstanding much. He could have ridden away with Juan without discomfort this very morning, to rejoin the outlaw band in the Gabilans to the north. Then why had he not?

Instead, when Juan spoke of their leaving, Romano had said, "Go on amigo, and I will join you later."

Juan had offered to stay until Romano felt like riding again, but to this Romano had demurred: "There is no need for you to stay, Juan. I am well! Just that I . . ."

It had been the solace of solitude that Romano craved, and perhaps Juan had recognized this need. With a cheerful "*Adios, amigo!*

Hasta la vista!" Juan had ridden away, leaving quite early in the morning.

In a way, Romano was glad that Juan had left, yet he knew quite well that had it not been for the loyalty of this one kind-hearted friend he himself would surely have died. For truly Romano had faced Death—had, as it were, shaken hands with Death.

The infected wound had become so putrid before the surgery that even that drastic treatment had almost failed, for the infection had already been coursing through his blood stream, poisoning his whole system.

Pain-racked, despondent, and sick to the very core of his being, Romano would have welcomed Death in those worst days of his illness; and had it not been for the conscientious care given him by Juan, he would indeed have died—and he knew it.

Juan had shot a *venado* and fed him venison broth, when the poisons racing through his system had robbed him of all desire for food. Juan had brewed herb teas and forced Romano to drink them, to cleanse his blood of poisons, and he had brewed other herbs to apply as hot poultices, to draw the inflamation from the still-infected wound.

Juan had even risked running into lawmen and had ridden over to Vasquez Canyon to buy supplies at Mancillas' store. With the needed flour, coffee, and frijoles, he had brought back a bottle of whiskey, to ease the pain for Romano. Yes, had it not been for Juan and his unfailing loyalty, Romano surely would have died.

In time, Romano's robust young body had thrown off the poisons, and his strength had returned. He could have ridden away with Juan this very morning had he desired to do so. Then why had he stayed?

In his moody introspection, Romano could not find an answer.

Without quite knowing why, he shrank from facing his erstwhile compañeros of the outlaw band. It had been a great blow to his ego that these compadres of the long trail had ridden off, leaving him to die alone in the mountains. With this abandonment by men he had thought of as loyal friends, blind trust in anyone was gone. And somehow, for the first time since joining the insurrectos, he felt that he had been a fool to leave the honorable life of honest men for the outlaw trail.

It was a dejected, crestfallen young bandit who so restlessly paced the mountain slopes that bright June day so long ago. The debonair young braggart of a few short weeks ago had changed, and in his place was a bewildered embittered young man, floundering through a quagmire of doubts and self-pity to—to he knew not what.

Now that Juan was gone, Romano felt desperately lonely, and he asked himself why he had not accompanied Juan when he left for the north country to rejoin the outlaw band.

In the weeks since Romano's injury, a great gulf had come between him and this one true friend in the outlaw gang, and Romano asked himself why this had happened.

Throughout those weeks of his illness Romano had found Juan to be both considerate and kind, yet, somehow, Juan's awkward sympathy had but made more poignant Romano's sense of his own misfortune. Was not Juan himself still virile!

Without consciously doing so, Romano let his wandering footsteps lead him to the meadow below the camp where Pancho, his saddle horse, was hobbled that he might graze without straying too far.

Often in these days since he had been up and around, Romano had sought out Pancho. A man may accept sympathy from a horse without embarrassment, but the sympathy of his fellow man, tinged with pity, can bring only a feeling of debasement.

Pancho nickered his welcome, then nuzzled Romano's arm to show his affection for the man who first had become his master, then his friend. The bay gelding was himself lonesome; with Juan's Grulla gone, there were no other horses anywhere near Beartrap Canyon. Although a few short months back Pancho had been of the wild mesteño bands ranging the Diablo Mountains, after the first bitter rebellion he had accepted as a friend the man who had robbed him of his freedom, and in his equine mind there were no resentments.

Romano loosened the floodgates of his own confusion, poured forth his own unhappiness to this one friend in whom he felt free to confide, and in this release of corked-up resentments against his own misfortune he found peace once again within his own soul.

Romano looked towards the lonely camp ground. Had it not been for his friend Juan, he would be lying there dead, his bones stripped bare by coyotes and buzzards.

One friend had stood by him in time of need, and so once again friendship could be important to Romano.

Romano thought of his mother, his stepfather, and the dozen half-brothers and half-sisters, all younger than he, in the small adobe casa down Santa Maria way, and in his heart he knew these kinsfolk at least would welcome him home and would be thankful that Death had not claimed him.

And Romano thought now of Miguela, his young wife, and of their two little boys, and of that tumbledown shack in the shanty-town outskirts of the sleepy little town of Ventura he had called home. He remembered that even now there should be a third youngster in his own family, for Miguela had been six months along with child the last time he had been home to see her, and that had been a good five months ago. In his heart he knew that Miguela would forgive him his neglect and welcome him home with loving arms, and would not reproach him for his neglect in the past.

Family ties which had not seemed important back in his carefree days as a roving bandido now took on meaning, and for the first time in over six years, Romano felt a twinge of homesickness.

The young man looked to the pine-clad hills back of the Beartrap Canyon, to the Craggs, so long a landmark to travelers, jutting from the mountain range to the west. He sniffed the crisp mountain air, and somehow, once again, he found life good. Should not life once again hold zest?—be meaningful?

It is self-pity, not misfortune, that tears a man down. This truth Romano saw, and in the seeing he shrugged self-pity away from himself as he might a threadbare coat.

Once again he had faith in himself, and with this renewed faith came also strength, courage, and pride. And having shrugged off self-pity, Romano was again eager to rejoin the world of men. Life was still before him. He did indeed have a choice as to his own future.

Romano knew he could rejoin the outlaw band if he so chose. His own courage and his loyalty to his compadres had never been questioned and he knew his companions of the outlaw trail would welcome him back as a member in good standing. But did he want to rejoin the band, to go back to that way of life? It was a dashing, carefree life, but always Death rode as your trail companion.

Or he could return to his own people, and to the life of a vaquero which could be rewarding in its own way.

Romano had an inherent skill with horses, and skilled horse-breakers were in demand. He knew he could be assured of a worth-while position as a horse-breaker on almost any ranch in California.

So, which fork in the trail should he take?

Today, Romano would make no decisions. Today his soul would drink in the strength of the wilderness solitude, that he should have the strength for right decisions. On the morrow he would decide his future. On the morrow he would set his feet on that fork in the trail which would take him to his future.

Having discarded his black mood of self-pity, Romano once again gave heed to his appearance, looked down on his own soiled, blood-stained, sweat-encrusted garments with keen displeasure. A man of pride should take pride in his own personal appearance!

He walked over to a pool formed by a basin of rock below the spring, and there he stripped and bathed. Then he washed his soiled garments and spread them on the rocks to dry in the sun.

Once again he had pride in his own body. Was it not still young, supple, and strong? Was there not much in life that he could yet accomplish? Turning twenty-four, there would still be many good years ahead of him, if only he used those years wisely.

Romano stretched to his full height, flexed his muscles, breathed deeply of the bracing mountain air. Life indeed was worth the living! Mother Earth gave strength to her children, if they would but turn to her!

Contentedly, the young man sprawled himself out in the grass to await the drying of his garments. And within his wayward soul, Romano had found peace of mind as well as hope for the future.

Early that June morning so long ago, long before the first rays of the rising sun had tipped the Craggs, the young man who for six years had led the adventuresome life of *un bandido bravo* broke camp, and was soon mounted and on his way. Pancho also was happy to be on his way, glad to be free of the hobbles which had held him back when the other horses ridden by the outlaws had left the glen.

The pine-scented air, the first rays of the rising sun, the sphinxlike Craggs somberly looking down on the wilderness, the stirring of wild life all about him, and his own stalwart young body now free of pain— Romano Garza rode proud in the saddle and took pride once again in his horsemanship. He had slept soundly and his mind was once again at peace with his soul.

Once again, for Romano, life was good.

The decision which the young man had put off the day before gave him no confusion this day. There was only one road for him now—the right road. Romano and Pancho were heading home, back to his family, and to the prosaic work-a-day world of honest men.

For Romano Garza, there was now no temptation to rejoin the outlaw band. That one last brush with the law had been enough to dampen forever any craving for adventure outside the law as far as Romano was concerned. As for that noble cause which had in the beginning drawn him into these extralegal activities, somehow its noble purposes had been prostituted by ambitious men for their own gain, and now that cause was badly tarnished by injustices inflicted in the name of justice.

The crease where a bullet had hit the fork of Romano's saddle, the stain of long-since-dried blood on the saddle, these reminders of his recent ordeal Romano hardly noticed. And yet...

In his daredevil flight from the posse, Romano Garza had been the victim of one of those weird one-in-ten-thousand freaks of mischance.

Though bullets had whizzed past him quite closely in that first wild exchange of gunfire, following that unexpected encounter with the lawmen, Romano had not been hit. Pancho was fleet and soon outdistanced his pursuers; and once out of range of accurate gunfire, Romano had congratulated himself that soon he would be completely out of harm's way. Then it was that misfortune overtook him.

Angling up the steep slope of a ridge he had to cross to escape the posse completely, for a time riding broadside to the by-now distant lawmen, Romano felt safe enough. In the past, he had faced far more hazardous situations and always had come through them unscathed.

Leaning forward in the saddle to help Pancho keep his footing, his own eyes on the treacherous rock-strewn trail, Romano had been contemptuous of the long-range rifle fire which kept wild bullets striking the hillside around him. Then one of those random rifle bullets had struck, hitting the fork of his saddle at an angle, and had glanced off.

It had been this flattened ricocheted bullet which had been Romano's undoing.

*   *   *

For Romano Garza, the homecoming had been as a balm to his troubled soul. Arriving at his mother's home in Santa Maria, he had been welcomed warmly by his kinsfolk there. His mother had wept as she kissed him, and she insisted that she had said prayers for his safety every night during those six years that he had been with the *insurrectos.* His stepfather had grasped his hand warmly and assured him of his welcome back into the family circle. His half-brothers and sisters had looked upon him as a hero, returning from a great adventure. And kindred friends from his boyhood had sought him out, welcomed him home; to them, he was a soldier whose valour was a matter of much pride to all loyal *hijos del pais.*

Then the ride south to Ventura, and to a warm welcome from his wife, Miguela, who not once reproved him for his neglect during the five years of their marriage.

There were also shy advances from little Jose and Diego, his sons, though truly the little boys had scarcely any recollection at all of their father. And there was the introduction to little Romana, his infant daughter, whom he was seeing for the first time. In the wayward soul of Romano Garza there was a kindling of paternal pride, knowing as he did that these three children would be his only offspring.

Lady Luck, who for a time had deserted Romano Garza, once again smiled benignly upon him. For as luck would have it, the vigilantes did not recognize him as having been among the holdup men of some months earlier, and hence he was free to seek gainful employment without the risk of being apprehended. It would mean that he must now set aside the name of Garza, which had been the name of his blood father. However, he could take the surname of his stepfather for no one was likely to connect that name with the outlaw band.

Romano had little trouble in finding a worthwhile job; his skill with horses was its own letter of recommendation, and employers did not ask too many questions as long as a man did his work well.

With zest Romano began work as a horse-breaker and vaquero. With zest, faith, and determination, for it would be in excelling other men in these rugged professions that Romano would prove his inherent manhood to himself as well as to other men. Did not the rigorous life of the vaquero require strength, courage, and skill? Was not the vaquero, of all men, a man whose manhood was proven beyond question by his work?

Romano gained friends, many friends; and in the simple pleasures of his people—the fiestas, the bailes, and the various contests of skill, he found keen enjoyment. Once again he had pride in the supple strength of his body, and when his comrades held contests of skill and daring, he always took part. Had he not great skill in these sports, even back in the years of his boyhood? And since his return to the life of the vaquero, did he not gain additional trophies?

There was a fine silver buckle, won in one competition as the best *lazador* of the district, and, even more important, that superb saddle, prize to the first man able to ride El Diablo Negro, the black outlaw horse who had thrown so many riders at fiestas over the country. To Romano, these trophies were of far greater importance than the loot of his outlaw years.

And for Miguela and the children there was a pleasant cottage, a haven to come home to. Even though his work on the big ranches required that he be away from his home much of the time, Romano had discovered that the joys of a home and family far outweighed the tinselly pleasures of the cantinas.

With the passing of the years, which take from a man the vigor of youth, Romano bought a small ranch in the southland, where he could plant an orchard and a small orange grove, and where he could raise a few head of cattle and horses—a parcel of land he could call his own, where he and the faithful Miguela could spend their sunset years, where they could entertain kinsfolk and friends, and could enjoy their several grandchildren during vacation time.

For Romano and Miguela, these were good years.

With the passing of the years, Romano could speak of his having been an *insurrecto* in the losing battle to regain Alta California from the gringos, with no fear of retaliation from the gringo lawmen. For with the passing of time, even the Americanos came to look upon the derring-do of the California bandidos with a touch of pleasant nostalgia. The bandidos, like the vigilantes, the claim-jumpers, drifters, gamblers, whore-ladies, and gringo highwaymen, were a part of that colorful past, so quickly lost in the shadows of times long gone, but not completely forgotten.

With understandable pride Romano would recount his own deeds; for had he not ridden with the Great Tiburcio Vasquez back in those halcyon years of *insurreccion*, before the gringos had completely conquered the land of Alta California and made her law-abiding?

Then had he not for a time ridden with that other brave *capitan de insurgentes* Reginaldo Santos? And had not he himself, Romano Garza, been wounded in that last battle between the gringos and Santos' *rurale* band?

Of these things could Romano speak with pride—not with shame; for in his own mind, and in the minds of his fellow countrymen, he had been a soldier fighting for a cause—a lost cause, it was true. Nonetheless, is not any soldier who has fought bravely, regardless of the fortunes of war, deserving of respect?

FOOTNOTE: "Romano Garza" and "Juan Montaña" are not figments of fiction. Both men were real, and both, at various times during the 1920s and '30s, were back in the La Panza country, reviewing old scenes and doing a little prospecting. By then they were along in years, and each was accompanied by younger men of their own families.

Both men spoke rather complacently of having been of the *revolucionarios*, and of early association with Tiburcio Vasquez and his band. However, since there are probably present-day descendants of both men, I have for this story deliberately masked identities, using for names aliases they themselves admitted using while riding the outlaw trail, rather than the names they were going by in later years.

AND WHISKEY FURNISHED THE FUEL

In a rude shack in a canyon surrounded by the La Panza Mountains there dwelt a young woman of considerable beauty, and the name that she went by was Chata Chavez, though what her name had been in infancy when she was christened, was anyone's guess. And what was the means of her livelihood here in this remote canyon? Well, truthfully, there appeared to be none—except perhaps her beauty.

The time was the year 1879, or thereabout, and the place was called by some the Vasquez Canyon, and by others simply the Mines.

Of the men who came calling at this remote canyon cabin—and there were many such callers—two men were dominant in vying for the lovely Chata's favors; and when either of these two were about, other men stayed away from the cabin.

Librado Corona and Francisco Valenzuela were friends of long standing, friends tried by the fire of mutual peril and found to be trustworthy, compadres of the trail, and congenial drinking companions. Yet, they were also rivals, and rivalry in itself breeds some degree of distrust.

Corona and Valenzuela had each been a trusted lieutenant in the *insurrecto* band of the estimable Tiburcio Vasquez, and each had been accountable to the great leader himself, but to him only and to none other. And now, with the memorable Tiburcio hardly four years

in the grave—his neck having been snapped by the hangman's rope—
the men who had once composed his band of followers were scattered,
leaderless, seeking refuge in out-of-the-way places.

It was the cherished dream of several of Vasquez' lieutenants to
organize another band of insurrectos, to step into the now-vacant
boots of the notorious Vasquez, as it were. And of these ambitious
lieutenants, none were more zealous than Librado Corona and
Francisco Valenzuela.

Though these two men still traveled together for mutual protection
from the gringo lawmen—and in an emergency involving either man,
the other would unhesitatingly have come to his aid—each man had
come to view the other's ambitions with an understandable degree
of suspicion. Then, to add to this rivalry between Corona and Valenzuela for prestige among their peers, there was also a growing rivalry
between them for the favors of the lovely Chata Chavez.

It was this rivalry between two prideful men over a beautiful woman
which sparked the flame, and it was whiskey that furnished the fuel.

*   *   *

"Hola! Doctor Esteel! Hola! Come queek! Come queek to the
door!"

A loud pounding on the cabin door and a man's excited shouts
awoke Dr. Still from a sound sleep somewhere around midnight.

Aware that some emergency had brought the caller at this time of
night, the doctor arose and lit a candle; then, clad only in his night-
shirt, he went to the door. There he came face to face with a very
worried man.

"Doctor Esteel, come queek! I shoot one man!" the midnight caller
said, then hastily amended his statement. "One man—he—he shoot
heemself!"

Emergency calls to patch up the loser in some knife or gun fight
were nothing new to Doctor Still back in those robust years when
men settled their feuds without recourse to formal law. He hastily
donned his clothing and saddled a horse kept tethered near the cabin
for such emergencies; then, with the little leather satchel containing
his surgical instruments hooked across the saddle horn, he hurriedly
left in the company of the midnight caller.

Mrs. Still was worried, for law had not yet come to the Mines,
there in Vasquez Canyon. She hurried over to the cabin of Angelito

Acuña, a good friend and neighbor, and she asked him if he would follow the departing men lest the doctor were being drawn into an ambush.

Angelito grabbed his rifle, procured his own mount, then rode on down the canyon in the direction the doctor had gone, aware that he was riding towards the old outlaw camp, still in use at times by men wanted by the law.

As for the women, there was nothing they could do but await the return of their men and hope for the best.

Having arrived at the camp of the wounded man, Dr. Still found him weak from loss of blood, though conscious and sitting up.

An examination of the wound disclosed that the bullet was still in the man's shoulder, lodged deep and in such a way that it could not readily be removed. However, until the bullet was removed it would be a constant irritation, and a source of infection. It would have to come out, and soon, if the man were to live.

Tersely, Dr. Still explained the situation to the injured man: He would have to cut in deep to get the bullet out; and beyond a snort of whiskey, there was nothing in the way of painkiller available to ease the ordeal for the patient. The wounded man would have to bear the pain of the probing and cutting if he hoped to live.

The injured man answered sardonically, "A man's hide and a peeg's hide, eet is all the same under the knife! Cut deep eef you have to, Doctor Esteel! The pain of the cutting, I can take eet!"

Deftly the doctor set about removing the bullet, and in time this was accomplished. Then the wound was cleaned and bandaged to reduce infection and prevent further hemorrhaging. Stoically the injured man bore the pain of the probe and the knife, and scarcely a grunt or a moan left his lips. Nor had it been needful for his companion to steady him during his ordeal.

When the operation was completed, the patient remarked jokingly, "Doctor Esteel, do you not find a man's hide ees like a peeg's hide when you cut into it? Eh, Doctor?"

Satisfied that he had done all that he could for his patient, Dr. Still spoke to both men, telling them that the injured man had a good chance for recovery if he would take proper precautions. However, under no circumstances should he be moved until the wound had closed over, for any severe jolt could start a hemorrhage, and already he had lost too much blood to risk further bleeding.

Having given these instructions, Dr. Still and Señor Acuña mounted their horses and returned to their cabins and to their interrupted sleep.

The following afternoon, Dr. Still rode back down the canyon to the campground the two men had shared, to see how the wounded man was faring. There was no camp. Both men were gone.

Presumably, with the first break of dawn, the uninjured man had loaded their camp supplies onto a pack horse, saddled the riding horses for both, then helped his injured comrade to mount. Then apparently both had ridden away to seek a campsite deep in the mountains where no one could check on their movements.

Word of the shooting went the rounds, first among the prospectors along Vasquez Canyon, then by way of the mail carrier to the San Joaquin Valley. Then on his return trip, Joe Arana, the mail carrier, brought back a message from the Sheriff of Kern County: "Hold those two men for questioning! I will send some men over for them just as soon as I can locate the posse out looking for them!"

The man who had been shot was identified as Librado Corona, recently released from San Quentin, and again wanted by the law for questioning; and his associate was identified as Francisco Valenzuela, on the wanted list on various charges over in the San Joaquin Valley.

However, the message from the Sheriff of Kern County had come too late. Both men had disappeared completely, leaving no clue as to their whereabouts.

FOOTNOTE: This story comes under the heading of family history, for Dr. Still was my grandfather, and often I have heard my folks tell of the time Grandpa was called out in the middle of the night, to cut a bullet from the shoulder of a man shot in some argument, only to discover a few days later that both the injured man and his compañero were notorious outlaws, wanted by the law in Kern County at the time.

Presumably, Valenzuela and Corona had had some whiskey-inspired dispute while sharing the same camp, and Valenzuela had shot Corona; then, realizing what he had done, he had gone for the doctor who was then living a mile or two up the canyon. And always the punch line of the story had to do with the young outlaw, seriously wounded and in considerable pain throughout the probing and cutting, trying to keep up his own *macho* self-image by joking about how a man's hide and a pig's hide were the same under the knife.

This incident took place not long after the Still family moved into the La Panza Mines, in the summer of 1879.

I am indebted to my Uncle Mentley Still for the details incorporated into this story.

History records that Librado Corona was the man arrested with Tiburcio Vasquez in Greek George's roadhouse on that fateful May 14, 1874—arrested while holding the infant of La Señero de Greek George in his arms. And there were those unkind enough to suggest that Corona had grabbed the baby up to use as a shield against the lawmen's bullets. Maybe so; maybe not. He may simply have been holding the baby at the time the lawmen broke into the house unexpectedly. He was but a neophyte bandit, eighteen years old, and a recent recruit into the Vasquez band.

Old prison records reveal that Librado Corona spent five years in San Quentin for his own part in the extortion of $800 from the aging Italian sheepman Alesandro Repetto (presumably Corona's first criminal activity up to the time of his arrest). He was released from San Quentin on May 9, 1879, and apparently ran afoul of the law soon thereafter.

According to the records, Corona was born in Mexico, and at the time of his arrest he had just turned eighteen. He was described as under average height, of slender build and boyish appearance, and of lighter complexion than many of his fellow countrymen.

In spite of his boyish appearance, Corona was said to have been deadly with both pistol and knife if cornered and engaged in a fight.

As to the outcome of Corona's little argument with his bosom pal Valenzuela, well...

Some months after Dr. Still removed the bullet from Corona's shoulder, someone riding through what was known in later years as the Beartrap Canyon came upon an abandoned campsite where two men had apparently camped for a time. In the bushes near this campsite there were old blood-soaked bandages, apparently thrown away as a wound was given fresh dressing.

Presumably, Valenzuela had taken his wounded compadre to a remote spot and there set up camp, caring for Corona until he had recovered sufficiently to ride away. Somewhat later, Librado Corona was seen and recognized by several who had known him in the past; so presumbly his wound had healed without complications.

There is a heartening epilogue to this tale of the long ago—it has been said that in his mature years Librado Corona forsook the life of an outlaw, married, settled down to earn a legitimate living, and in due time raised a family. There are, it has been said, descendants of Librado Corona living in California today, descendants who can speak of their ancestor with respect—can even brag a bit and tell how, in his rebel youth, Corona had been a trusted lieutenant of that romantic *revolucionario*, the Great Tiburcio Vasquez himself.

In the previous story, I have deliberately masked the identities of Romano Garza and Juan Montaña, to avoid possible embarrassment to present-day descendants. However, circumstances place Librado Corona in a somewhat different light. His name and his known association with Vasquez are matters of public record, hence there seems to be no reason not to use his name here. His having been arrested with Tiburcio Vasquez is mentioned in just about every book written on the life of Vasquez—has in fact given him a notoriety perhaps out of proportion to his probable involvement with the outlaw band.

As told in a previous section of this series, after the Tres Pinos robbery in which three unarmed men were killed, Vasquez and his followers split up, going separate ways to avoid leaving too obvious a trail. Shortly thereafter, Vasquez enlisted several new recruits, including Librado Corona.

Running short of ready cash, and hearing that the sheepman Repetto had sold some sheep, Vasquez sent Corona to the sheepman's ranch to size up the situation.

Posing as a transient shearer, Corona asked for a job; and once on the ranch, he managed to introduce Vasquez and Chavez as acquaintances seeking jobs also. Thus Vasquez and Chavez were able to gain entrance. Learning too late that Repetto had already deposited the money in the bank, Vasquez forced him to make out a check for $800, then send his nephew to Los Angeles to cash the check, threatening to kill the older man if the youth refused to go.

This episode may well have been Corona's initiation into outlawry, and possibly his only crime up to the time of his arrest about one month later.

IN PERSPECTIVE

Before ending this chapter on the Vasquez Gang, it might be well to point out a few facts about how life was lived back there a century ago, to gain a perspective on the activities of the California bandidos of the 1870s, and perhaps to place the reformed bandidos, who in later years re-entered the realm of law-abiding men, in a more understandable light. To start with, one should take the over-all picture:

During the Civil War years, California was pretty much on her own, and all too often the only law enforcement was of the vigilante variety. Then the Big War was over, and to California came a horde of newcomers, many of them discharged soldiers from both the North and the South, uprooted and restless.

Then came the overland railroad, completed in 1869, bringing with it an influx of rowdy gandy dancers, discharged from the railroad when the work was finished, to add their numbers to an already disproportionately large number of inherently lawless men drawn into California by promises of quick riches. These men, coupled with the miners already entrenched in the Mother Lode country, tended to squeeze the native Californiano and the more recent immigrants from Mexico out of Northern California. The seaport town of San Diego also had come under the dominance of the upstart aliens, leaving Central California as the last stronghold for the Spanish Americans in Alta California.

Under these circumstances, is it any wonder that the *hijos del pais* should view the aliens with distrust?

In their own eyes, and in the eyes of many of their fellow countrymen, the bandidos were soldiers, not criminals. And perhaps it is as soldiers that these rebellious ones should be judged.

Certainly, back in those disrupted times following the Civil War, formal law was faulty at best. It was erratic in application and all too often partisan, with those entrusted to law enforcement favoring their friends and manipulating the law to their own personal interests. Also, although there had been some attempt by the more responsible men to curb vigilante action, such law enforcement was still occurring openly throughout the 1880s, and *sub rosa* well into the present century.

It is hard to come up with any action on the part of the bandits themselves that in retrospect would seem more reprehensible than that episode of the Coon-dogs lynching the youth Miguel Lugo. They called Miguel a horse-thief, only to learn when it was too late that the horses he had been accused of stealing were in fact his own. It was an inexcusable, grisly, lawless act, all in the name of law enforcement.

There had been justification for the vigilante action in San Luis Obispo in 1858, which resulted in the hanging of seven men under a kangaroo court form of justice. At the time, wanton murders were being committed with ever-increasing frequency, and the legal agencies could not or would not move against the murderers. Someone had to take drastic measures to bring a desperate situation under control. But in the case of the Coon-dogs, there was absolutely no justification for taking the law into their own hands.

True, distance and the rugged Santa Lucia Mountains, plus an unexpected stampede of strangers into the La Panza Mountains following the discovery of gold there, had made it difficult for the Sheriff of San Luis Obispo County to police the eastern half of the county, and outlawry was on the increase there. However, once the Coon-dogs had taken the accused youth into custody, they should have taken him back to San Luis Obispo and turned him over to the legal authorities. His claims to the horses could then have been checked out, and if he had in fact stolen the horses, he would have been brought to trial. If convicted, he would have been punished, even though a legally convicted horse-thief usually got only five years in prison instead of being hanged, which the more ardent advocates of law and order considered the only cure for horse-theft.

The men in control of the Coon-dogs on that expedition were not of the vagrant class. There were mature, influential men in that band, men who professed a desire for law and order in the new land. Yet it is hard to come up with a more flagrant breach of the law than their own actions in lynching a youth without benefit of trial.

It should be pointed out that the Californianos had their own internal problems as well as their problems with the gringo newcomers. The bandidos were not particular about their victims. They robbed the *hijos del pais* as enthusiastically as they did the gringos.

Also, before bidding a final *Adios, amigo. Vaya con Dios* to the estimable Tiburcio Vasquez, let it here be noted:

Contrary to popular notion, Vasquez was not launched on his outlaw career through American injustice. He brought on himself his own first conviction and prison sentence when he and a compadre descended upon the corral of a fellow countryman, one Luis Francisco, and there did "felonously steal, take, and carry away, against the peace and dignity of the people" one mule and nine horses, with an estimated total value of $435.

Understandably, Señor Francisco was vexed when he discovered the loss of his property, and forthwith he hied himself to the local law enforcement agencies and swore out a complaint; and shortly thereafter, Vasquez was apprehended under circumstances which left little doubt as to his guilt. Vasquez pleaded guilty and threw himself on the mercy of the court. He was given a five-year sentence which, considering the temper of the times, was a moderate punishment, for in those days horse-thieves were usually hanged, impartially, and without regard to race, religion, or national origin.

It was not American lawmen bribing his lady love into betraying him, as legend has it, that ended Vasquez' career. It was a trusted lieutenant within his own band, the cuckolded Leiva, who blew the whistle on him. And it was Vasquez' own lack of gallantry in extorting that $800 from the Italian sheepherder that pinpointed his whereabouts, making it possible for the lawmen to corner him.

And finally, it was one of Vasquez' own fellow countrymen who sealed his doom. Having reviewed the case after conviction, California's native-born governor, Romualdo Pacheco, refused to grant executive clemency.

Part VI

WOE UNTO THE EVILDOER; FOR HIS END SHALL BE CUT OFF!

More tales from the past in which more miscreants and malefactors meet an inglorious end.

WOE UNTO THE EVILDOER

"Woe unto the evildoer! For his end shall be cut off, and his soul shall be consigned to eternal damnation! To a pit of fire and brimstone! and to an eternity of awesome torment! To a Hell that hath no ending..."

The grim voice of the minister thundered on as his captive audience squirmed, yet dared not leave. This was no ordinary Sunday preaching where one could walk out with impunity, or stay and snooze through the sermon. This was a funeral service, and some degree of sorrowful respect had to be shown the recently departed.

True, the departed had been something of a rogue, a miscreant who had earned little respect from his peers during his checkered sojourn on earth. He had led a shabby life, and had met an inglorious end. For Death had come in a saloon brawl in which one of the participants had drawn a knife, jabbed it between the ribs of our friend, and then himself departed in the confusion, to escape undetected. At least no one had chosen to identify the knife-wielder when the lawmen arrived and questioned those still present in the saloon.

"Woe! Woe! Woe unto the evildoer! His end shall be cut off! I shall smite the evildoer! So saith the Lord God Almighty!" The minister smote his left palm with his right fist to emphasize this point, then went on: "Let the woefully misspent life of this our misguided friend whose earthly shell lies here before us—his unhappy soul now facing the Judgment Seat, to be consigned to that awesome pit of the Damned! Let the grievous fate of this our wretched friend be a warning to all!" The minister paused to let this sink in, then continued:

"Again I say: Woe unto the evildoer! His end shall be cut off! His name shall be stricken from the Book of Life!"

He paused again, then: "Was not the end of this our sinful friend who lies here cut short while he was still in the prime of manhood? In the prime of his life, his end was cut short by the Lord God Almighty who in His great wisdom chose to destine this man to the darksome pit of fire and brimstone, as a warning to all that sinful man must one day face his Maker!"

To ten-year-old Willie, the only one of the assembled mourners who truly mourned for the departed, this enthusiastic consigning of the soul of the deceased to the fires of Hell did seem to be going too far. After all, the minister had been called upon to eulogize the man— not to consign him to Hell!

Maybe the miscreant *had* been a bad man, but he wasn't an *all*-bad man! At least not from Willie's point of view. When sober, he had been an affable fellow who liked kids, who had in fact spent hours on end entertaining the kids of the town with his tales of derring-do.

But Willie dared not express his views, for back in those good old days, children did not question the wisdom of their elders. Not out loud, they didn't!

The preacher droned on: "Again! Again, I say—I repeat! Woe! Woe unto the evildoer! His end shall be cut off..."

FOOTNOTE: This story had its origin in some of the reminiscences of my uncle Will Still, going back to the years the Still family spent in El Pueblo de San Luis Obispo (1867 to 1872).

As a lifetime Methodist, Uncle Will held to an unyielding belief in a good hot Hell for the evildoer, should such evildoer fail to repent in time for Salvation. Still, to Uncle Will, this enthusiastic consignment of the man's immortal soul to the Fiery Pit by the minister who had been asked to deliver the eulogy did seem to be overdoing.

In defense of the preacher: Steeped for a lifetime in the grim Calvanist doctrine of Predestination and Eternal Damnation, where even the Very Elect might fail the test on the Day of Judgment, the minister no doubt felt that since this particular evildoer was past any chance of help, his misspent life should be put to use as a warning which might save some other erring soul from the pit of burning brimstone. And perhaps if there were more fire-and-brimstone preachers scaring the living Hell out of evildoers now, we might have less crime on the streets today.

In this story, we have considered the afterlife of evildoers, as viewed by an earlier generation. But then, perhaps these evildoers who were so enthusiastically ushered into Hell, with its warm climate and congenial company, were not so badly off. How about those evildoers whose deeds were so horrendous that not even Satan wanted anything to do with them and refused them the sanctuary of Hell, after they had been turned away from Heaven, forcing these miserable shades of the departed to haunt throughout eternity the scene of their gory crimes?

One such case was the murder in the Mission.

MURDER IN THE MISSION

A century ago, the murder of a family in the old Mission San Miguel Arcangel was a very popular topic of conversation, and it was said that bloodstains could be seen on the walls and floors for many years after the crime. This was blood which had spurted from the trembling bodies of the victims, who had been attacked while slumbering and had literally been chopped to death with an axe. And to add substance to this legend, even then in the making, the spectral forms of the unholy quintet who had perpetrated this atrocious crime were scaring unwary wayfarers who chanced to be passing the gloomy Mission buildings on a moonlit night.

The story behind this legend of murder and ghosts has come down through the years in many versions, including various spellings of the family's name. What was the true story?

In his *History of San Luis Obispo County* (published in 1883), Myron Angel tells us that a Mr. Read, an Englishman, gained possession of the old San Miguel Mission buildings sometime before 1847 and established his family there, having brought them up from South America.

With the discovery of gold in 1848, Read took off for the Sierras to mine, returning that fall with several thousand dollars' worth of gold dust. He was hospitable and loquacious, and took pleasure in exhibiting his wealth.

In October of that year, a party of sailors, deserters from a ship of war lying in the harbor of Monterey, stopped for the night in the Mission, eating supper with the Read family. Then sometime during that night, the whole family, including the young children of the household, was slaughtered.

A day after the murders had been committed, John M. Price and Francis Z. Branch, themselves returning from the mines country, stopped at the Mission. They had known Read, and they were worried when no one made an appearance, so they searched the buildings

until they came upon the bodies. They then went on to San Luis
Obispo to report the crime.

A posse formed and pursued the murderers, overtaking them at
Carpenteria (near Santa Barbara). In the ensuing fight, one of the
posse was killed, and others were wounded. The murderers themselves were all killed. One of them jumped into the ocean and tried
to swim away, but was shot before he could get out of rifle range, and
"sank to rise no more."

According to Mr. Angel, the Read family consisted of Read himself, his pregnant wife, his daughter, his son-in-law, three children,
and an old Negro retainer, all murdered that fateful night—eight persons killed in all.

Here we have an account written by a reputable historian some
thirty years after the incident took place. Mr. Angel gave credit to one
of the men who had discovered the crime, John M. Price, for the details as given in the book, and that is the true story of the murder in
the Mission—or is it?

In *San Luis Obispo and Environs*, an updated version of local history compiled by Annie Morrison and published in 1917, there is an
account of the murder of the Read family in the old Mission San
Miguel, apparently based on the Angel account, for it follows that
version fairly closely. The victims are identified as Mr. Read, his wife
and infant daughter, Read's daughter and son-in-law, their three
children, a women who had come to act as midwife, and the old Negro
retainer, all killed by a band of renegade sailors who had stopped at
the Mission for supper.

In this version the eight persons murdered in Angel's story have
increased to ten, with the addition of the midwife and the baby.

History of San Luis Obispo County, edited by A. V. Kell, published
in 1939, says that in December of 1848 there came to the Mission San
Miguel five sailors who had deserted from a man-of-war in Monterey.
In this account Reed showed the sailors a bag of gold obtained from
a sale of sheep to the miners. The sailors went on to Paso Robles, but
returned the following night and murdered Reed and his family.

Here the persons murdered are listed as: Reed himself, his wife and
infant son, his brother-in-law, named as Jose Ramon Vallejo, Josefa
Olivera the midwife, her daughter and son (the latter four years old),
and three servants, including a five-year-old Indian boy.

This is a sharply different arrangement of characters from that given in Angel's account—ten persons killed, counting the baby. (In the Angel book, the wife was near confinement.)

The editor of this book admits there are various versions of this incident, one version holding that Midwife Olivera escaped the massacre, and another version saying that it was the Indian boy who escaped.

In *California Missions*, by J. Berger, published in 1941, the story is that the San Miguel Mission was sold to Petronillo Rios and William Reed in 1846, by then governor Pio Pico. This account goes on to say that in 1848 a party of five adventurers murdered the Reed family, ten persons who were at the time occupying the padres' quarters in the old Mission buildings. And, it goes on, the five murderers were tracked down—one was shot, one drowned, and three were executed following capture.

In *The Salinas*, by Anne B. Fisher (1945), there is still a different account of the incident. Mrs. Fisher got her material from interviews with old-time residents of the Salinas Valley.

According to this version, Petronillo Rios and William Reed (an English sailor) bought the Mission San Miguel from Governor Pio Pico for $300. Then gold was discovered, and Reed and Rios left. After their return, three renegades Reed had met in the gold fields came by. Reed bragged too much, and the renegades massacred the whole family. In this telling of the story, the persons killed were William Reed, his expectant Indian wife, her eight-year-old brother, an aging midwife, her daughter, this daughter's child, and two little boys who were sons of Reed. Also killed were a Negro servant, an aging sheepherder, and the sheepherder's young grandson.

Here we have eleven persons killed, and a sharply different arrangement of characters. Of these, one little boy escaped the slaughter, wandered into the mustard fields, and died from exposure.

In this account, the renegades number three, and when overtaken by the posse near Santa Barbara, two were shot, and "The Irishman" surrendered but was shot soon afterward. The man who discovered the bodies is identified as Captain Pryce of Los Osos Rancho.

Missions of California, compiled for P.G. & E. Co. (1970) contains still another version of the story. This account says that Petronillo Rios and William Reed bought the San Miguel Mission from Governor Pico in 1846, paying $600 for the property. In 1848, Reed went to the gold fields, brought back some gold dust, and also sold some cattle and sheep. Then in December (1848) five deserters from a British man-of-war had dinner with the Reeds and learned of Reed's good fortune. They left, but slipped back at night and murdered Reed, his family, servants, and visitors. Eleven persons were killed, but no names are given in this account.

A posse pursued the murderers and intercepted them near Santa Barbara. One killer was shot, another jumped into the ocean and drowned, and three were hanged. "For years there were legends of ghosts prowling the ruins of the Mission."

The story as handed down by descendants of Petronillo Rios names the murder victims as William Reed, his wife, their three-year-old child, Mrs. Reed's young brother, an older woman acting as nurse (or midwife), her married daughter, this daughter's young child, a Negro servant, and a sheepman and his grandson. (Some versions say that this sheepman was a Basque or Portuguese who chanced to be traveling through with his grandson and took lodging for the night, while other versions say he was an Indian sheepherder working for Reed.

Another version of the story as handed down through the years has "an Indian family" as the victims slaughtered in the Old Mission, possibly confusing this incident with some other from those lawless years.

There have been many accounts of this murder in the old Mission San Miguel in books and in magazine and newspaper articles printed through the years, as well as in the recollections of descendants of early residents of the area. Details vary. The name of the murdered family has been given variously as Read, Reed, Reid, Ried, and even Rede; the number of persons slaughtered ranges from seven to fifteen, and the bloody villains from three to seven, with five the number most often accepted.

The persons comprising the Reed household vary sharply in the telling, both as to their number and their relationship to the head of the household. Some versions say that Señora Olivera, the midwife, was William Reed's mother-in-law, and that there were members of her family in the massacre.

The murderous malefactors have been identified as British sailors from a man-of-war they had deserted; American sailors or soldiers who had deserted; and mongrel renegades who had followed Reed from the gold fields for his poke of gold.

Some versions go into gory detail and tell how the older members of the household were chopped to death with an axe while they slept, and how the younger children were "grabbed by their feet and their brains bashed out against the pillars and walls of the old Mission."

Should this tale from the long-ago be discounted as but a bit of folklore—an incident which probably never took place at all—simply because of the erratic reporting of it?

No one has ever questioned the basic story of the slaughter of a family within the walls of the old San Miguel Mission buildings by a pack of renegades whose motive was presumably robbery. However, it would appear that either those assigned the grisly task of removing the victims' bodies from the buildings and burying them failed to write down an official account identifying the bodies or, if such an official record was made, it has been misplaced or lost.

It is hard for modern researchers, who have grown accustomed to the fine reference libraries, the stacks of newspapers, magazines, etc., and the detailed but tedious courthouse records from which to sift their information, to realize just how meager were records of any sort under frontier conditions.

In most cases, those trying to reconstruct the frontier past must rely on accounts written sometimes as much as thirty to fifty years after the incident took place, accounts which when set down relied less on written records than on survivors' memories—memories already growing hazy with the passing of the years.

Under such conditions, details were bound to get scrambled, but that does not mean the incident did not take place.

Heck! I sidetracked from the theme I started on, namely the ghosts of those murderers who used to haunt the Old Mission grounds a century ago. What ever happened to them?

Wayfarers speeding past the Old Mission San Miguel in their high-powered cars don't have time for ghosts; so our spectral friends have in recent years been woefully neglected. However, unless the Ol' Boy down below has relented and taken their guilt-harried souls home to Hell, they are probably around somewhere, and will again make their appearance on moonlit nights when folks slow down enough to see them.

And now, having learned what happens to the immortal souls of unregenerate evildoers, let us look at what happened to the mortal bodies of some of the murdersome miscreants in those robust years now long gone and almost forgotten. To start with—the grisly tale of an insignificant man who rides the tail of a comet.

AN INSIGNIFICANT MAN RIDES
THE TAIL OF A COMET

"He does but ride the tail of a comet! An insignificant man who seeks importance by claiming an association with a more illustrious man!" Hugo the bartender spat a *quache* of tobacco juice into the nearest spittoon, wiped his walrus mustachio with the soiled dishtowel he held in his hand, then went back to wiping dry the drinking glasses on the bar in front of him.

"He claims to have been a trusted lieutenant of Joaquin! Bah!" Hugo spat again, wiped his mustachio, and went on: "Joaquin Murrieta would have wiped his backside on such as he, then would have thrown him away as unworthy of being used for a second wipe!"

"The man had me fooled," the gringo newcomer acknowledged. "He was a most convincing raconteur! Especially about his own daring exploits!" Then the gringo laughed. "True or false, his tales of derring-do were worth a bottle of tequila!"

"Abdulo el Tigre he called himself when first he came into the Santa Maria Valley about ten years ago." One of the barroom loungers entered the conversation. "His claim then was that he had been one of Joaquin Murrieta's band of *insurrectos*; and since the estimable Joaquin had by then departed Alta California and was not around to deny the claim, there were many who believed him."

"Abdulo el Tigre!" Another bar-lounger exclaimed, then laughed as though *el tigre* were funny. "He has proven to be a most uninspiring tiger! Abdulo el Asno is what everyone calls him now!"

"Abdulo?" The American's tone implied a question. "That name sounds more Turk than Spanish or Indian."

"Abdulo's sire was a Saracen sailor who jumped ship in old Yucatan, and his dam was a barmaid of our people," Hugo explained. "At least, that is Abdulo's story, and it is probably true."

"It is probably the only truth in all his *cuentos fantastico!*" The bar-lounger who had spoken first laughed, then went on, "His *cuentos de hadas* (fairy tales) do keep him in liquor, and when hungry enough, he can always find work enough for a meal. Though, of a truth, he would rather starve to death than to hunt for a worthwhile job!"

Hunched down in his chair at a table in a corner, Abdulo drank his tequila alone, for no one had seen fit to join him when he offered to share the bottle which the American had ordered placed on his table. If he did overhear the conversation at the bar through the jovial din of the barroom, he gave no sign. On his swarthy hawk-nosed face there was reflected all the deep-rooted resentments that the outcast feels towards all mankind.

True, Abdulo had no one to blame but himself. When he first came into the Santa Maria Valley, he had been received in a comradely manner, had always been invited to join the celebrants in the local cantinas; and his rather grandiose accounts of his own exploits may even have been given some credence by his new acquaintances.

Abdulo had been endowed by Nature with a superb animal body which seemed to stand up remarkably well under his indolent, dissolute way of life. Also, he had a shrewd mind, capable of devising clever ruses, and a glib tongue which usually got him out of difficult situations. In short, Abdulo el Tigre was a man whose every appearance would seem to fit in with his self-assumed role of *un bandido bravo*.

Four-flushers, however, cannot fool their audiences forever, and men who must work for a living in time grow tired of buying dinners and drinks for a man who rarely works.

In time, Abdulo's plaint that work was scarce fell on deaf ears. Other men found work, so why not Abdulo! And now, with the Big War between the States drawing working men into the army, Abdulo's whining plaint that work was scarce was even less valid than it had been in the past.

Throughout the years since coming into the Santa Maria Valley, Abdulo had been arrested for petty offenses on several occasions, and one of those times he had served six months on the chain-gang. His reputation as a ne'er-do-well had spread from Santa Maria to other communities; and with the passing of time, Abdulo became a suspect in even more serious crimes, though as yet nothing serious had been proven against him.

He was like a sheep-killer dog who may already have acquired a taste for blood—so said men who knew sheep, dogs and men.

These derelictions of Abdulo, *hijo del Sarraceno*, were recounted for the Americano's benefit by the men at the bar, quite indifferent that Abdulo himself was in the barroom, within hearing distance—if indeed he could comprehend what was said in his present state of intoxication.

"A great man blazes his own pathway across the heavens—a comet in his own right!" Hugo the bartender was in a philosophical mood. "On the other hand, an insignificant man, instead of emblazoning his own brilliance through noteworthy deeds, rides the tail of a comet."

*   *   *

Sick to the stomach yet impelled by morbid curiosity, the Americano watched the gruesome proceedings. His four American companions also watched, but having been raised on the frontier, they had acquired some degree of callousness. Nonetheless, even these hardened frontiersmen found it somewhat revolting to watch without protest as men skinned the still-twitching carcass of another man.

This time at least, the impromptu execution of an evildoer had not been because of high-handed gringo prejudice against the native Californianos. To their credit, the five Americans in the party which had tracked down the murderer had done their level best to convince their Sonoran fellow-avengers that the captive miscreant should be taken back to Santa Maria and there given a legal trial. But to no avail, for the Americans were outnumbered seventeen to five by the Sonoreños.

The victim of the crime had been a Sonoran, an elderly man—a kindly, inoffensive man, well-liked in the community. And his death had come through no fault of his own; no fault that is save only that he had worked hard and had been frugal. It had been rumored around Santa Maria that the old man had a small hoard of gold hidden in his isolated cabin, gold coins saved from his productive years towards the needs of advancing age.

The old Sonoreño had been brutally beaten, his arm broken, and then left for dead. Howver, there had still been enough life left in his broken body when he was found for him to name his assailant before he died; and the name that the dying man had given was Abdulo, *el hijo del Sarraceno.*

To the Sonorans living around Santa Maria, this had been a crime against one of their own people, and the hot blood of Old Spain, mingled with that of the prideful Yaqui, demanded vengeance—immediate vengeance. It had been they who had organized the band to track down the killer, and it had been with some reluctance that they had allowed any of the Americanos to accompany them as they left on their mission of vengeance.

The guilt of the wretched Abdulo could hardly be questioned, for the old man had named him before he died, and others had seen him in the general vicinity of the cabin shortly before the crime had been committed. Then to add to this initial evidence against Abdulo, the tracks of a shod horse had been located back of the old Sonoran's cabin, and those tracks had led directly to a hastily made camp in the Huasna country. And in that camp, taken by surprise, was none other than Abdulo, son of a Saracen.

Even more damning, personal items known to have belonged to the old man, along with several hundred dollars in gold coins—gold coins which Abdulo most certainly had not come by through legitimate channels—were found on Abdulo's person.

On the strength of such overwhelming evidence of guilt, and for such a heinous crime, there was not a court of law in the land that would not have convicted Abdulo and given him the death sentence. Abdulo the misfit richly deserved hanging and, aware that it would be useless to further insist that the murderer be taken back to town for an official trial, the five Americans had agreed to a vigilante-type trial on the spot. Then, with the trial over, the Americans had agreed to an immediate execution of the condemned man.

Here again a conflict of wills had taken place. The Americans had insisted that Abdulo be hanged, the official form of execution. The Sonorans, however, wanted a slower, more painful form of death, more in keeping with their own Yaqui heritage.

The Americans had prevailed to the extent that the condemned man had been given a degree of hanging. However, the Sonoreños had insisted on performing that ceremony by themselves, not entrusting it to the gringos.

The Sonorans first stripped Abdulo stark naked, then put one loop of a reata around his thick bull-neck and the other end of the rope across a limb, then pulled the groveling wretch up till his toes barely touched the ground, and held his arms to prevent his easing the choking effects of the tightened noose.

When strangled into a state of near unconsciousness, Abdulo had been released from the noose and laid out on the ground. Then, although the man obviously was not yet dead, the Sonorans started skinning him.

A skinning knife had been inserted near the navel, then run completely around the body, severing the skin into two separate portions, with one team of skinners peeling the hide of the torso upward—like a sweatshirt being removed. Meanwhile, the other team of skinners were peeling their portion downward, much as though they were removing a pair of trousers.

At this point, Abdulo had regained consciousness, let forth a shriek and almost jerked away from his captors, but was restrained.

The American newcomer protested, but received a curt *"Callarse la boca, Gringo!* El Viejo did not recieve a speedy death at the hands of this mad dog! So why should the dog receive a speedy death at our hands!"

"You had better keep your lip buttoned, friend!" one of the Americans warned, *sotto voce.* "As you can see, our *paisano* pals can play rough when they are riled!"

The shrieks subsided to a gurgling intake of breath, as shock brought unconsciousness; and in time the skinners had the skin of the upper torso peeled up to the neck where it was severed along the line of the chin, then pulled across the head, then the arms peeled down, severing the skin at the wrists, leaving an inside-out hide resembling a long-sleeved sweater or undershirt.

Meanwhile, the other team had peeled the skin of the lower body downwards, stripping the skin across the thighs and calves without slitting it, then severed it at the ankles, leaving the body completely skinned except for the head, hands, and feet.

There was still a jerking of the limbs and a gurgling sound in the throat, but whether this was from any awareness of pain or merely the reflex actions of a body still pliant, the American newcomer could not tell.

Grimly the American thought back to that evening when he had first met Abdulo, had listened half believing to his dramatic tales of his adventures as a member of Joaquin Murrieta's band of insurrectos.

What was it that Hugo the bartender had said? Instead of emblazoning his own brilliance through noteworthy deeds, the insignificant man rides the tail of a comet.

Joaquin Murrieta had been the comet, his deeds of daring already becoming a legend. Abdulo had been the tail rider, his only brilliance what little reflected glory he could get through claiming to have once been part of Murrieta's band. But there all resemblance ceased.

There had been something of gallantry about Joaquin, something to inspire the respect of other men in spite of his outlaw status. But there had been no redeeming qualities in Abdulo the outcast. In life he had been an insignificant man relying on reflected glory; in death he suffered the degradation of being skinned like an animal.

There was none to grieve the passing of Abdulo, *hijo del Sarraceno.* No, not one.

In death, Abdulo, son of a Saracen, was to achieve a fame he had not known in life, but alas! it was not the memory of daring deeds that brought him this fame. Rather, it was his durable hide that would, for a time, be a reminder of his sorry misspent life.

It has been said that the skinners took the hide of Abdulo home with them and there put it on stretchers, much the way a trapper does the hide of a varmint, to keep its shape while that hide is being cured. The tubular hide, having been turned inside out while on the stretchers, was thus processed without having to be split open.

Stretched, cured, and properly tanned, the hide of Abdulo resembled a buckskin undershirt and drawers; and by making a slit at the throat, ankles, and wrists, to allow head, feet, and hands to pass through these restricted areas in a human hide, the leathern garments could be donned by living men. Fortunately, Abdulo had been a large barrel-chested man, and in the stretching the hide had achieved an even greater circumference than it had had while on its original owner.

A small man could don these garments of human hide over winter-weight red flannels; a medium-sized man could wear them over a summer-weight union suit; but a big man had to strip right down to his own bare hide before he could wriggle his frame into these weird garments, made from human hide and seamless. However, once inside, the wearer found the garments skin-tight but shaped properly to the contours of his own body.

At least, that is the way certain old-timers used to describe the buckskin shirt and drawers made from human hide.

FOOTNOTE: Back in the 1920s, an old Sonoran who had lived much of his life in the Santa Maria area told, as an incident from his own youth, this tale of "the son of a Saracen" who had paid for his slaying of an aged Sonoran by being hanged and then skinned. He spoke as though his own stepfather had been among the band of avengers. And he told of the unique garments made from that hide.

And now, having touched upon the subject of articles made from human hide, perhaps we may be pardoned if here we digress from the basic theme of the California bandido and present the saga of the everlasting hide of Big-nose George Parrott.

THE EVERLASTING HIDE OF
BIG-NOSE PARROTT

Back in the late 1870s, a bold bandit known as Big-nose George Parrott and his band of bully-boys were giving the Union Pacific Railroad a bad time in the Rocky Mountain states, derailing trains and in general making themselves a public nuisance. Then, to compound their unpopularity, they ambushed and killed a popular deputy sheriff and a detective for the railroad, and then escaped the posse.

A short time later, a member of the Parrott gang was arrested, but was taken away from the lawmen and lynched by a group of vigilantes.

About two and a half years after the railroad detective and the deputy were killed, Big-nose George Parrott was captured and lodged in the jail in Rawlins, Wyoming. And true to form, Big-nose did the wrong thing at the right time to increase his unpopularity.

Lodged in jail, with only one man keeping watch, Big-nose faked a violent illness, and when the deputy opened the cell door to investigate, Big-nose slugged him, then took off down the street. He was recaptured, however, and escorted back to jail.

Vexed at this antisocial behavior on the part of their reluctant guest, the good citizens of Rawlins broke into the jail, took Big-nose away from his jailers, then escorted him outside and on down the street to the nearest telegraph pole.

Someone threw a rope across the cross-arm of the pole, then a slip-noose was placed around the neck of Big-nose Parrott, and in true frontier fashion, the miscreant was hauled up at the end of the rope, "a-kickin' and a-swingin' his arms like a dawg-gawn jumpin'-jack;" for it would seem no one had the foresight to bind his wrists and ankles before hanging him.

With one hand holding the rope above his head to ease the strangling noose, Big-nose swung back and forth, like the pendulum of a clock, his eyes glued to the telegraph pole. In time, the not-so-easily discouraged badman managed to swing his body over against the pole and grab hold, then started to shinny up the pole.

Alas for this noble attempt to escape the lynch-mob! Before he

could shinny up to the temporary safety of the cross-arm of that telegraph pole, one of the vigilantes made a flying leap and grabbed the
escapee by the ankle and held fast, pulling Big-nose down and away
from the pole, holding to the ankle until "Pore Ol' Big-nose quit a-
kickin'" and hung limp at the end of the rope.

Satisfied at last that the badman was sufficiently dead to take down,
the vigilantes loosened the rope and lowered the body, laying it out in
the street. But now that the varmint was dead, what was to be done
with the body? *That* was the question everyone asked.

As it happened, there was in Rawlins at the time an aspiring young
doctor, fresh from an Eastern medical college and eager to advance
his skills with the scalpel.

Here was a fresh cadaver, ready for immediate dissection, with no
kinfolks or friends on hand to claim the body for burial. And so the
earthly remains of Big-nose George Parrott were turned over to this
worthy young medical student, in the interests of scientific advance-
ment.

That the physiognomy of Big-nose George Parrott not be forgotten
by future generations, the young medic first made a lifelike image of
the deceased bandit, then proceeded with the dissection of the cadaver.

First the young doctor carefully skinned the lynched man, that he
might study the muscular arrangement while it was intact; then he set
about opening the body cavity and removing various organs in order
to have a better understanding of the workings of the human innards.
Then with this internal dissection completed, the ambitious medic
decided he would have a look at Big-nose George's brain—if any.

And so this budding young scientist procured a meat saw from the
local butcher shop and proceeded to saw the skull into two pieces,
removing the top of the skull at about eyebrow level so that the brain
might be fully exposed while still in its chamber.

Having completed his scientific studies, the young medic viewed
the remains, by now pretty well disconnected.

The muscles and viscera had served their purpose and would soon
become a foul-smelling mess, so it seemed prudent to dispose of these.
However, certain of the more interesting organs might be worth pre-
serving in formaldehyde for future study. The skeleton also might be
worth saving. This left only the carefully-skinned hide, of little value
scientifically, since human hides can be studied on live humans. But
still, the hide was too good to throw away.

The bones of Big-nose George were in fact cleaned of clinging flesh, dried, then stored in the basement for further study. These bones were unearthed in 1950, when a construction crew located them in the basement of a building being torn down. They were well-preserved, having been stored in an empty whiskey barrel. There could be no question that these were the bones of George Parrott, for the brainless skull was topless.

Topless? What do you mean by topless? you may ask.

The skull in the old whiskey barrel had no top, the skullcap having been sawed off at about eyebrow level.

Then what became of the skullcap of Big-nose George?

Polished, the skullcap of Big-nose reposed on a table in the doctor's office, a noteworthy conversation piece for many years, serving the useful purpose of ashtray and receptacle for discarded trivia.

In his later years the good doctor bequeathed it to his secretary, and this worthy lady felt it was worth passing on to future generations. And so this skullcap ashtray was presented to a museum, to become a conversation piece once again, but to a larger assortment of viewers.

What of the hide of Big-nose George?

Rather than waste such good leather, the doctor had turned over the hide to an expert tanner, then he had the tanned hide made up into useful articles. He kept one of those articles, a medical kit, to carry his instruments and medicine in while making house calls.

The skin of Big-nose George's thighs was converted into a pair of ladies' high-top shoes—quite in fashion at the time. Unfortunately, none of the young ladies of the doctor's acquaintance could be induced to wear the shoes; so these shoes made of human hide were relegated to a showcase in the window of the Rawlins Bank, kept on display along with other memorabilia from Wyoming's lusty beginnings.

No part of Big-nose George's hide was wasted. Every last bit was turned into some useful article: gloves, billfolds, hat bands, watch fobs—you name it. There was even a most ingeniously designed seamless purse, a real conversation piece, to hear old-timers who claimed to have seen this purse tell it.

And so Big-nose George Parrott achieved a fame of sorts, but not for his deeds of daring, for as a bandit leader working on the railroads, George Parrott and his men fell woefully short of the accomplishments of those railroad immortals, the James brothers, the Youngers, and the Dalton Boys, whose deeds of derring-do these misfits had tried to emulate.

No, it was not his daring deeds but rather his durable hide that was to bring everlasting fame to Big-nose George Parrott.

FOOTNOTE: The saga of Big-nose George Parrott has been recounted through the years, not only as a subject of fireside tales but also in print—in books and in numerous magazine articles.

The physiognomy of Big-nose George will not be forgotten, for a cast was made of that death mask and presented to a museum, to go on display so that the visage of Big-nose would not be lost to future generations.

Some of the articles made from George's durable hide did survive a finicky generation and were eventually donated to museums along the route of his earthly career.

Pictures of the plaster cast made from the death mask, along with those high-top shoes made from his hide, have appeared in various periodicals, as have photos of the skeleton in the whiskey barrel, complete with the topless skull, giving some degree of authenticity to the saga of Big-nose George Parrott. There was even a ballad written about him and his predicament as he tried to shinny up the pole, "but slipped an' kicked, an' died."

As with most legends out of the past, details get scrambled in the telling; so it is suggested that anyone desiring absolute historical accuracy would do well to contact one of the historical societies in Wyoming or some other state where Big-nose and his band "worked on the railroad," and where details may have been traced out more thoroughly.

And now for another macabre tale from the long ago, the legend of the superb specimen.

THE SUPERB SPECIMEN

Back in those robust years of the American frontier, a certain evildoer was apprehended and sentenced to be hanged.

This particular rogue had been an outstandingly handsome man—tall, broad-shouldered, muscular, lean-hipped, and virile. He had, in other words, been a superb physical specimen of the genus Homo sapiens, and it did seem a crime to consign so noteworthy a body to the earth, to be eaten by worms.

This matter was discussed heatedly by the vigilantes as they prepared for the hanging, their viewpoints perhaps a bit out of kilter due to an over-indulgence in hard liquor. Then one of them came up with an idea that appealed to his fellow vigilantes, though probably not to the subject of their discussions.

The hanging was carried out on schedule. Then, as soon as the miscreant ceased his struggles and hung limp, the vigilantes took down the body and turned it over to an aspiring young taxidermist. He had taken part in the lynching and had quite happily agreed to carry out the suggestion that such a superb specimen be preserved for the edification of all.

This perfect specimen was skinned, carefully, the way a cougar or other wild animal to be mounted would be skinned, and the hide was carefully processed. The flesh was stripped from the skeleton, then the bones processed so that they too might be used without risk of spoilage. The skeleton was then reassembled, and over it was placed a papier-mache substitute for muscles and sinews, carefully sculpted to the exact measurements of the bandit at the time of his death. Then over this papier-mache musculature was placed the properly cured hide of the miscreant.

Glass eyes, a bit of coloring on cheeks and lips—and behold! A statue so lifelike in appearance that a breechclout had to be placed around the loins of the reassembled specimen lest his lifelike appearance shock the delicate sensibilities of the beholder. At least, that is the way the story went.

So that all might enjoy viewing this superb example of the taxidermist's skill, it was secured to a pedestal and placed on display near the bar in the local den of iniquity, to compete for attention with the saloon's other attraction, a lifelike, life-sized, full-figure oil painting of a buxom naked lady.

Alas! Art is not always appreciated. The respectable ladies of the town, hearing of these art exhibits, took a dim view of what seemed to them a flagrant violation of decency. And so the women plotted among themselves how to rid the community of all sources of evil.

In the wee small hours of a moonlit night, after the place had closed and the proprietor had gone home for the night, the women descended upon this saloon. They chopped their way in, smashed all the whiskey bottles and hacked open the stored barrels of whiskey, letting the contents spill over the floor. Then, to top off their crusade against sin, these worthy ladies made a bonfire and consigned to it both the offending oil painting of the naked lady and the unique example of the taxidermist's art.

Thus came to a fiery end a magnificent specimen of the human race.

FOOTNOTE: Was there ever really such a specimen preserved for a time through the skill of a taxidermist? Or was this a bit of fiction invented in the fruitful brain of a spinner of big windies?

Frankly, I do not know. One sure thing is that the gentleman who told the story certainly kept a straight face if he were telling a tall tale!

But enough of the macabre. Let us get back to something more conventional—like the hanging of Rafe Jackson.

THE HANGING OF RAFE JACKSON

Rafe Jackson was not too worried as he pulled the saddle from the back of his sweaty horse, then hobbled him so that he might graze along the river flat without wandering too far during the night. However, before turning the horse loose to graze, Rafe critically examined his mount's front hoof.

The horse had a damaged front hoof which required a specially shaped shoe to correct it—a crooked shoe—but this imperfection in no way impaired his ability to travel. He had traveled along at a good clip all day, and there was no sign of lameness even after the day's journey.

Rafe would have preferred a sound horse. But a man with a pack of rowdy vigilantes hot on his trail cannot be too choosy when he must acquire a fresh mount on short notice. Rafe's own horse, exhausted and going lame, had given out a few miles south of San Luis Obispo, and Rafe had traded the lame horse for one he found grazing in a pasture, the only available horse gentle enough to be caught in the open.

In spite of that vigilante pack out after his scalp, Rafe was not too worried as he spitted on a willow stick the rabbit he had shot, skinned, and gutted, then placed it over the campfire to cook. He was confident that in taking the little-known trail going east from Santa Margarita, he had made good his escape.

The posse would naturally think he had kept to El Camino Real and would go on up along the old Mission trail on the assumption that his goal was San Francisco. By the time the vigilantes realized he had given them the slip, he would be long gone and could lose himself in the mining camps of the Stanislaus.

While waiting for the rabbit to roast, Rafe Jackson counted the money he had with him. Over $3,000 in gold and greenbacks. Not bad! Not bad at all!

True, that wad of money now in Rafe's possession might well have cost a man his life. But that was not Rafe's own worry as he appraised his present wealth.

A sore-headed son-of-a-bitch had accused him, Rafe Jackson, of double-dealing in a poker game down in Santa Barbara and had imprudently reached for his gun. And so, of course, Rafe had had to shoot the bastard. It was as simple as that.

With his own gun out and smoking, Rafe had scraped up all the money on the table there in that gambling hall, then took off hell-for-leather, heading north along the old Mission route, well on his way before the patrons of the gambling hall got their wits together and formed a posse to run him down.

Hell! He'd survived worse predicaments! Rafe dismissed the vigilantes from his mind as he tore the roasted rabbit apart and began to eat. He had had no food since leaving Santa Barbara in the afternoon of the day before, and he was damn hungry!

Rafe Jackson was wolfing down the rabbit when his hobbled horse whinnied. Rafe looked around and saw mounted men converging on his campsite from all directions.

Too late Rafe realized his folly in building a fire. That curl of smoke had pinpointed his camp, giving his pursuers a chance to surround the camp before he saw them.

Rafe knew he was cut off from any chance of escape, and to try to shoot it out with the vigilantes was tantamount to committing suicide. His only hope would be to brazen things out. After all, the other galoot had gone for his gun first!

As the vigilantes closed in on the camp, one of them dismounted and examined the hoof of Rafe's horse. "This is the horse we've been following," the posseman stated. "We've caught the right son-of-a-bitch! No mistake about it!"

"That varmint he done shot down in Santa Barbara will probably live—doggone it!" another member of the posse remarked pessimistically. "By the time we get the bastard back to Santa Barbara, there won't be anything to hang him for!"

"Wow! Look at this wad of dinero!" Another member of the vigilante pack, in frisking Rafe for hidden weapons, had found the roll of greenbacks and the gold coins in his money belt. "It sure would be a crime to let this double-dealing bastard get away with a wad like that!"

"Horse-stealing is enough to hang the bastard for right here and now!" Another member of the pack had to get in his say. "Hang the bastard, then us gents splits the dinero!"

"Hang the horse-thief!" another rowdy yelped. "Three thousand dollars split between the twelve of us! Over $250 apiece! Not bad!"

"If us gents don't hang the bastard, somebody else will!" someone sagely observed. "Why not hang the bastard right now and get it over with!"

And so Rafe Jackson's saddle was placed on the back of the horse with the crooked shoe, and Rafe himself, wrists tied behind his back, was heisted up into the saddle.

The horse was led to a nearby cottonwood tree, and there Rafe Jackson was hanged, his body left swinging in the springtime breeze, there in the old Estrella River Valley. He was left unburied, as a warning to all malefactors to mend their ways.

FOOTNOTE: This is one of those shadowy tales out of the past where too much time has elapsed for anyone to verify the story.

As a boy I remember hearing old-timers tell of a Rafe Jackson, hanged by vigilantes over in the Estrella Valley of eastern San Luis Obispo County, for a shooting he had been involved in down Santa Barbara way. He was tracked down because the horse he had stolen had a crooked shoe, making the tracking easy when he left the more traveled route for the Old Outlaw Trail.

This was an incident from those turbulent years while a civil war was brewing back East and the only law enforcement for California was of the vigilante variety.

Presumably, since both the lynchers and the man they lynched were from outside the county, the incident was never given the attention it might have been given had local people been involved.

And now, another shadowy tale from the almost forgotten past, a tale in which more evildoers come to an inglorious end—a tale in which drastic measures were taken lest zorruelos grow into zorrazos.

ZORRUELOS GROW INTO ZORRAZOS

"Dirty dog of a gringo!" The youth slapped the old man across the face. "Tell us, old man, where you have hidden your money! Or we shall break your *other* arm!"

"And break both his legs also!" The other youthful delinquent snickered as he put added pressure on the old man's arm. "He will talk if we break enough bones!"

The old man's face was twisted with the pain of his bruised and broken body; blood from his battered nose stained his greying beard; and his right arm hung limp at his side. He tried to rise from the chair but a vile oath from El Malo and a twist to his left arm by El Zompo forced him back.

"Tell us, old fool, where you have hidden your money!" Malo snarled. "If you do not, I shall give Zompo a nod, and he *will* break your other arm!"

"And your legs too!" The burly lout called Zompo twisted the old man's arm across the back of the chair. The bone above the elbow snapped as too much leverage was applied.

"That—that tobacco can. The can back of that coffee can..." The old man sank back in his chair, the pain having robbed him of all thought of resistance.

El Malo got the indicated can and dumped its contents on the table; and from the scattered pile of tobacco there emerged perhaps $100 in greenbacks and gold coins.

Having counted the money, the youthful tough spat disgustedly on the victim to show his vile mood. "They say, old fool, that you must have over one thousand dollars hid here in your cabin! Where is it? No lying! If you do not tell us where your money is hidden, we *will* kill you!"

"I swear that is all the money I have in the world! I have no more!" The old man's eyes reflected his suffering; not only had Zompo broken both his arms in trying to force him to tell where his money had been hidden, but also several ribs had been broken in that first scuffle before the boys overpowered him. "Take the money and leave. I have no more money! I swear I have no more!"

"Liar!" El Malo jerked the old man from his chair, threw him to the floor, then began a senseless stomping and kicking of his victim, continuing the stomping until the writhing form grew limp.

Disgusted that their escapade had not netted them more loot, El

Malo and his clumsy companion set about a thorough ransacking of the cabin, but uncovered no more money. Giving up the search at last, the youthful delinquents gathered up as much of the old man's personal effects as appealed to them—his watch, pocket knife, hunting knife, rifle, and revolver, which were about the only things of real value in the cabin.

Aware they themselves would be logical suspects should the body of the old man be discovered soon, the young ruffians decided a few weeks of camping out in the mountains might be in order; so they gathered up a pack of blankets, cooking utensils, and grub enough to last them several weeks. This added burden made it necessary for them to appropriate the old man's pack mule, for the horses they were riding were aged and in poor condition and would not last for long under any added burden.

No qualms of conscience assailed these youthful malefactors, no regrets that a murder was now added to other crimes they had in the past committed. Nor was there any real fear of discovery, for the old man had been something of a hermit, living far off the beaten trails. There was little chance that anyone would discover the murder soon. It might be many months before anybody rode by the isolated cabin and discovered the body.

Unworried that any agents of vengeance might track them down, the two young killers whom for this story we shall call El Malo (the Bad One) and El Zompo (the Clumsy One) made their camp deep in the Sierra Pelona, confident that in leaving the scene of their crime they had masked their trail well. No compassion, no regrets assailed them for the aged recluse lying dead back there in his cabin. Their only emotion was keen disappointment that they had failed to uncover that rumored cache of over one thousand dollars, said to have been hidden somewhere around the cabin.

This was not the only crime these two *zorruelos* (fox whelps) had committed during their brief life span. Crime had been their heritage from early childhood.

At the tender age of nine, El Malo had watched as an angry mob hanged his father for stabbing a man to death in a barroom brawl. Then his mother had taken on a lover who had coached the boy in thievery and in depravities of the most loathsome nature. As for Zompo, his own mother quite frankly admitted she herself did not know who had begat the boy, for her means of livelihood had come from pleasuring many lovers, often several during a single night.

From these blighted beginnings, each boy had found that in crime he could get both the excitement he craved and a livelihood without the tedium of working for wages. So far, it would seem, Lady Luck had been with them, for as yet they had received no serious punishment for any of the crimes they had committed. However, their reputation as miscreants was making them unwelcome wherever they went.

Within the past few months, the boys had been ordered to leave El Pueblo de Los Angeles, the place of their birth, then Ventura, then Santa Barbara.

It was in a Santa Barbara saloon that Malo had chanced to overhear some barroom loungers discussing the old hermit and the cache of money he was presumed to have hidden somewhere around his cabin. And so, instead of going north along El Camino Real, the route the boys appeared to have taken when ordered out of Santa Barbara, they had turned back at San Marcos Pass, circling back through the mountains until they located the old hermit's cabin.

Did I say Lady Luck had been with the two youthful miscreants? Well, Lady Luck is a perverse Jezebel at best, and this time she chose to ignore the young delinquents completely. Only hours after the crime had been committed, a chance traveler passed the old recluse's cabin and found the battered body sprawled on the floor.

It did not take the discoverer of the crime long to alert the residents of Santa Barbara to the murder which had been committed in the hills back of town.

Quickly a vigilante posse was formed, comprised of most of the Americans living in the district, and also men of the old Spanish-California families. And with this posse went a full-blood Yaqui, noted for his skill as a tracker.

Although in their youthful arrogance the boys believed they had masked their trail well when leaving the old man's cabin, it did not take the Yaqui long to unravel the trail, and once the direction the fugitives had taken could be established, the vigilantes had little trouble in following them.

By evening of the second day, the vigilantes had located the boys' camp. Unsuspecting of any posse on their trail, the youths had carelessly laid their weapons aside and were lounging around camp. Thus they were taken into custody without any resistance on their part.

The youthful malefactors denied any knowledge of the old hermit, or any part in his slaying. But their denials fell on deaf ears, for the old man's mule had been found grazing in the meadow with the boys' saddle horses.

Even more damning were various items found in the boys' possession, items which were identified by members of the posse as having belonged to the old man. Add to this bit of evidence just over one hundred dollars in greenbacks and gold, the acquisition of which the boys could not explain, and a trail which had led the posse directly from the old hermit's cabin to the campsite in the Sierra Pelona, and any court in the land would have convicted the youths for the murder of the old man.

"Don't kill me... Don't kill me... " Bereft of his usual arrogance, El Malo pleaded with his captors. "I beg of you, don't kill me! I am too young to die. Too young... "

Tears of terror and self-pity glistened on the ashen cheeks of the youthful delinquent El Malo, and his nose dripped—dripped like the nose of a little boy who dreads a spanking he knows will come.

Nor was Malo's companion in crime taking the situation with any greater fortitude. Blubbering "Take me home to mi madre," Zompo's hulking shoulders shook with racking sobs he could not control. "Madre mia... madre mia... madre... "

The men of the posse looked at the two captive youths. They looked at each other, and then away. They avoided the gaze of their companions, lest the eyes betray the workings of the mind.

In an avenging mood, men may hang mature men without qualms; for mature men are assumed to have acquired the responsibility of maturity. But to hang two boys whose upper lips scarcely bore the first downy hint of coming manhood...

Responsible men do find repugnant the prospect of enforcing the death penalty on youthful criminals, even though the brutality of their crimes warranted the supreme punishment.

"Zorruelos grow into zorrazos!" one of the possemen, a Sonoran, remarked sardonically. "Why wait for these whelps to grow to maturity before exterminating them!"

"That is true," another member of the posse admitted. "Turn these punks loose now and they will kill again."

"Sooner or later, they will have to be hanged!" another posse-man said grimly. "Hanging them now will save the life of their next victim!"

In a somber mood, the vigilantes heisted the blubbering boys onto their horses and led the horses to a spreading cottonwood tree, and there the fox whelps were hanged.

FOOTNOTE: Here again is one of those provocative tales from a time long gone, a tale which seems almost to have passed from memory, as those involved passed across the Great Divide.

This story came by way of an old-timer, a Spanish-Californian, and it would seem that a fairly large proportion of the avengers were in fact *Californianos* and *Sonoreños*.

That expression, "Zorruelos grow into Zorrazos"—? In the vernacular of the old-time Spanish-Californian, the term *zorruelo* (fox whelp) was applied to juvenile delinquents, and the term *zorrazo* (big he-fox) to more mature miscreants.

Part VII
LEGENDS
IN THE MAKING

More stories from the past where details have grown dim with the passing of time, and where verification is hard to come by. Call them fireside tales; call them folklore; call them "big windies" if you want to. Here goes.

JUAN DE DIOS SANTOS

Juan de Dios Santos, known also as El Lobo, did not blame his companions for having left him wounded, to work out his own salvation as best he could or, failing, to face his doom alone. He who had been christened John of God a Saint in early childhood by devout parents, then in manhood had earned the nickname the Wolf, would have done likewise had he himself escaped the posse's bullets and a companion been wounded.

It had been every man for himself in that inglorious routing when the band of *revolucionarios* Juan Santos had been with was taken by surprise in their unguarded camp in the Cuyama Valley.

With grim determination, Juan de Dios Santos urged his weary horse to even greater effort, and in the wolf soul of this man who should have been a saint of God was the gloomy foreboding that this was to be his last ride. It was as though Death on his invisible black charger rode by the side of the wounded bandit, Death's presence felt rather than seen.

At the first opportunity to pause and rest his by-now winded horse, Juan Santos tightly bandaged the wound where a bullet had shattered a rib as it tore on into his body. The bullet was lodged deep inside, so deep there could be no way for him to remove it. But even this bandaging did not completely stop the blood which oozed from under the bandage and ran down his side.

The respite was not for long; always there was the risk that the posse had picked up his trail, and El Lobo dreaded capture even more than death. Sheer willpower alone held this wolf to the saddle, for already a black blankness sometimes engulfed him, blotting from his mind all conscious thought.

It was the wolf's instinct for direction rather than any conscious knowledge of landmarks that took the wounded outlaw to a remote canyon deep in the rugged Sierra Madre, a canyon in which there were many caves where a wounded wolf might hide.

There was, however, conscious thought in the mind of the rider when he stripped saddle and bridle from Cuervo, his horse, for in the innermost being of this wild wolf of a man was still manhood, and knowing that Death had marked him, he would not leave his friend Cuervo tethered, to die slowly of starvation.

Taking his bedroll and saddlebags with him, El Lobo sought out a remote cave for his dying; the wolf instinct in him demanded that he die far from mankind. His instinct told him that his own death must not be witnessed by the unsympathetic eyes of the curious.

With reverent hands El Lobo, who had been christened Juan de Dios Santos, took from his saddlebag a small, exquisitely carved figure of the Madonna which he had salvaged some months previously from the ruins of the Old Mission Nuestra Señora de la Soledad. He set this holy relic from the days of the Mission padres in a niche in the rock wall of the cave, where in his dying hours it might offer him the solace of a promised Hereafter. And in the dissolute soul of El Lobo was a prayer such as he had been taught in his early youth.

*   *   *

To the boys, on that bright spring day sometime in the 1880s, this was just an outing, a hike in the mountains, with some not-too-interesting caves to be explored. Having hiked most of the forenoon, they had eaten their lunch at a spring far up one of the canyons, then set about their exploration.

A shout from one of the boys drew his companions to a cave where he was standing, a rusted rifle in his hands.

"Spooky in here!" the youth said, indicating the cave behind him. "Dead man's bones, and no telling what!"

"Pirate treasure cave?" another lad put in hopefully. "Let's have a look."

Exploration of the cave disclosed a human skull, along with bones scattered about, presumably the rest of the skeleton. But there was little else of interest, certainly no cache of pirate treasure.

The passing of thirty years can blot out much. Little was left of clothing and saddle-bags—a rusted hunting knife with a stag-horn handle, some scattered cartridges, some mother-of-pearl buttons, and a silver belt buckle. These things the boys examined curiously.

Nothing except the belt buckle seemed worth the bother of carrying home. The rifle and the knife had been so close to the mouth of the cave that rain had hit them, rusting them beyond salvage.

The skeleton was dismissed as unimportant. Just an Injun or a greaser who'd died back here in the mountains so many years ago that he didn't count any more. It was common enough to find skeletons in remote caves back in the 1880s.

A small, exquisitely carved Madonna found in a niche in the rocks was also dismissed as unimportant—just a cute trinket to be carried away, passed around while the day's outing was fresh enough to be of interest, then set aside—and forgotten.

FOOTNOTE: As a boy, I remember hearing of an outlaw, one Juan de Dios Santos, who disappeared into the mountains after being wounded in a skirmish with lawmen. Then some thirty years after his disappearance, the skeletal remains of a human body were found in a cave "somewhere in the mountains back of Santa Barbara" by some boys who had been on a hiking trip. The remains were tentatively identified as that of the outlaw Juan de Dios Santos. However, I have been unable to verify this legend.

Was there ever a Juan de Dios Santos who died a lonely death deep in the mountains? *Quien sabe, amigos! Quien sabe!*

There were many embittered men among the *Californianos* who, having refused to acknowledge defeat, went the outlaw trail in those early years following Mexico's relinquishment of California to the United States. And for many of these rebellious men, that trail led to a lonely death and an unmarked grave.

As one of the legends passed down by the Spanish Californians, this story of Juan de Dios Santos seems worthy of being preserved and passed on as a part of the folklore of a people. The same can be said for the story which follows, the legend of a redheaded son of a Scotchman known as El Rojo.

EL ROJO, HIJO DE ESCOCES

In dealing with old legends—those stories which have come down through the years by word of mouth rather than by way of "official records"—there are a few facts of life which must be dealt with. In relying on memory alone, the narrator with the best of intentions all too often is apt to confuse dates (even to the extent of a generation or more), run elements of unrelated events into one story, and confuse personalities so that one person is credited with the actions of another. This would seem to have been the case with the legend of El Rojo, Hijo de Escoces. This rather intriguing tale, as told by some of the older of native Californianos, went something like this:

Muchos años ago, a British ship docked in one of the Mexican seaports for repairs and to take on supplies. The ship remained in port for several weeks.

While this British ship was at dock, the sailors were given liberal shore leave to find relaxation in the *cantinas* of the seaport town and, for those fortunate to find someone willing, a bit of the feminine companionship men long at sea crave so desperately. Among these fortunate ones was a persuasive young Scot with fiery red hair, whose ardor won the heart of a young girl of Spanish and Aztec blood.

In due time the ship set sail, and our redheaded Scottish tar sailed away, leaving his love to bear their son in shame and to rear him under the stigma of illegitimacy. The boy bore a double stigma as he had inherited the flaming red hair of his sire, marking him as being of alien blood.

This lad, son of the Scottish sailor, grew into stalward manhood, a prideful young man who from early boyhood had rebelled against the restrictions a class-conscious society had placed against the illegitimate offspring of foreigners. In time he broke away from the *gente de razon* completely, drifting into the wilderness where for a time he threw in his lot with the roving Apaches, learning their ways, and himself teaching the Indians something of the skills of the white man.

Although he had earned the respect and good will of the Indians, this redheaded son of a Scotsman was restless and resentful over his alienation from the world of white men; and so, in time, he left the Indians for the roving freebooter life, at times back in the settlements of New Spain, at times returning to the friendly Apaches. And in time he came to be known as "El Rojo, Hijo de Escoces," and whatever the surname of his sire might have been, it was forgotten with the passing of the years.

In time, El Rojo had a following of Cholos, men of mixed blood, like himself, who had become outcasts from a more circumspect society. Eventually El Rojo formed this band of mongrels into a rebel army, with the avowed purpose of reclaiming their rightful heritage as free men. And in their rebellion against the established order, El

Rojo and his followers became marked men, to be hunted down and exterminated—like *lobos* and *gatos del monte.*

In retaliation, El Rojo and his band took to robbing the settlements of the *gente de razon,* and to waylaying and robbing chance travelers along the old emigrant trail where it passed through the province of Sonora on the way to the newer settlements of Alta California. And now his earlier amicable relationship with the fierce Apaches was a lifesaver for our friend El Rojo. For whenever the avenging soldiery set out in pursuit of the bandits, El Rojo and his band would head northward, seeking sanctuary among the Indians of the Arizona desert.

As the depredations of the outlaw band became more bold, efforts to capture or kill the various members of the band became more intense. In a last-ditch effort to destroy the renegades by any means possible, a bounty was placed on the scalp of El Rojo, Hijo de Escoces.

Forced to leave the older settlements of Mexico, El Rojo and his band moved northward, continuing their raids on the emigrant caravans as they passed through the deserts of Sonora, or along El Camino Real in Alta California, then disappearing into the uncharted wilderness when pursuit by the soldiers made things too hot for them along the more traveled routes.

Then gold was discovered in Alta California, and for men outside the pale there was a chance for a new beginning in the wild mining camps, where a man's past could be forgotten.

Adept in learning various languages, El Rojo took a new identity, and in his later years he led a circumspect life as a rancher under the laws of the *Americanos.*

This in essence is the legend of El Rojo, Hijo de Escoces, as told by various old-timers among the native Californians—a rather provocative tale of a redheaded devil-may-care Robin Hood of the Devil's Highway and his merry cholo band.

Some forty or more years ago my mother was trying to trace out some of the old legends of the early-day California bandits, and from several of the old-timers then living came this tale of El Rojo, son of a Scotsman. Many also said that El Rojo eventually became an honest man and settled in the Cuyama country, where he applied for what is now known as the old Cuyama land grant.

Here, it would appear, is one of those instances where two separate personalities have been confused into one person, and where various incidents involving these two men have been fused into one story.

The Cuyama land grant was indeed applied for by a man named Rojo who held much influence with the Indians, but here any similarity between this early settler of the Cuyama Valley and El Rojo the *bandido* would seem to end.

In the Spanish language, *rojo* is an adjective meaning "of a reddish hue," and it can be used as a nickname much as Americans use the nickname "Red." However, in Spanish Rojo (or Rojos, or Rojas) is also a surname, quite common and in good standing, and has nothing whatsoever to do with the color of a man's hair or his complexion.

Records indicate that one Jose Maria Rojo (a man who was influential with the Indians of the Cuyama Valley) did in fact apply for the land now known as the Cuyama land grant, a Mexican grant which was eventually patented by the estate of Don Cesario Lataillade. However, it would seem that Jose Rojo's relationship with the Indians was more that of a trader before he took up the land. Apparently he had some knowledge of medicine and some skill in setting bones, and he was accepted by the Indians as a medicine man of some importance.

There is no evidence at all that this hardy pioneer of the Cuyama Valley had any connection whatsoever with El Rojo, Hijo de Escoces. There is nothing to indicate Don Jose Rojo ever had any connection with any of the bands of outlaws who used the rugged mountains surrounding the Cuyama Valley as escape routes during the heyday of the California bandido.

FOOTNOTE: Does this puncturing of the legend that the Cuyama Valley's first white settler was a notorious highwayman necessarily disprove the legend of El Rojo, Hijo de Escoces? Does the fact that no one seems able to establish positively that any redheaded son of a Scotsman ever existed necessarily prove that he, like Santa Claus, was but a figment of someone's overactive imagination?

There must have been some basis for the tales of this redheaded *bandido bravo*, for these stories came down from the generation that could still remember California's turbulent growing pains, and these people were sincere in recounting the legends as they remembered them.

Why discount an interesting story just because no one can offer proof of its origin? Let's keep our redheaded son of a Scotsman alive in the legends of the Californianos.

THE LEGEND OF THE PICKLED DUTCHMAN

Back in the not too distant past, the legend of the pickled Dutchman was a favorite topic of conversation around the campfires of vaqueros and harvest crews, and even in the more refined atmosphere of family homes when other topics of conversation wore thin. It was a rather gruesome tale of how the unoffending German handyman was slaughtered by the irascible rancher, who cut his carcass up into chunks and then pickled the meat in a pork barrel. This "pickled pork" of human flesh was fed to travelers who chanced to stop by for a meal, and to a harvest crew that was stationed at the ranch for a time.

Different versions of how this nefarious crime was discovered have come down through the years. Among them are that a vaquero stopped at the ranch to water his horse and discovered a human shoulder blade and thighbone in the mud below the trough, rooted up by hogs using the overflow as a wallow; that a human nipple was discovered on the rind of a slab of pickled "pork" fished out of a barrel of salt brine; and that a harvest hand, guzzling a plate of stew, came up with a human fingernail in his spoon. There were other versions, also, too numerous to mention here.

Grisly as this tale was, it seemed to have appealed to people of an earlier generation, and as the story was passed on, it took on sharply varied versions. For this series of legends, I shall narrow the story to one version, pieced together from the recollection of my uncle Mentley Still, and from notes my mother took down some forty years ago in interviews with the old-timers of the Carrisa Plains area then living.

It all started one day when Windy Smith, who had a little ranch in the Temblor Mountains, stopped at La Panza to have Doc Still patch up some wounds he had recently received, wounds which were painful but not fatal.

To put things mildly, Windy was perturbed. Johnnie had tried to kill him! What was more, Windy bet Johnnie had already killed poor ol' Heiney! Even worse, Windy bet Johnnie had been feeding Heiney to the harvest hands! That salt pork Johnnie had served for dinner sure tasted mighty peculiar!

With little prompting from Doc Still, Windy told his own version of the story.

Windy had stopped by Johnnie's place to gab and had stayed on for dinner. He had noticed that Ol' Heiney who had been working as a chore-man for Johnnie for the past few years at "$10 a month and keep" had not returned from his presumed trip to Bakersfield where he had gone, as Johnnie had told the neighbors, to wet his whistle.

Windy had noticed also that Heiney's beloved meerschaum pipe was lying on the mantel over the fireplace, and he had commented on the fact that Ol' Heiney never went anywhere without his pipe.

Johnnie had gotten angry and told Windy to shut up if he knew what was good for him! So, for the time being, the subject of Ol' Heiney had been dropped, and Windy sat down at the table to fill his plate with frijoles flavored with slices of salt pork.

After dinner, as he was preparing to leave, Windy had wittily remarked that he thought maybe Johnnie had killed poor Ol' Heiney to save paying him his back wages.

Then Johnnie had gone plumb loco and grabbed up a pitchfork and come at Windy, wild-eyed and yelling bloody murder!

Windy Smith had made a run for the old workhorse he had been in the habit of riding and managed to scramble into the saddle, but not before he received some rather embarrassing punctures. (As one old-timer put it, "Johnnie had jabbed Windy where he couldn't sit down for a week!")

Fortunately for Windy, his leather coat and chaps had prevented serious damage to his person. Reining his mount down the trail, he set out hell-for-leather, coaxing the horse into a run. However, as Windy's phlegmatic old plowhorse lumbered down the canyon, Johnnie had raced back into the house for his pistol. He took a shot at Windy and winged him, but fortunately it was just a flesh wound which, cleaned and dressed, would cause him no serious trouble.

Though not fatally wounded, Windy had spent a sleepless night in his cabin. So, with the coming of daylight, he had again saddled his old horse and set out for La Panza, to get the doctor to treat his injuries. However, by his own admission, he had had to stand up in the stirrups all the way there because of his painful wounds.

Having done all he could to ease Windy's suffering, Doc Still then prevailed on Windy to ride on into San Luis Obispo with the mail carrier to report the incident to the sheriff and give his reasons for believing that the old German roustabout might have been murdered.

And so, ensconced on a pillow which Mrs. Still had thoughtfully given him to ease his injured dignity as the old buckboard jounced along over the rough road, Windy Smith set out with the mail carrier for the county seat town, there to make his report.

Representatives of the law did make a trip out to Johnnie's ranch in the Temblor Mountains and searched the premises. They found various articles which were identified by neighbors as having belonged to the old German. They also located in the ranch storeroom a barrel of salt pork that looked mighty suspicious.

And so, Johnnie was arrested and ordered to stand trial on a charge of murder.

Johnnie's brother, a prominent rancher with a good deal of influence in the county, procured the services of a slick city lawyer. This lawyer had Johnnie take the Fifth Amendment and refuse to answer all questions put to him.

Johnnie was brought to trial, and witnesses were put on the stand to testify about that barrel of peculiar pork which allegedly had been found in Johnnie's storeroom.

Here again the city lawyer turned the tide by asking each witness on the stand if he were "absolutely positive that the pork in the barrel was in fact human flesh, and not the flesh of a hog."

Thus pinned down to a positive statement, the witnesses would hedge, giving the jury reasonable grounds for doubt.

Johnnie was acquitted. (Some versions of the story had it that he was sent to an asylum for a time.)

After that, Johnnie became a recluse, living for a time in a cave up around Cayucos. Later he was converted by the Salvation Army, and in time, as the case faded from public attention, he drifted into obscurity.

It is here that legend takes over, as those who had eaten at Johnnie's table between the time Ol' Heiney disappeared and the time Johnnie was arrested began comparing recollections about that "peculiar pork" they had eaten.

FOOTNOTE: Here again it is well to forget names. "Johnnie" was the scapegrace son in an otherwise respectable pioneer family, and in retrospect it would appear that he was on the borderline of insanity. Certainly his attack on Windy Smith with the pitchfork would indicate he had homicidal impulses when aroused. Also, the circumstances around the disappearance of the old Dutchman would strengthen the belief that he had been killed. Not only were personal items that had belonged to Ol' Heiney found on the ranch, but no one had seen him around Bakersfield, where he had supposedly gone.

As to the verdict: Back in frontier times there were none of the refinements of science to prove or disprove the contention that the "pickled pork" found in Johnnie's storeroom might in fact be human flesh; at most, the evidence against Johnnie had been circumstantial.

Having had a reasonable doubt in their minds, planted there by the slick city lawyer, the jurors were justified in asking for an acquittal on the grounds of insufficient evidence.

For those curious enough to delve for the story, the official version of the trial might be found in old courthouse records of the 1890s. But, Heck! Legends are best when passed on as they were handed down, for thus they gain life and color. Disappointingly, once disinterred from lifeless records, legends become but skeletons—musty bones—and of little interest to anyone.

TO THINK THAT MINE OWN WIG SHOULD BEAR WITNESS AGAINST ME

The friendly tavern keeper grinned benignly as the dimly lighted barroom of his establishment in the little settlement of Santa Margarita began to fill with loud-mouthed but paying customers. This jovial innkeeper had two noteworthy features: his cheerful grin and his sleek black hair.

A hush fell over the crowded barroom as the local sheriff and a half-dozen deputies came in. They liked to wet their whistles as they discussed the latest caper of the jolly highwayman who for the past two years had been holding up the stage as it crossed La Cuesta on its way between the Salinas Valley and the Coast.

The jolly bandit had two noteworthy features when described by his victims: a jovial chuckle emerging from behind his black mask as he pocketed the loot, and sleek black emerging from under his old battered felt hat.

The pattern of the holdups was becoming monotonous. The jolly bandit would emerge, mounted, from behind a rocky point or a clump of brush, his rifle pointed at the stage driver, who would prudently stop his horses right then and there.

The passengers would be ordered out of the stage, then told to place their valuables in a canvas sack which the jolly bandit would toss down; then someone would return the sack to the masked man, who would thank the donors and ride away, chuckling with good humor.

Always, it would seem the jovial bandit knew which of the passengers had valuables on their persons.

Alerted that another holdup had taken place, the local law enforcement men would rush to the scene of the crime and there pick up the trail, only to lose it in the rugged slopes and canyons of the Santa Lucias.

        *   *   *

The jovial grin on the face of the jolly bandit was hidden by a black silk scarf which he used as a mask, but the paying customers were aware of the jolly mood of the highwayman, for he chuckled merrily as the canvas sack containing the passengers' valuables was handed back to him.

The bandit's garb was faded coveralls such as were worn by transient railroad hands. No doubt they had been donned for the occasion and would be discarded as soon as the bandit was out of sight on the stage. His mount was nondescript, an aging horse, blackish-brown in color, with no distinguishing features, and he had been smeared with mud to further confuse any possible identification of the bandit through his mount.

The passengers could remember only two features: That jolly chuckle, and the sleek black hair peeking from under his slouch hat.

With a cheerful, "Adios, amigos! Replenish thy pocketbooks before thy next journey!" the benign bandit wheeled his horse sharply about, then rode away, leaving the robbed passengers standing by the side of the stage. But, alas! As better men before him had done, the over-confident highwayman underestimated his quarry.

A brash young man whose pistol had dropped to the seat when the bandit ordered the passengers to get out of the stagecoach hastily retrieved his gun and pumped six shots in the general direction of the fleeing bandit. The shots were not too effective, it is true, but one bullet did knock the hat from the head of the fleeing robber before he disappeared around the bend in the road.

The stagecoach driver ordered the passengers back into the coach, saying that the sooner the sheriff was notified of the robbery the better chance the law would have in tracking the miscreant down, then muttered under his breath, "Not that notifying the sheriff will do any good!"

This jolly bandit had outwitted this particular sheriff far too many times in the past.

Having been notified of the holdup by the stagecoach driver, the sheriff and several of his most trustworthy deputies set out for the scene of the crime—not that the trip would do any good! The trail would be easy to pick up at the start, then would be lost in the rugged Santa Lucias—as it had always been in the past.

A waste of time in making the ride, the sheriff muttered to himself. But, Hell! A good sheriff has to make a good show if he expects to be re-elected!

The place where the holdup had occurred was easily located, for the stage driver had given a good description of the spot. But then, the scenes of previous holdups had also been easily located. The trail of the fleeing bandit was easily found—but then, it had been thus in all the previous holdups in which the jovial highwayman had taken part.

Always it was later that the trail was lost, after the fast tracks had reached the rough country behind the open road. It was as though the highwayman knew every inch of the mountains and could weave his way through terrain other men would consider impassable.

Always in the past, the men of the law had been forced to give up the chase in gloomy confusion, not knowing which direction the wanted man had taken.

But, Hell! The rules of the game must be adhered to, even though defeat was a foregone conclusion!

In true western story fashion, our friend the sheriff picked up the trail, signaling his deputies to follow. But he did not go far before he jerked his mount to a halt.

"What the Hell! What the hot hopping hairy Hell!" the sheriff ejaculated. "What the hairy hot Hell!"

Our masterful guardian of law and order swung his bony frame from the saddle, stooped, squinted, grunted an unintelligible monosyllable, then picked up an object from the ground, scrutinizing it closely. In bewilderment, if not in downright consternation, our friend the sheriff viewed this unexpected bit of evidence. Was it a clue to the crime?—a battered felt sombrero shot so adroitly from the head of the fleeing bandit that his scalp had been peeled right off his thick skull?

"So the lousy son of a bitch wore a black wig!"

This trite observation from one of the deputies brought the sheriff back to reality. "But, who the hot hopping hairy Hell wears a sleek-haired black wig! *That* is the question!" quoth our sleuth. "Just you answer me *that* question, or forever keep your big damn mouth shut!"

None of the deputies could answer the sheriff's question, so all rode along in silence as the sheriff traced the bandit's trail on into the Tasajara Canyon, then lost it when the fugitive's tracks disappeared along a rocky spur of the mountain.

Once again the fox had outwitted the hounds. Disgusted, the sheriff motioned his men to turn back. By now the jolly bandit was long gone and there was little chance of unraveling his trail.

Glumly, the posse rode into the little town of Santa Margarita, tired and hungry, but loath to make their appearance without a captive, knowing they would be ribbed over letting the jolly bandit elude them once more.

"Let's wet our whistles at the tavern before going on to San Luis," remarked the deputy whose astute observation had brought the order for silence. "So much *not* talking done made my throat dry."

"Guess I could use a snort my own self," the sheriff admitted. "That there scalp—wig—done got me buffaloed!"

*   *   *

"What the Hell! What the baldheaded hairy hot Hell!"

In blank consternation did the sheriff look at the bald head of the jovial tavern keeper. "Don't tell me you are as bald as a billiard ball!"

Sheepishly the tavern keeper admitted he had been hiding under a wig for some time. Then he remarked that he had had to send the wig away to be cleaned.

Silently the sheriff pulled the black wig from his pocket, then he glanced from the wig to the shiny bald head of the tavern keeper. A genial innkeeper whose sleek black hair was gone, and a sleek black-haired wig shot from the head of the jolly highwayman—even the dullest Sherlock Holmes should be able to put those clues together.

"Sir! I suspect you are the jolly bandit!" exclaimed the sheriff. "Try this wig on for size, sir! If it fits, it will mean ten years in the hoosegow for you, my friend!"

With a sheepish grin on his face, the jovial innkeeper donned the wig. It fit like a glove.

Lady Luck had been kind to the jolly highwayman for so long, but at last Miss Fortune had taken her place! So thought the unhappy innkeeper as the sheriff led him away, and in his heart he railed at Miss Fortune.

Madam Fortune, thou art truly a cruel bitch! To think that mine own wig should bear witness against me!

FOOTNOTE: This tale from days long gone had its base in an actual incident. The wry misfortune of the jolly highwayman who for some time held up the stage as it crossed La Cuesta has been recounted in several histories of San Luis Obispo County. The jovial tavern keeper avoided detection for quite a while. Then a brash young man who had been on the stage took a pot-shot at the bandit, dislodging his wig, and thus brought about the downfall of the jolly bandit.

THE INGLORIOUS END

"These raids have netted us little! Paltry peon wages only!" Joaquin Murrieta—he of the same name as his kinsman, the glorious Joaquin of tradition—spoke to Jose Valenzuela, his compadre. "Let us forego these piddling holdups of cantinas and grocery stores and try now for something really important!"

"Your plan, compadre?" Valenzuela inquired.

"Let us rob the stage bringing the gold from the bank in Monterey to the Almaden Mines for their payroll," Murrieta suggested. "Our six compadres are chafing for action."

"These our compañeros! Bah!" Valenzuela spat contemptuously in the general direction of the rag-tag band who had recently accompanied the two when they raided a roadhouse. "They are but sheep! Not wolves!"

"With masks on their faces, they will pass for wolves!" Murrieta snickered. "The stage driver and the armed guard will think twice before offering resistance to so large a band of masked men. And once you and I have the gold in our hands, let the sheep scatter!"

Joaquin Murrieta the Younger and his compadre, Jose Valenzuela, sat apart from their henchmen. Although Murrieta and his partner had enlisted the aid of these nondescript recruits, neither one had much confidence in their valour. However, despite the obvious deficiencies of these followers, Murrieta was confident his plan would work out satisfactorily. And so he and his compadre set the scheme in motion.

This plan, as laid out by Murrieta, proved to have been most ingenious, and the Almaden stage was robbed with precision. In their black masks, waving their big pistolas, the sheep appeared to be fierce wolves, so the stage driver and the armed guard offered no resistance.

Instead, they meekly surrendered the gold and the mail bags to Murrieta and Valenzuela, who collected the treasure themselves, not trusting their confederates with any part of the day's take.

In high good spirits over the lucky outcome of the holdup, the eight bandidos left the scene of their crime. But it would seem that Lady Luck had turned against them. They had gone but a few miles from the scene of the holdup when they met the Sheriff of Monterey and a posse of rambunctious deputies, still seeking these men for one of their earlier raids.

The panicked bandidos scattered; and herein could be seen the wisdom of Joaquin Murrieta. For the panicky sheep in their wild flight from the posse so confused the Sheriff and his men that both Murrieta and Valenzuela were able to make their own escape into the mountains, with all the loot still in their possession.

The gold was heavy, however—far too heavy to carry on a long trip. It would be conspicuous, and if found on their persons, it could well prove a death warrant for our friends Joaquin Murrieta and Jose Valenzuela.

And so, Murrieta and Valenzuela buried most of the gold in the Diablo Mountains, retaining only enough for their immediate needs.

"Paisano, amigo," Murrieta said to his friend and fellow countryman. "One day we shall return here and retrieve our hidden wealth. In the meantime, it should be safe buried here in the mountains of the Devil."

"But should one of us die before we can return to claim our buried gold," Valenzuela said, "what then should the man who survives do about the money?"

"Then the whole of the wealth shall belong to the survivor," Murrieta said. "Let that be understood."

The two compadres shook hands to seal this most sacred pledge between them. Then they rode away together, to participate in the excitement and profits of more raids against the annoying gringos. In the furor of a bandido's adventuresome life, Joaquin Murrieta and his compadre, Jose Valenzuela, forgot the gold they had buried in the mountains of El Diablo.

Robbing the rich and retaining the loot proved to be a most profitable enterprise. Within a few years, Murrieta and Valenzuela had wealth enough cached away that they could afford to retire from their arduous and occasionally risky profession.

Even more pertinent, the climate of Mexico was probably healthier than that of California for men with a price on their heads in Alta California.

And so, bidding a fond *adios* to the land which had been so kind to them, the two bandidos hied themselves to Mexico, where their gold might buy them much pleasure. Nor had they need to seek out the gold they had buried in the mountains of the Devil.

Safe in Mexico, Joaquin Murrieta met a comely young vixen whose beauty appealed to him, and so he took this fair young lovely to wife, although I greatly fear without legal formalities or ecclesiastical sanctions.

This luscious young woman—whom for this story we shall call Luisita—took great pleasure in the gowns and bright baubles the freehanded Joaquin lavished upon her. There were silken gowns and fine hand-embroidered linens, gorgeous silk scarves, and shawls imported from Spain. There were also necklaces of pearls, and others of hand-carved coral beads, to adorn her lovely neck; jeweled brooches to adorn her lovely bosom; diamond and sapphire rings for her slender fingers; and ruby pendants for her shell-like ears.

Thus did Joaquin bedeck the lovely Luisita, that she might be the envy of all the other women.

The rich raiment pleased mightily the vain little soul of Luisita. She gloried in the appreciative stares of the men and the jealous glares of the women.

As for Joaquin Murrieta, it was with possessive pride that he lavished gorgeous gowns and glittering gems on his lovely Luisita, for was he not the proud possessor of the most fragrant flower of all womankind?

But, alas! Good fortune does not last forever! In time, the free-spending Murrieta had spent his last centavo. He found himself flat-broke after so many years of affluence. It was then he remembered that cache of gold hidden deep in the Devil Mountains of Alta California for all these years.

Jose Valenzuela was now dead. The whole amount of the buried treasure was now rightfully the wealth of Joaquin Murrieta, in accordance with the agreement he and Valenzuela had entered into when they had buried the gold.

"The spoils of my other ventures have now all been spent, Luisita my beloved wife!" Joaquin Murrieta announced. "Now I must replenish my wealth lest we both suffer the indignity of starvation! I must enlist the aid of a trustworthy compañero, then return to the land of the Californianos to recover the treasure I have buried deep in the mountains of El Diablo!"

Tearfully, Luisita begged that Joaquin not leave her, fearing that once gone, he might never return.

"Don't leave me, my beloved!" she implored. "To be parted from you, my lover, my husband, would bring me to a sorrowing grave!"

"Do not weep for me, my beloved wife, *mi dulciana*!" Joaquin took the weeping woman into his arms. "I will be thinking only of you all during my trip, counting the days until I return to you, my beloved sweetheart!"

"Then stay, my beloved!" Luisita sniffled. "Stay with me always!"

Joaquin ran his fingers through the raven tresses of his love. "I go only to retrieve the treasure so that I can once again buy you jewels and clothes."

Now this promise appealed mightily to the covetous soul of Luisita; but with this awakened desire for more finery, there came a fear also.

"Joaquin, my lover, my husband, I fear that in that faraway land of Alta California you will find another young woman as lovely as I; and it will be on her that you will spend the treasure of the Diablos! It will be she for whom you will buy things! And it will be your lonely Luisita whom you will leave behind, to wait for you and cry!"

"Woman! Do you not trust me!" Joaquin was fast becoming impatient. "I am your lover! Your husband! Your man!"

"I shall make this trip to Alta California with you, my beloved husband." This brilliant solution had just entered Luisita's conniving little brain. "Then I can be at your side when you dig up the treasure of the Diablos!"

"Silence, woman!" Joaquin exploded with wrath. "Silence, she-fox! This is a journey for men only! I, the man, shall go! You, the woman, shall stay here!"

Seeing Joaquin's wrath and fearing that should he leave in anger he would never return, Luisita became conciliatory. "You are right as always, my beloved husband. Do as you think best. You are the man and you make the decisions."

"That is better, woman!" Joaquin said grumpily. "Keep your place, woman!"

"I will await your return, caro mio," Luisita said, "and every night

I shall say a prayer for your safe return." But under her breath she muttered, "And the Devil's curse be upon you, my faithless lover, should you not return upon schedule!"

Joaquin Murrieta took into his confidence a young friend, telling him of the buried fortune in the Diablo Mountains, and offering him a share of the gold if he would help retrieve it. And so the two compañeros set out on their mission, taking the long and difficult trail up across the deserts of Sonora. But from the start, it seemed that Madam Misfortune was to haunt them, making it more difficult to retrieve the treasure.

After much hard luck in crossing El Camino del Diablo, Murrieta and his companion reached Alta California, then made their way on up into the Cantua Canyon country.

Starting from the scene of that stage holdup of so many years ago, Murrieta retraced with great care the route he and Valenzuela had taken afterwards, and in time he located the spot where the two had buried the gold.

Alas! The treasure was gone! Someone had found the cache of gold coin and taken it away. Only a hole in the ground was left to indicate where the loot had been buried.

Had the lawmen, hot on the trail of the fleeing bandits after the holdup, been able to track Murrieta and Valenzuela to the place where they had hidden the gold? Had they suspected the loot had been buried and been able to find it?

Hardly. This hole in the ground had been but recently dug.

Had Jose Valenzuela, before his untimely demise, foolishly taken some other person into his confidence? And had that other person violated so sacred a confidence by coming here and stealing the gold?

Or perhaps had he himself, while in his cups, talked too much—maybe a great deal too much? For within his own soul, Murrieta knew that when he was drunk he all too often bragged foolishly.

Well, no matter! The gold was gone, and there was no way now to retrieve it. There was nothing left for Murrieta and his compadre to do now but return, empty-handed, to Mexico.

Had the vindictive Luisita, impatient over the delayed return of ·her long-overdue lover, convinced herself that her man had already recovered the treasure and even now was spending it on another love? Even now might Luisita be praying her spiteful curses for the down-fall of Joaquin?

Truly, Lady Luck continued to frown on Murrieta, turned her back upon him completely and would not aid him.

For this Joaquin Murrieta—the not-so-glorious kinsman of the veritable Joaquin of legend—not only was there the keen disappointment of finding the buried treasure gone, but Fate was to send him other misfortunes as well.

Hardly had this Joaquin and his youthful compañero left the scene of their keen disappointment when ill fortune struck again. The horse ridden by Joaquin went lame, and it became necessary to acquire another mount so they could get back to Mexico.

Without the money to buy a horse, Murrieta found it necessary to acquire his mount from the remuda of one of the ranches in the Diablo Mountains. Again the cynical Señora de la Fortuna aided, not Murrieta but his adversaries. The theft of the horse was quickly discovered and a hastily formed posse set out on the trail of the bandits.

As Murrieta and his campañero fled ingloriously, the pursuing avengers fired on them and Joaquin was wounded. A well-aimed rifle ball pursued the fleeing bandit, hit the back of the saddle, and went through the cantle of the saddle to lodge deep in the fleshy portion of his buttock.

Fortunately the two bandits had already achieved the partial protection of rough country, and shortly their pursuers gave up the chase and turned back. Fortunately also, Murrieta was in country familiar to him from those years when he and his compadres had used the Diablo Mountains as a hideout, before he himself had retired from the honorable career of *un bandido bravo.*

Murrieta led the way to a cave which would have to serve as a refuge until his wounded rump healed sufficiently for him to ride once again.

With groans of anguish and humiliation did this Joaquin Murrieta submit to the painful ordeal of having the flattened bullet dug out of his injured buttock. Fortunately there were no serious complications. The bullet was out, the wound was cleaned and dressed, and in due time it would heal enough for the bandits to ride on.

Within the anguished soul of this Joaquin there was much bitter resentment that Fate should have been so unkind.

To have made that long tortuous journey up across the forbidding Highway of the Devil to the Mountains of El Diablo, only to find the buried treasure gone, was bad enough. But this last misfortune—this wounded rump!

Why could not Fate have been more kind? If she insisted that he must receive a wound, then why, oh why, could it not at least have been in a more romantic place?

A wound in the chest or shoulder, the scar of which he could show with pride, would have been an honor! But this! This wounded rump!

To have been shot in the rear as he fled an enemy!

What an inglorious end!

FOOTNOTE: Lest the reader think that the writer has been fabricating these stories completely and without regard to genuine folklore, perhaps here a *cuento* of *bandidos bravos* as written down by a native *Californiano* himself might be of interest. It is from a letter written thirty years ago by an old-timer. This man's own first-hand memory encompassed those turbulent years of transition between the time that Central California was largely of the Spanish-American heritage and culture, and the days of Anglo dominance.

The following is an excerpt from a letter written by Don Jose Blanco, dated July 22, 1947:

Since they [Murrieta and Valenzuela] were in Calif. it happen that [they] were scouting around trying to find a place to raid, and it happen [that] the stage [drove] by. They agree right now to go and stop and rob the stage. They agree and prepare in a minute, and they holt it up, and [they] went through also two mail sacks and two boxes of seal gold coin, close to the Almaden Mines. Stage had along two cattle buyers.

They [Murrieta and Valenzuela] each had a sack of the mail bags [and] of coin. They broke open the box [of coins] and put [the coins] in the mail bags, and took it away.

They went to the rough country to get out of sight. It was an awful heavy load, so they decide to bury it [the gold]. And that is the way they buried it and forgot about it. So they did, and went along to where they started to go.

They talked the buried matter over, and they agree between themselves. Murrieta said to Valenzuela, "Pal" he say, "If I should happen to go first, you come and take mine."

Valenzuela said it was understood [that the survivor was to take the buried gold] and agreeable between the two pals. And they shook hands, and they forget it [the buried gold].

Years afterward, when they were in Mexico rich as they could be, Velenzuela passed. Well, it was up to Murrieta to come and get what they agreed to do if such were the case.

One day, he [Murrieta] told his wife, "My dear wife, I have to go to Calif."

Murrieta lit out and come and found the place, and while he was eying

around close to the spot, somebody shot him in the leg above the knee, and
cut the back of the neck [of Murrieta's saddle horse] about eight inches, and
made the horse awful sick with that awful cut. It [the bullet] went through
the cantel [cantle] of the saddle, through his [Murrieta's] thigh and then
[through] the front part of the saddle, and through the back of the horse's
neck, back of the ear.

(Ironically, here the story must end, for the last page of this particular letter was lost or misplaced many years ago. And so, we must
leave our hero with a wounded rump.)

This tale as told by Don Jose Blanco is a genuine *cuento*, one of
those tales vaqueros were wont to tell of an evening as they whiled
away the time around a campfire. These tales were picked up by
others, retold, often embellished in the retelling, and with the passing
of the years became the folklore of a people.

It was through these cuentos rather than through written records
that the lives and exploits of the various California bandidos were
kept alive.

And now, something on the life of Don Jose Blanco might be of
interest.

"Joe" Blanco was from one of the pioneer families of Central California, and he grew up in the Santa Margarita vicinity. Then in his
mature years, during the early decades of the present century, he and
his brothers operated one of the large cattle ranches of the Cuyama
area.

Don Jose's own boyhood was during those turbulent years when
Central California had little in the way of real law. He had a first-hand
memory of many of the incidents involving the outlaws and the vigilante action taken against them. And he knew personally several of
the reformed bandidos (men who in their youth had been at odds with
the law, but who in later years led law-abiding lives).

Although Don Jose's earlier education had been in Spanish, and
his mastery of English had to come later, he was of scholarly inclin-
ation, read a great deal, and had a rather wide insight into matters of
historic interest. He had in his possession a number of books and old
documents of genuine historic value.

In compiling this series of legends on the early days in Central
California, I have drawn on notes taken down from interviews with
Don Jose and on certain letters written by him some years back for
some elements in these stories, especially in some of the stories about

members of the Vasquez Gang.

As to those letters written by Don Jose, it should be born in mind that at the time he wrote them, he was a man of advanced age, his eyesight was failing, and his hand was getting a bit shaky. In places these letters are a bit hard to decipher, yet as a link to the past they are priceless.

REFERENCES

History of San Luis Obispo County, compiled by Myron Angel. First published in 1883. Reprinted 1966, with an introduction by Louisiana Clayton Dart.

Letters written by Walter Murray in 1858, explaining the actions of the Vigilantes. (Some of these letters are reprinted in the book.)

History of Santa Barbara, San Luis Obispo, & Ventura Counties, by Yda Addis Storke, 1891.

San Luis Obispo County & Environs, edited by Annie L. Morrison, 1917.

History of San Luis Obispo County, edited by A. V. Kell, 1939.

Sixty Years in Southern California, by Harris Newmark, 1930.

Cattle on a Thousand Hills, by Robert Glass Cleland, 1941.

History of California, by R. G. Cleland, 1922.

Great Stagecoach Robbers, by Eugene Block, 1962.

Pictorial History of California, by Paul C. Johnson, 1970.

Gold Rush Album, by Joseph Henry Jackson, 1949.

Great West, by Charles Neider, 1958.

Great American West, by James D. Horan, 1959.

Men to Match My Mountains, by Irving Stone, 1956.

California Missions, by J. Berger, 1941.

Romance of the Highways, by Commander Scott, 1947.

The Salinas, Upside Down River, by Anne B. Fisher, 1945.

California Vaquero, and other books in this California Vaquero series, by Arnold R. Rojas, 1953.

Missions of California, and other booklets published by Pacific Gas & Electric Co., 1970.

Californios, by Jo Mora, 1949.

The Hunted Bandits of the San Joaquin, by George Beers, 1875. Reprinted 1960, with an introduction by Robert Greenwood.

Crimes and Career of Tiburcio Vasquez, by M. F. Hoyle, 1927.

Life and Adventures of Joaquin Murieta, by Yellow Bird (John Rollin Ridge). First published in 1854 (with various revisions during 1860s and 1890s). Original version reprinted in 1954, with an introduction by Joseph H. Jackson.

Life of Joaquin Murieta (author unknown). Published in 1859, in the *California Police Gazette*. Reprinted 1932, The Grabhorn Press. Reprinted in 1969, by Valley Publishers, with introductions by Francis P. Farquhar, Raymund F. Wood, and Charles W. Clough.

Devil on Horseback, by Dudley T. Ross, 1975.

Junipero Serra, by Bernice Scott, 1976.

Monterey, by Augusta Fink, 1972.

El Camino Viejo, by F. F. Latta, 1936. (The old inland route).

Joaquin, Bloody Bandit of the Mother Lode, by William B. Secrest, 1967.

Mariana La Loca, by Dr. Raymund F. Wood, 1970.

Legend of Tiburcio Vasquez, by Ruben E. Lopez (in *Pacific Historian*, 1971).

San Luis Obispo County, Title Insurance booklet, 1960.

Kern County, Title Insurance booklet, 1961.

Sworn Statement, by Charles W. Weeks (army deserter), Feb. 5, 1874, on the Vasquez band.

Joaquin, Hero, Villian, or Myth?, by Remi Nadeau *Westways*, Jan. 1963).

Parade of Golden Years (San Luis Historic Society, about 1950).

Carrisa Plains, by Dennis Gardner (*California Traveler*, May 1967).

La Panza Gold Rush, by Dennis Gardner (*California Traveler*, June 1967).

Protected Valley, by Virginia Williams (Santa Margarita booklet).

Santa Margarita Country, by Russ Leadabrand (*Westways*, March, 1967).

La Panza, by Richard H. Dillon, published by William Wreden, 1960.

Legends of La Panza, by Richard H. Dillon (*Westways*, May 1961).

Other books, magazines, and newspaper articles.

INDEX